LONE STAR
Valor

D1608886

TEXANS OF THE BLUE & GRAY
AT GETTYSBURG

JOE OWEN

Battle of Gettysburg. Charge of the Confederates on Cemetery Hill. Niday Picture Library. *Alamy Stock Photograph.*

Lone Star Valor
Texans of the Blue & Gray at Gettysburg

Library of Congress Control Number: 2018967923

ISBN-978-0-9993049-5-2

Printed in the United States
Copyright © 2019 Joe Owen
First Edition

Please visit our website www.Gettysburgpublishing.com for information on all our titles.

Front Cover Image – **"Clubs Are Trumps"** *by Dale Gallo*n
www.gallon.com

Back Cover Images – **"The Angle"** ©*Mark Maritato*
www.maritato.com

Civil War Drum – Courtesy of the Library of Congress

A time to love, and a time to hate; a time for war, and a time for peace. –
Ecclesiastes 3:8

Dedicated to:

CTRSN KIMBERLY KAYE STILLWELL, USN,
MAY 12, 1965 – APRIL 16, 1985.
A dear friend and an outstanding sailor in every sense.
She served her country with Honor and Distinction.

3RD GREAT-GRANDFATHER, 3RD LIEUTENANT THOMAS S. HAYES,
AUGUST 27, 1821 – MARCH 11, 1912,
12th Battalion, (Day's) Tennessee Cavalry Regiment.

3RD GREAT-UNCLE, 3RD LIEUTENANT JOHN T. GROSS,
APRIL 22, 1836 – NOVEMBER 7, 1911,
57th Georgia Infantry Regiment.

2ND GREAT-GRANDFATHER, SERGEANT GEORGE A. WILLIS,
MARCH 29, 1829 – FEBRUARY 17, 1872,
8th Georgia Infantry Regiment.

3RD GREAT-GRANDFATHER PRIVATE WILLIAM DUNBAR GROSS,
AUGUST 28, 1820 – AUGUST 14, 1897,
6th Mississippi Infantry Regiment.

How many a glorious name for us,
How many a story of fame for us
They left: Would it not be a blame for us
If their memories part
From our land and heart,
And a wrong to them, and shame for us?

No, no, no, they were brave for us,
And bright were the lives they gave for us;
The land they struggled to save for us
Will not forget
Its warriors yet
Who sleep in so many a grave for us.

But their memories e're shall remain for us,
And their names, bright names, without stain for us;
The glory they won shall not wane for us,
In legend and lay Our heroes
Shall forever live over again for us.

- Abram Joseph Ryan

Foreword

Of all the soldiers present at the Battle of Gettysburg, perhaps none had a clearer understanding of the stakes than the men from Texas. After all, they had been through the crucible of independence before, giving them a practical, battle-forged experience in nation building that no other Confederates possessed.

Once a territory of Mexico, Texas declared its independence in 1835 and defended that claim in a revolution that lasted until 1836. For ten years thereafter, the independent Republic of Texas sat in the borderlands between an embittered Mexico, plotting revenge, and the United States of America, enticed by the rich resources Texas could bring to the Union. Finally, after much political wrangling and heated debate, Texas became the 28th state in 1845, although it took the Mexican-American War (1846-48) to settle the matter.

Today, we might rather glibly say, "Remember the Alamo!" repeating lines we've heard from movies, but in 1861 when the Civil War broke out, the Alamo remained a fresh and painful memory. The cost of independence, most keenly remembered there but felt on a dozen other Texas battlefields, struck a somber and all-too tangible chord. Texas did not vote to secede lightly. They, of any Confederate state, understood the potential cost in blood.

During the ensuing two years, the Texans paid that cost, too—most notably at Gaines' Mill outside of Richmond, where the Texas Brigade first earned its everlasting fame, and in the dreaded cornfield of the Miller farm at Antietam. Between 1861 and 1863, Texans from more than a dozen regiments left their blood in the soil of Virginia and Maryland.

Through the lens of hindsight, we can see the forces that conspired to bring the Confederate army to Gettysburg in early July 1863, and through that same lens of hindsight, we often see Gettysburg as a crucial turning point of the conflict. The veterans themselves—those from north and south—used that same lens to look back at the battle with special purpose and meaning. The newspaper articles and soldiers' letters home, Joe Owen has collected in this volume show Gettysburg through those two power lenses that, combined, offering a unique view of the most famous battle of the Civil War. While many of these articles have appeared in print before—most notably, as Joe points out, in the original newspapers themselves—they have never before been collected into a single volume. As such, this book will stand as a useful companion to Joe's other collections, *Texans at Gettysburg: Blood and Glory with Hood's Brigade* and *Texans at Antietam: A Terrible Clash of Arms, September 16-17, 1862*, both of which provide excellent compilations of similar letters and newspaper accounts.

For researchers, Joe's curatorial work makes an extremely useful contribution to the overall literature of the battle. For Civil War buffs, Texans, and other interested parties, this edited collection offers a special view of the battle from a group of men uniquely qualified to understand the stakes involved.

Also of note are the Union accounts Joe has included here. In the years following the American Civil War, much of America's attention turned westward, captured by the spirit of expansion. Texas had a powerful allure then, and many men—some alone, some with their families sought their fortunes in the Lone Star State just as men had done a generation earlier in the years before the Texas revolution. As former northerners, they had a perspective of their own that included a powerful understanding of the war's stakes too, which included a much different understanding of the power and meaning of liberty than the perspective their southern-born neighbors shared.

Lone Star Valor: Texans of the Blue and the Gray at Gettysburg, allows us to read for ourselves the words and ideas of the Texans at Gettysburg — south and north — whose differing experiences set them apart from everyone else on the field of battle.

Chris Mackowski, Ph.D.
Editor-in-Chief, Emerging Civil War
www.emergingcivilwar.com

Acknowledgements

I would like to thank Kevin Drake and Bernadette Loeffel-Atkins for their wonderful support in *Lone Star Valor: The Texans of the Blue and the Gray at Gettysburg*. American Historical Artist Mark Maritato, who generously gave permission for the use of his paintings, *The Angle – Armistead at Gettysburg,* and *Confederate Skirmish Line*, which is on the back cover. Also would like to thank artist Dale Gallon for use of *Clubs are Trumps* which is on the front cover. Much gratitude to John Hoopes, for the photograph of his great-great grandfather, Private William Abernathy of the 17th Mississippi Infantry Regiment. Heartfelt thanks to Chris Mackowski, founder and editor of the outstanding "Emerging Civil War" website. Chris's contribution, advice and support was invaluable.

My special thanks to John Heiser. John's knowledge of the Battle of Gettysburg, and editing advice was invaluable. A special thank you to Randy Drais and photographer Tom Miller, whose wonderful photographs greatly enhance *Lone Star Valor: The Texans of the Blue and the Gray at Gettysburg*. My thanks to Margaret Duckett, who graciously provided the photograph of Simon Abernathy, who was former slave of Private William M. Abernathy. Simon traveled to Gettysburg with Private Abernathy, and found him grievously wounded after the battle, and carried him back to safety. Thank you to the Alabama Department of Archives and History for providing the photograph of Nicholas Weeks of the 3rd Alabama Infantry. Thank you also goes to the State of Kentucky Archives for providing the photograph of General Thomas L. Rosser. Much appreciation to Howell Cobb, Ray Fincham, Harry Hogue, Stuart Whitaker, John Clay Elisor, Jill Ogline-Titus, Sherry Polan and Craig Riley. Each of these individuals gave permission to use their photographs of the soldiers or the monuments at Gettysburg NMP. My appreciation goes to noted historians and authors Michael C. Hardy and Scott Mingus Sr., also to Andy Hall and James M. Smith II, who assisted me tremendously. Thank you to Patricia Petersen Rich, who graciously provided the photograph of the Virginia Monument.

Most of all I would like to thank my wife Cathy and my parents Tom and Jean Owen, and the rest of the Owen family and friends for their constant encouragement and support.

Introduction

I t is estimated that over 165,000 soldiers fought at the Battle of Gettysburg, July 1-3, 1863. Regiments from every Southern state, with the exception of Kentucky and Missouri, which were considered border-states, fought at the battle under General Robert E. Lee in the Army of Northern Virginia. After the Civil War hundreds of these Confederate veterans, moved to Texas to escape Reconstruction, begin a new life, move closer to family, begin new businesses, or just for the adventure. The public interest regarding the events and battles of the Civil War grew significantly. Newspapers around the country and especially Texas began to fill the demand by publishing stories of the soldiers who fought in the war and the memories they carried with them. The Battle of Gettysburg, which was the turning point of the American Civil War also known as the High Tide of the Confederacy, was of particular interest. Reporters in Texas sought out veterans of this great battle that fought for either the North or the South in the hopes of bringing new stories and experiences to the public eye. These stories were often found on the front page of the local newspapers or letters home. The 50th Anniversary in 1913 and the 75th Anniversary of the battle in 1938 aroused the nation's interest about the Battle of Gettysburg and the veteran reunions.

In 1912, Mamie Yeary published her classic book, *Reminiscences of the boys in gray, 1861-1865.* The book was based on the interviews she conducted either by written correspondence or in person with the Civil War veterans that were still living in Texas. Hundreds of these veterans, both North and South fought at Gettysburg and told her their stories of the battle. Their stories ranged from a few sentences to several pages long. Their stories are in *Lone Star Valor: Texans of the Blue and the Gray at Gettysburg.*

Two stories of African-Americans are told. One is a slave who carries his master's wounded body from the battlefield, and the other is a Union artillerist, which is a poignant example of the causes of the Civil War and why the Battle of Gettysburg took place, a free black who was a soldier in the Army of the Potomac, and the other a slave serving his young master from Mississippi.

There is only one article from a soldier of Hood's Texas Brigade. It is not intended to be a slight to the soldiers who fought under the Lone Star Flag of Texas in the immortal Texas Brigade. Instead, *Lone Star Valor: Texans of the Blue and the Gray at Gettysburg*, is intended to tell the stories of the other Texans who fought at the Battle of Gettysburg who were in the other Confederate regiments, and moved to Texas after the Civil War. Fifteen stories of Union soldiers who fought at the battle and moved to Texas after the Civil War, their stories are included as well as stories of civilians who lived in Gettysburg during the battle and moved to Texas are told.

All these stories combined, from civilians to the soldiers, are bound together by one common thread, the memory of those three days in July 1863. The Texas veterans never forgot the blood and sacrifice of their comrades. The bonds of these brothers-in-arms lasted a lifetime. The devotion of duty to the cause in which they believed is evident in their stories. The articles of the soldiers and civilians are transcribed just as they were when published by the newspapers; the reminiscences are transcribed as they were found in their letters and diaries.

It was an honor to find and share their stories about the largest battle and reunions in United States history.

Joe Owen
Blanco, Texas

STORIES OF THE BLUE & GRAY AT GETTYSBURG

Key

For historical accuracy and true to the reminiscences of the Battle of Gettysburg as told by the Texans, each story is transcribed as originally written in the letters, newspaper articles and interviews.

Brief summary of article or letter

Name of soldier

Regiment

Residence of soldier (as necessary)

Name of newspaper (as necessary)

Date of newspaper (as necessary)

Article headline (as necessary)

Gettysburg. View of the hills on the left of our position from the Rebel artillery, last rebel shot. Alfred R. Waud
Library of Congress.

CAPTURED AND RECUPERATED IN THE HOSPITAL

WILLIAM M. ABERNATHY
17TH MISSISSIPPI INFANTRY
McKinney, Texas
The Democrat
Galveston, Texas May 23, 1895

Colonel W. M. Abernathy

Hon. W. M. Abernathy of McKinney, colonel and inspector general Northeastern division of Texas, was private, company B, Seventeenth regiment of Mississippi infantry, Barksdale's brigade, McLaw's division, Longstreet's corps, Army of Northern Virginia, in 1862; participated in the campaigns of 1862, 1863, 1864 and 1865; was wounded three times and left because of wounds in a hospital at Gettysburg; carried to David's Island, New York, and exchanged as being too badly disabled to serve: rejoined his command and was detailed as courier at Longstreet's headquarters in the latter part of 1864 and surrendered at Appomattox.

INTENSITY AT THE PEACH ORCHARD

WILLIAM M. ABERNATHY
17ᵀᴴ MISSISSIPPI INFANTRY

McKinney, Texas
The Democrat
October 5, 1899

His Flag Now.
An Interview With W. M. Abernathy
He Stands by the President and the Flag.

McKinney, Texas, September 30. – Ex-Confederate W. M. Abernathy, whose name was mentioned in the Fort Worth notes in *The News*, makes a statement, giving some facts regarding the Gettysburg battle. He also wants it understood plainly that he is loyal to our president and army. He says:

"I am glad to see Col Cummings has corrected the statement in *The News* that he and

Private William Abernathy,
17th Mississippi Infantry Regiment. John Hoopes.

I belonged to the Seventeenth Massachusetts at the Battle of Gettysburg. Even here in my office I have hung up a record showing I was a member of the Seventeenth Mississippi and surrendered with Lee at Appomattox, we had a hard time explaining to J. Pearson Welch, Warden and some others the color of the regiment to which I belonged. Now, I guess I can go to the fair on ex-Confederate day.

"Yes, I was at Gettysburg, and the colonel has not told all. We were supporting Moody's battery and it lost so many men that volunteers were called for to help them man their guns. The colonel's cheery voice, 'Come along, boys,' was the first to answer. Lundy Gunn, a brawny sergeant of Company A, was second. Well before Cummings ceased speaking a dozen were running to the guns. If all good ex-Confederates get to heaven I'll beat the colonel there for he will have to rummage around the Pennsylvania fields for his hand before it starts.

"My old comrade is mistaken about fighting the Seventeenth Massachusetts that day. I walked over the ground and examined their monuments some two years ago. The first troops we encountered were from New Jersey. They were formed along the Emmitsburg Pike. Their monuments are in the peach orchard. Here we had another tough fight. Lieut. Ramrean was shot through the left arm and part of his right hand shot off. He still cheered on the boys. After driving back the Indianans, I noticed him; he had been shot through the mouth. He was still in front waving that old black hat, blood oozing from his mouth. There were no well men helping the wounded that day. The wounded men went to the front and Jim R. was leading the left of the company in the charge on the Excelsior brigade and their batteries. They too, have monuments to commemorate the valor of the New York Excelsior's.

"About six hundred yards back of the New York Excelsior monuments is where our brigadier Barksdale, was killed. A marble tablet marks the spot. Back nearly the same distance the line of monuments to a Wisconsin command. Here they stopped our brigade to finish the job next day which they didn't do.

"I am coming to Dallas fair not to glory having helped drive those who carried the flag there. It's my flag now. I made peace at Appomattox. I am ready to jubilee when our boys carry it in triumph over in the Philippines. I am with our president. We will never lower it one inch or carry it back now one step."

DEVOTION FROM A FORMER SLAVE

WILLIAM M. ABERNATHY
17TH MISSISSIPPI INFANTRY
McKinney, Texas
Weekly Democrat-Gazette
January 31, 1907

Simon Abernathy, former
slave of William Abernathy.
Margarett Duckett.

Greetings From Old Servant

Hon. W. M. Abernathy sends the following from his bed of sickness.

"Quite a number of people asked me about my old servant Simon in Mississippi. I have had his letter several days and now let him answer:

"My Dear Friend – I received your letter and check on Christmas eve. I must thank you for remembering me. It does my heart good to hear from you as much or more than my presence. I am quite well and was glad to hear you and your family was the same. Well, you and I are one more year nearer our eternal home where I trust we shall meet and know each other. Please always kindly remember me to Mrs. A and the children. I am over always your faithful,

"Simon."

Who knows, old Simon, we are one year nearer the knowledge. Meantime, from my bed of sickness, I pass up rheumatic old Simon's greetings and good wishes to the *Courier-Gazette* and *Democrat Gazette*, their readers, our friends, and especially to that faithful comrade Joe T. Hannaford, Morrilton, Ark., whose name brings a smile and a God blessing. He sought me at Gettysburg and found me down but faithful Simon was already beside me, grieving piteously."

TRIBUTE TO "BILLY" ABERNATHY

WILLIAM M. ABERNATHY
17TH MISSISSIPPI INFANTRY
McKinney, Texas
McKinney Daily Courier-Gazette
August 17, 1911

Battle of Gettysburg. Engagement in the Peach Orchard.
Library of Congress.

W. M. Abernathy; An Appreciation.
Ft. Worth Lawyer Pays Fine Tribute
– Tells Of Old War Times. Many
Fights, Narrow Escapes, And Record Of Great Morality Among Their Company.
Ft. Worth, Tex., Aug 16, - To the *Courier Gazette*:

Some kind friend has sent me your paper of Aug 9, containing sketch of my old-time friend, neighbor and messmate in the Virginia army, Hon. W. M. (Billy) Abernathy, noting his sudden death on the 8th inst. I call him Billy, for such was he ever known to us of the Early Grove mess in Marshall County, Miss., where we enlisted in April 1861, as neighbor boys (not in 1862 as the sketch has it.) We were in it from the first and for half a century he has kept the faith as a true son of the South, than whom none braver or better under the flaming red cross to glory and victory. We stood together on that fatal 2nd of July, 1863, looking down into the valley of death in the Peach Orchard at Gettysburg from 8 o'clock in the morning till about 4 p. m., in the afternoon, on Seminary Ridge, awaiting the order to rush down on Sickles with his bloody angle of 10,000 men in blue with munitions of artillery and all the latest improved arms, which our single thin gray line was ordered to break and scatter, but at a cost of 275 of the 448 men in ranks of our regiment, 17th Mississippi Infantry. I was sergeant major of the regiment and numbered the guns going in, outside of the officers. In two hours these 275 were put out of action and when the night came there was gathered in a single tent on that field of glory all the field and staff of the regiment except Dick Jones, killed dead on the field – that is. Col. Holder wounded in the groin, Lieut. Col. Fizer wounded in the head, Sergt. Major Cummings, a similar wound in the hand and the orderly of the Col. Brown Jones, disabled also. When shot I was making for a battery in front which I failed to reach, but Billy heard the order to go for it and was among the captors of this death dealing machine of war and was shot off one of the cannons of the enemy after waving his hat in victory astride it.

Since Billy came to Texas, I have met him now and then at reunions and heard from him by letter often. In one of these he told me of the last days before the surrender how our company of originally 125 (B, 17th Miss,) was reduced to but seven at the wind-up, and that one day shortly before this, they went bathing and every one of the seven showed on their bodies honorable wounds received in defense of the constitutional liberty of our beloved Southland.

Billy was in every march and fight with his command from the first great battle of the war at Manassas (which the federals name more appropriately for them, Bull Run) fifty years ago last July, till the last shot at Appomattox, April 9, 1865.

He wrote me once of how these boys wept when they were told the war was at an end and without our gaining what we went out to battle for and that they smashed the guns against trees and stumps rather than suffer the disgrace of grounding arms. You may search the records of that great war and no company sizes up with a better showing for courage and fidelity to the cause than our little company of boys – Co. B, 17th Miss. Regiment, Barksdale's Brigade, McLaws' Division, Longstreet's Corps, Army of Northern Virginia, R. E. Lee, General.

Billy was well known to Marse Robert as one of his most trusted couriers and his children will certainly cherish this noble example of so worthy a sire as one so near to the greatest commander in all the annals of history for ability and morality and humanity.

Mississippi was the storm center of the great upheaval and these Mississippians will ever be proud of having acted so long and faithfully their part in maintaining local self-government and Home Rule, a cause that is never lost.

C. C. Cummings

AN IMPORTANT QUESTION

GEORGE N. ALDREDGE
14TH TEXAS (CLARK'S) INFANTRY & 2ND
TEXAS (CHISUM'S) PARTISAN RANGERS

Dallas, Texas
Galveston Daily News
May 28, 1904

Judge Aldredge of Dallas, with a companion, was attending one of the great World's Fairs many years ago. The two visited a panorama of the Gettysburg battle. The man explaining it to the sight-seers was one-armed and dressed in the Union uniform. "Ladies and Gentlemen," he said, "there in the right-hand corner is where our brave boys met the shock of the enemy and drove them back in confusion. To the right in that wheat field, the carnage raged for hours, but finally our brave boys drove them back into the woods beyond, but with a terrible loss of life on both sides. There is the foreground you see the stone which marks where Gen. Armistead of the enemy fell, and that stone marks the point of the salvation of the Union. There they came on in frantic rage, but we mowed them down by the hundreds, nay, by the thousands." Thus he went on, and finally added: "Ladies and Gentlemen, if there is anyone present who wants to ask me any questions I would be pleased to answer.' At this the Judge stepped forward and said "Who were we fighting?" Sometimes, in one enthusiasm of indorsement or statement, we may overlook an important thing.

A Lingering Wound

Isaac Allen
13ᵀᴴ Mississippi Infantry
Stephenville, Texas
Stephenville Empire
December 8, 1883

Isaac Allen, better known as Pap Allen, a veteran of the Confederate war and who received a wound at the famous Battle of Gettysburg, July 2, 1863, is now unable to turn himself in bed from the effects of the wound. No trouble from the wound was experienced until the twenty-third of last October. He was shot in the thigh. Mr. Allen lives on Col. Eulcomb's place, and has been known as an industrious, energetic man, never failing to make a good crop. We deeply sympathize with him in his affliction, and hope that relief may soon come to him.

A Strong Spirit

H. S. Arnold
6ᵀᴴ Mississippi Infantry
Copperas Cove, Texas

The campaign through Maryland and into Pennsylvania had been made and after the Battle of Gettysburg had been fought, with all its loss, the spirit of this man was as strong and he was as valiant as at any time during the struggle. All he wanted was for the people at home to remain loyal and true and the armies of the South could not be crushed. This was the spirit that pervaded the army and which made it necessary for the North to resort to numbers and to have a continuing flow into their ranks to overwhelm the armies around Richmond.[1]

Pickett's Charge from a position on the enemy's line looking toward the
Union lines, Ziegler's grove on the left, clump of trees on the right.
Edwin Forbes. *Library of Congress.*

Remembering Chancellorsville and Pickett's Charge

G. E. Barringer
28ᵀᴴ North Carolina Infantry
Farmersville, Texas

Born Feb. 27, 1834, Mount Pleasant, Cabaras County, North Carolina. Enlisted in the Confederate

---

1   Mamie Yeary, *Reminiscences of the boys in gray*, (Book), 1912, p.26.

Army in the fall of 1861, at Mount Gillead, Montgomery County, North Carolina, as a private in Company E, Twenty-Eighth North Carolina Regiment, Gen. Lane's brigade, Gen. Wilcox's division, Gen. A. P. Hill's corps, Army of Northern Virginia. My first Captain was W. P. Barringer, and first colonel was Jas. H. Lane. Was slightly wounded at Turkey Ridge, below Richmond. Was currier under Gen. Lane. Was in the battle of Chancellorsville, had my horse killed; was also at Gettysburg, where the second horse was killed. Was in Ream's Station, Turkey Ridge, Jones' Farm, near Petersburg, and many other small engagements. There were two couriers at each battle, and one was on reserve. It seemed that Gen. Lane preferred me to the other courier because I always got there. Our brigade lost 900 men in the charge at Chancellorsville. Gen. Lane's brother and I were lying behind a small black jack stump and Lane asked me to move over a little as the shells were all coming on his side. I moved about four inches and just then a grape shot struck him between the shoulders and went entirely through his body. The shock threw him about ten feet, and when I went to him he said, "You can do me no good," and was dead. I came home to get another horse and the army started to Pennsylvania. I overtook them on Sunday before the Battle of Gettysburg. I saw Picket's charge. We tried the same charge but did not get to the breastworks. We went further to the left. We had to go through a field. We came back from Pennsylvania to Fredericksburg and were cut off by Sheridan's army. I was not surrendered, nor paroled. Came to Texas Jan. 3, 1871.[2]

THE GALLANT CHARGE AND LOSS OF THE MISSISSIPPIANS

A. H. BELO
55TH NORTH CAROLINA INFANTRY

Houston, Texas
Galveston Daily News
June 9, 1893

Texas Abroad

B. B. W., of Macon, Miss. In a recent issue of your valued journal was an editorial headed "The Memory of Gettysburg," wherein you, as I believe, justly say: "We have never been able to see why Gettysburg should have been regarded as such a triumph for the federal arms." Yet in my humble opinion, you fall into error – an error, an injustice, I have never before known outside of the Virginia press – when you seek to make Pickett's charge the most daring, heroic and disastrous of Lee's troops on the memorable 3d of July.

There were in the assault made on Cemetery heights other commands of the Army of Northern Virginia who not only went as far and sustained as heavy losses as Pickett's division of Virginia – notably, Davis' Mississippi brigade, whose position in that charge was to the immediate left of the Virginians, and whose colors of one or more regiments were being waved in close proximity to the federal earthworks on the heights while Pickett's men were already in defeat. The Virginians, as intimated, had correspondents at hand to herald their great prowess and chronicle their wonderful losses in wounded and slain, while the Mississippians with equally as heavy slaughter, if they did not suffer any greater loss, were the first to beat a retreat, and yet to the outside world and Virginia correspondents, were "not in it." Davis' Mississippi brigade came out of the charge with every regimental officer killed or wounded, leaving regiments commanded by line officers, captain and lieutenants.

Among the wounded were our present able and faithful governor and intrepid soldier, Colonel John M. Stone of the Second; the late lamented Colonel Reuben O. Reynolds of the Eleventh, who, after a career as soldier and statesman, suppressed by none, has "crossed over the river;" Colonel Andrew M. Nelson of the Forty-second, a faithful soldier and upright man, who also has passed to the shores of eternity; Colonel Andrew M. Nelson of the Forty-second, a faithful solder and up right

---

2   Ibid., p. 41.

man, who also has passed to the shores of eternity; Colonel J. K. Connolly and Lieutenant Colonel A. H. Belo of the Fifty-Seventh North Carolina, attached to the brigade of Mississippians, and as gallant a body of men as ever honored any state. Colonel Belo is now the distinguished editor and proprietor of *The Galveston News;* and last – not least – that the true soldier and Christian gentleman of your city. Captain John W. Dillard of the Second Mississippi. To have attacked Meade in the impregnable heights of Gettysburg was, in my humble opinion, the one and only serious mistake in the military history of the Immortal Lee, which mistake he admitted and assumed, and when the true history of the memorable charge on July 3 at Gettysburg is recording it will be seen that there were other than "Pickett's division" who "fought nobly" attested, as is claimed for these Virginians by decimated ranks.

THE HEROIC 55ᵀᴴ NORTH CAROLINA INFANTRY REGIMENT

A. H. BELO
55ᵀᴴ NORTH CAROLINA INFANTRY
Galveston, Texas
Galveston Daily News
September 14, 1895

A Sketch of the Fifty-Fifth North Carolina Regiment Written by Lieut. Charles M. Cook. Organized at Camp Magnum in the early part of 1862. Its position in the Fight At Gettysburg.

The regiment as it marched from the railroad depot to take its place in the lone, with its bright arms gleaming in the sun of that beautiful day, with quick, martial step, its company officers splendidly dressed, as if for a grand parade, its field officers mounted on fiery charges, and its magnificent band playing first "Dixie" and then "Maryland, My Maryland," presented one circumstance of war, that is its pomp, and if not its most impressive, certainly its least horrible showing. Little did it occur to any of us that the aspect of this organization would be so completely and so unhappily changed within a few weeks.

The regiment crossed the Potomac with the army of northern Virginia in fine spirits, and when it reached Cashtown on the night of the 29ᵗʰ of June, it was in splendid condition. The regiment marched out of Cashtown early in the morning of the 1ˢᵗ of July going down the Chambersburg turnpike toward Gettysburg. We came in sight of the town about 2 o'clock a.m. The union forces were on the ridge just outside of the town and formed across the turnpike to dispute our advance. Marye's battery was placed General Heth on the south side of the turnpike and opened fire on the enemy. Davis' brigade was immediately thrown into ling of battle of on the north of the road and ordered to advance. Archer's brigade was formed on the south of the road and was ordered forward about at the same time. There was a railroad that had been graded but not ironed which ran nearly parallel with the turnpike and about 100 yards from it. The Fifty-fifth regiment was on the left of the brigade, and owing to the character of the ground was the first one to come into view of the enemy, and received the first fire in the battle. It was a volley fired by the Fifty-sixth Pennsylvania regiment commanded by Colonel Hoffman from Cutler's brigade. Two men in the color guard of the regiment were wounded by this volley, The regiment immediately returned fire and inflicted considerable loss upon the Fifty-six regiment. The Eleventh Mississippi regiment was on detail duty that morning so we had only three regiments of our brigade, the Second and Forty-second Mississippi regiments and the Fifty-fifth North Carolina. The regiments in our front were the Seventy-sixth New York, the Fifty-sixth Pennsylvania and the 147ᵗʰ New York of Cutler's brigade. After the enemy's position became known by their fire, our brigade charged them in magnificent style. The left of our regiment extended considerably beyond the right of the enemy's line, and not the proper time our left was wheeled to the right. The enemy fled from the field with great loss. From the beginning of this engagement it was hot work. While the regiment was advancing, Colonel Connelly seized the battle flag and waved it aloft. This drew upon him and the color guard the fire of the enemy and before he fell badly wounded in the arm and hip. His arm was later amputated. Major Belo, who was near him at the time, rushed up and asked him if he was badly wounded? Colonel Connelly replied, "Yes but do not pay any attention to the Mississippians." After the defeat of the forces in front of us, the brigade swung around by the right wheel and formed on the railroad cut. About one-half of the Fifty-fifth regiment being on the left extended beyond the cut on the embankment. In front of us there then was the Ninety-fifth and Eight-fourth New York (known as the Fourteenth Brooklyn) regiments who had been supporting Hall's battery, and were the other two regiments of Cutler's brigade, and Sixth Wisconsin of the iron brigade, which had been held in reserve when the other three regiments of that brigade were put in to meet Archer's advance. Just then the order was received to retire through the railroad cut, and that the Fifty-fifth North Carolina cover the retreat of the brigade. The federal regiments in front of us threw themselves into line of battle by a well-executed movement, notwithstanding the heavy fire we were pouring into them, and as soon as their line of battle was formed, seeing a disposition on our part to retire, charged. They were held in check, as well as could be done, by the Fifty-fifth regiment covering the retreat of the brigade: A part of their regiment was in the road cut at a great disadvantage. One of the federal officers on the embankment, seeing Major Belo in the cut, threw his sword at him, saying: "Kill that officer and that will end it." The sword missed Major Belo, but struck a man behind him. Major Belo directed one of the men to shoot the officer, and it was done. This somewhat checked their charge, and we fell back to another position. The loss of the regiment was very great in killed and wounded, and a large number were captured in the road cut. From that time until 3 o'clock in the afternoon we were not engaged. About that time Early came in with fresh troops from the left. We formed in line with them on their right and were hotly engaged in the battles that afternoon driving the enemy before us and capturing a number of prisoners. At sundown we were in the edge of Gettysburg and the regiment was placed behind the railroad embankment just in front of the seminary. In the afternoon Lieutenant Colonel Smith, while the regiment was waiting in reserve, walked toward the right to reconnoiter and was mortally wounded and died that night. Major Belo was also seriously wounded in the leg just as the battle closed that evening. Davis' brigade during the night was moved from the position on the railroad cut near Seminary to a piece of woods across the Willoughby run west of the mineral springs, and there rested during the 2d. On the night of the 2d it was moved to its position on the confederate line known as seminary ridge, on the right center, and stationed in McMillan's woods, our division being on the left of Longstreet and our brigade, being the left center of our division. General Heth had been wounded on the 1st and General Pettigrew was in command of our division. General Pickett's division of Longstreet's corps was on the right of our division and occupied a position just in the edge of Spangler's woods. And it was from these positions that we moved out to that last fatal charge on the afternoon of July3. Our division was not supporting Longstreet as had been repeated published but was on line with his troops. Our regiment had suffered so greatly on the 1st that in this charge it was commanded by a captain, and some of the companies were commanded by non-commissioned officers. But the men came up bravely to the measure of their duty and the regiment went as far as any other, on that fatal charge, and we have good proof of the claim that a portion of the regiment led by Captain Satterfield who was killed at this time, reached a point near the Benner barn, which was more advanced than that attained by any other assaulting columns. Lieutenant T D. Falls of company C, residing at Fallstown, Ashland county, and Sergeant Augustus Whitey of company E, residing at Everett's in Martin county who with Captain Satterfield, have recently visited the battlefield, and have made an affidavit as to the point reached by them. The place has been marked by the United States commission. There was eighteen regiments and one battalion from Virginia, sixteen regiments from North Carolina, three regiments from Mississippi, three regiments from Tennessee and one regiment and one battalion from Alabama in the advancing columns.

The contention between Pickett's division and Heth's division, the latter commanded then by Pettigrew, has doubtless arisen from the following:

The portion of the enemy's forces just in front of Pickett's division was behind a low rock wall which terminated at a point just about opposite of Pickett's left. About eighty yards to the rear of this point there was another stone wall which commenced there and ran along by Benner's barn toward the cemetery, and the enemy, instead of containing his line to the right from the termination of the first wall through the field, dropped about eighty yards to the second wall and continued his line behind that. So, to have reached the enemy in our front' we must have marched eighty yards beyond a continuation of their line from point, where Pickett reached the enemy in his front. Some of Pickett's men passed over the first line of the enemy and a few of them reached a point some forty yards in the rear of the line and near the federal battery.

Some of our regiment reached a point within nine yards of the rock wall in front of us. That was seventy-three yards beyond a continuation of the line of the first wall, and allowing two yards for the thickness of the first wall, beyond the rock wall to points reached by some of Pickett's men and running a line parallel with the first wall so as to strike the most advanced point reached by Pickett's men, and continuing beyond to the advanced point reached by the men of the Fifty-fifth regiment, it will be found that the latter points is thirty-one yards in advance of that line.

The Fifty-fifth regiment was a part of the rear guard on the retreat, and in the attack made upon them at Falling Waters they lost several killed and wounded. The loss of the regiment at Gettysburg amounted to sixty-four killed and 172 wounded, including the few casualties at Falling Waters and the number of captured about 200, added to these, made an aggregate of more than one-half the number of men in the regiment. All of the field officers and all of the captains were either killed, wounded or captured. Lieutenant M. C. Stevens of company G was the ranking officer and commanding the regiment on the retreat until it reached Falling Waters, when Captain Whitehead had sufficiently recovered from his wound to take command. Captain R. W. Thomas of company K, however, returned to the regiment soon after we went into camp on the Rapidan and commanded the regiment with great acceptability until Lieutenant-Colonel Belo's return the following winter. In the official report of his division at Gettysburg made by General Heth, and found in the records published by the United States government, Colonel Connelly, Lieutenant-Colonel

Brigadier General Henry Heth. *Library of Congress.*

Smith and Major Bello are particularly mentioned for gallant and meritorious conduct, but Colonel Connelly was so severely wounded that he was never able again to command the regiment. This was a great loss, for he was not only brave and loyal in his support of the southern cause, but his sentiment and conduct were so chivalrous, that he impressed all men and officers of the regiment with his on lofty ideas, and Lieutenant-Colonel Smith was dead. The very soul of honor, he was older and less impetuous than Colonel Connolly, but gentle and refined as a woman; he was conscientious and painstaking in the discharge of every duty and enforced among men the same rigid rule of attention to duty he was prescribed for himself. No hasty utterance and no unclean word ever escaped from his lips, and by his daily life he taught us what a beautiful thing it is to be a Christian gentleman.

Colonel Belo returned to command in January 1864, but he had not entirely recovered from his wound received at Gettysburg. It was made on the leg by a fragment of shell, and in his determination not to be captured he fell back with the army from Gettysburg. A portion of the time he was in much danger of capture that he exposed himself greatly and by the time he reached Winchester the condition of the wound was so serious that for several days it was feared amputation would be necessary.

A. H. Belo, 55th North Carolina Infantry Regiment.
Library of Congress.

THE FARTHEST ADVANCE AT PICKETT'S CHARGE

A. H. BELO
55TH NORTH CAROLINA INFANTRY
Galveston, Texas
Galveston Daily News
June 21, 1896

Battle of Gettysburg

In October last Dr. Wyeth, now of New York, and Colonel A. H. Belo visited Gettysburg, and Major William Robins of the United States battlefield commission devoted two days in taking them over the battlefield. It was noticed that Major Robins had placed three stakes to commemorate the points reached by Lieutenant T. D. Falls, Captain Satterfield and Sergeant J. A. Whitley. These gentlemen have been recognized as having attained the utmost point reached by any Confederate in that fatal charge. Lieutenant Falls was asked to furnish such data on the battlefield as occurred to him and to make a little drawing showing the Benner barn and the locations of the various points of interest on the battlefield. In reply Lieutenant Falls has favored The News with the following letter, giving an account of the visit of himself, Colonel John K. Connally and Sergeant J. A. Whitley to the memorable battlefield of Gettysburg.

A Visit to Gettysburg.

Fallston, N. C. June 1, 1896. Colonel A. H. Belo. – My Dear Friend: having promised you a sketch of our visit to the historical battlefield of Gettysburg, I acknowledge it was certainly the Fifty-fifth North Carolina regiment, for the enemy's line broke our front, and had the line on our right came up we would have carried the day. But just at this juncture Pickett's men broke and fell back, and we, being flanked on the left also, were compelled to retire. After retreating some seventy-five yards I was wounded and captured.

The $1,500,000 which is said to have been expended by the government on this battlefield in the erection of monuments, shafts and statues, makes the place present a grand spectacle to the eye of the visitor as he goes dashing over and around the whole scene on the modern electric cars.

Yes, thirty-two years have fleeted away since that grand and most horrible event, and here and there we meet a survivor whose head and beard are frosted on account of years, some, no doubt, on account of tolls, privations and hardships endured during the four years of warfare. But alas! How many of us will be seen walking about thirty-two years hence. Time flies, but eternity never ends. Is it not of vital importance when the long roll beats to be ready to answer to our name. Let us pause and think. Respectfully.

T. D. Falls

A Letter From Sergeant Whitley,

Sergeant J. A. Whitley of Everetts, N. C., was asked to send The News an account of his recollection of the point reached by him at Gettysburg. The following extract is taken from his letter, writing from Everetts, N. C., under the date of June 8:

"As to the three days' fighting at Gettysburg, our regiment, the Fifty-fifth North Carolina, was a part of the first line. We were supported by the second and third lines. We charged across the field and crossed a road about one hundred yards from the Federal works (a stone fence). Our line was cut down to a mere skirmish line when we got to the works, about thirty feet on the right of that old barn. Our flag had fallen a few yards back. The Yankees had run back to a second stone fence, a hundred or more yards. There was not a Yankee to be seen. We had whipped and repulsed them at this point. I looked back for our support and saw them in full retreat, at least 150 yards from me. Captain Satterfield was the only man I saw near me on my left. He and I started a few paces back, when a shell from our batteries that were protecting the retreat of the second and third lines fell just in front of him, exploded and literally tore him to pieces. I fell behind a small elm, and was soon ordered to surrender. I am satisfied we had whipped the Yankees and if our support had come up we would have gained a victory. It was a great mistake to retreat after the enemy had run. I can only speak for our part of the line. I know that there was not a Yankee behind that rock fence when I got to it. I hope the history now being prepared will do us justice, for many of us have never yet received justice in history."

Fifty-Fifth North Carolina
History of Regiment and Officers-Positions Occupied at Gettysburg.

The Fifty-fifth North Carolina regiment was organized the 6th day of May, 1862, at Camp Mangum, near Raleigh, N. C. The companies composing the regiment were company A, from Wilson county, William J. Bullock, captain; company B, Wilks county, Abner S. Caloway, captain; company C, Cleveland county, Dickson Falls, captain; company D, Cleveland county, Silas D. Randall, captain; company E, Pitt county, James T. Whitehead, captain; company F, composed of men from Cleveland, Burke and Catawba counties; Peter M. Mull, captain; company G, Johnson county, J. P. Williams, captain; company H, Alexander and Onslow counties, Vandever Tegue, captain; company I, Franklin county, Wilson H. Williams, captain; company K, Granville county, Mauris T. Smith, captain.

John K. Connally of Yadkin county was elected colonel; Abner S. Caloway, captain of company B, was elected lieutenant colonel; and Captain James T. Whitehead of company E was elected major. William H. Young of Granville county was appointed adjutant.

The regiment spent several weeks at Camp Magnum drilling and went from there to Kinsten, N. C. Lieutenant Colonel Caloway resigned and Major Whitehead died. Captain Maurice T. Smith was made lieutenant colonel. And A. H. Belo of Salem, who commanded a company in the eleventh regiment, North Carolina volunteers, was made major. Colonel Smith was killed at Gettysburg, and Major Belo became lieutenant colonel, and upon the resignation of Colonel Connally on account of severe wounds, Lieutenant Colonel Below became colonel. Adjutant Young resigned in November 1862, and Henry T. Jordan of Person county was appointed adjutant and was captured at Gettysburg. whose place was filled by Lieutenant C. M. Cook until the surrender at Appomattox. The senior captain being also a prisoner, there was no other regular field officers appointed.

The regiment did full service during the summer, fall and winter of 1862 in eastern North Carolina, Petersburg and Black Water, Va., where it formed into a brigade with the Second, Eleventh and Forty-second Mississippi regiments. General Joseph R. J. Davis was assigned to its command. About June 1, 1862, the regiment with the brigade was ordered to join the army of Northern Virginia. When the Fifty-fifth regiment left the cars at Hamilton's crossing, near Fredericksburg, to take its place in its brigade in Heth's division, A. P. Hill's corps of the army of Northern Virginia, it was both in respect to its discipline and its appearance, one of the finest regiments in the army. Colonel Connally was a fine tactician and was without a superior as a disciplinarian. He was admirable on the field in his handling of his regiment. He had faithfully improved the time spent in eastern North Carolina and Virginia, and while at Petersburg drilling. The regimental band, composed of seventeen pieces, led by Prof. Charles E. Jackey, endured at Heidelburg, was a very fine band. The men of the regiment were well clad and the ranks of each company were full. It was well officered and all had full confidence in its field officers.

The company officers were splendidly dressed, as far as a grand parade, its field officers mounted on fiery chargers, and its magnificent band playing first "Dixie" and then "Maryland My Maryland," presented one circumstance of war, that is its pomp, and if not is most impressive, certainly its least horrible. Little did it occur to any of us that the aspect of this organization would be so completely and unhappily changed within a few weeks. The regiment crossed the Potomac in fine spirits, and when it reached Cashtown on the night of June 29 it was in splendid condition. The regiment marched out of Cashtown early on the morning of July 1, going down the Chambersburg pike toward Gettysburg, and came in sight of that town about 9 a. m. The union forces were on the ridge, just outside of the town, and formed across the pike to dispute our advance. Marye's battery was placed by General Heth in position, and opened fire on the enemy. Our (Davis') brigade was immediately thrown into line of battle on the north side of the road, and was ordered forward about the same time. The Fifty-fifth regiment was on the left of the brigade, and owing to the character of the ground was the first to come into view of the enemy and receive the first fire. Two men in the color guard of the regiment received wounds by this volley.

The Fifty-fifth immediately returned the fire, inflicting considerable loss upon the Fifty-sixth Pennsylvania regiment. The regiments were the Fifty-sixth Pennsylvania, Seventy-sixth New York and the Hundred and Forty-Seventh New York of Cuther's brigade. After the enemy's position became known by their first fire, our brigade charged them in magnificent style. The left of our Fifty-fifth regiment extended considerably beyond the right of the enemy's line, and at the proper time Colonel Connally seized the colors (Sergeant Galloway being shot down) and bore them aloft, at the same time wheeling the regiment to the right. This conspicuous display of the Colonel's military strategy and of his gallantry drew upon him and the color guard the fire of the enemy, and he fell badly wounded in the arm and hip. His arm was afterward amputated. Major Belo, who was near him at the time, rushed up and asked him if he was badly wounded. Colonel Connally replied: "Yes, but do not pay any attention to me; take the colors and keep ahead of the Mississippians.

The enemy fled from the field with great loss, and while in hot pursuit of them by our brigade a flanking column appeared from out of the woods west of the seminary and to our right. The brigade swung around by the right wheel and formed on the railroad cut, about one-half of the Fifty-fifth regiment being on the left extended beyond the cut on the embankment. In front of us there then were the Ninety-fifth and Eighty-fourth New York, known as the Brooklyn regiments, who had been supporting Hall's battery, and were the other two regiments of Cutter's brigade and Sixth Wisconsin of the Iron brigade, which had been held in reserve, when the other regiments of that brigade were put in to meet Archer's advance on the right. Just then the order was given to retire through the railroad cut and that the Fifty-fifth North Carolina cover the retreat of the brigade. The Federal regiments in front of us seeing a disposition on our part to retire charged. They were held in check by the Fifty-fifth North Carolina regiments as well as could be done, a part of the regiment being in the railroad cut and at a great disadvantage. One of the Federal officers in the embankment, seeing Major Belo in the cut threw his sword at him, saying: "Kill that officer and that will end it." Major Belo directed a man to shoot the officer, which was promptly done by Zaph Lawrence of company C, the officer rolling down the embankment at Lawrence's feet.

This somewhat checked their charge and we retired through the railroad cut to another position. The loss of the regiment was very great in killed and wounded and a large number were captured in the railroad cut.

From that time until 3 o'clock in the evening there was a lull. About that time General Early came in with fresh troops from the left. We formed in line with them on their right and drove the enemy from that field and at sun down we were on the edge of Gettysburg and the regiment was placed behind the railroad embankment just in front of the seminary. Just at this juncture, while taking this position a fragment of a shell struck Major Belo in the leg, inflicting a very painful wound.

In the afternoon Lieutenant Colonel Smith – while the regiment was waiting in reserve – walked toward the right to reconnoiter and was mortally wounded and died that night. Our (Davis) brigade was moved during the night from its position on the railroad near the seminary to a piece of woods across Willoughby Run, west of the mineral springs, and there rested during the 2d. On the night of the 2d it was moved to its position on the Confederate line, known as Seminary Ridge, and stationed in McWillow's woods. One division being on the left of Longstreet and our brigade being the left center of our division. General Heath being wounded on the 1st, General Pettigrew commanded our division. General Pickett's division of Longstreet's corps was on the right of our division. And it was from these positions that we moved out to that last fatal charge on the afternoon of July 2, 1863. Our division was not supporting Longstreet's as has been repeatedly published, but was on line with his troops and the Fifty-fifth regiment had suffered so greatly on the 1st that in this charge it was commanded by a captain and some of the company's non-commissioned officers.

But the men came up to the measure of their duty bravely, and the Fifty-fifth went as far as any other on that fatal charge, and we have good proof of the claim that a portion of the regiment led by Captain Sutterfield who fell within nine yards of the enemy's stone wall with colors in hand, reached a point near the Benner barn which was more advanced than the position attained by another of the assaulting column. Lieutenant T. D. Falls of company C, residing at Fallston in Cleveland county, and Sergeant Augustus Whitney of company E, residing at Everetts, Martin county, N. C., who were with Captain Sutterfield, have recently visited the battlefield and have made affidavits as to the point reached by them. The place has been marked by the United States commission, and a map drawn showing the points reached by these men of the Fifty-fifth regiment in relation to other known objects on the battlefield, such as the Benner barn and the bronze book, which marks the high water mark of the struggle for southern independence.

The contention between Pickett's division and Heath's division, the latter commanded by Pettigrew, has doubtless arisen from the following: The portion of the enemy's forces just in front of Pickett's division was behind a low rock wall which terminated at a point just about opposite of Pickett's left. About eighty yards to the rear of this point there was another stone wall, which commenced there and ran along by Benner's barn toward the cemetery, and the enemy, instead of continuing his line to his right from the termination of the first wall, and through the field, dropped eighty yards to the second wall and continued his line behind that. So to have reached the enemy in our front, we must have marched eighty yards beyond a continuation of their line from the point where Pickett reached the enemy on his front. Some of Pickett's men passed over the first wall and a few of them reached a point some forty yards in the rear of the line and near the Federal battery. Some of our regiment reached a point within nine yards of the rock wall in front of us. That was seventy-three yards beyond a continuation of the line of the first wall, and adding to that the forty yards beyond the rock wall to the point reached by some of Pickett's men, and running a line parallel with the first wall so as to strike the most advanced point reached by Pickett's men of the Fifty-fifth North Carolina regiment, it will be found that the latter point is thirty-one yards in advance of that line.

In regard to the foregoing Lieutenant Falls writes: "The above is a part of Cook's history of the regiment, all of which is correct. I have omitted some minor incidents that he gives and supplied some he does not give. In addition to the above statements it must be added that the Fifty-fifth had broken the enemy's line and never thought of falling back until we received the order from our right to fall back. It was then we discovered that Pickett's men were retreating in bad order and the enemy in pursuit. The Fifty-fifth had the enemy driven from behind the wall, but to save being cut off by Pickett's pursuers we were forced to retreat, and after retreating some seventy-five yards I was wounded by a cross fire from the enemy.

"Furthermore: When Colonel Connally, Sergeant Whitley and myself visited the battle field the 3d day of last July, we met at the wall three ex-United States soldiers of the Forty-second New York, who came there that day (the thirty-second anniversary of the battle) to view the old scenes, who said they stood immediately opposite where Captain Satterfield fell and that we came to a point (pointing down within ten feet of the rock wall) and that they had thinned out our lines until it was but a mere skirmish line; that as their shell and shot would ploy furrows through our ranks they were as quickly closed up and that we came rushing on undaunted. Such gallantry they never had witnessed as that displayed by the Fifty-fifth on that charge of 1500 yards across the open plain.[3]

CONFEDERATE VICTORY WAS NOT MEANT TO BE

A. H. BELO
55TH NORTH CAROLINA INFANTRY
Galveston, Texas
Galveston Daily News
February 25, 1900

The Battle of Gettysburg
Reminiscence Of The Sanguinary Conflict Related By One Who Was There.
Stirring Scenes And Valiant Deeds. – Major Robbin's Letter About the Gettysburg of Today.
Lent from Archives of Camp Sterling Price.
   (*Extracts from the minutes of the meeting of Sterling Price Camp, Jan 19, 1900.*)
   Comrade A. T. Watts stated that in response to the request of the camp he had called upon Comrade A. H. Belo and solicited him to prepare for the benefit of the camp a paper meeting his experiences of the Battle of Gettysburg and presented as the reply a very interesting history related to that battle and the part enacted by the Fifty-Fifth North Carolina infantry, which was under his command. The paper is so much consequence as history and so interesting in the detail that the adjutant was instructed to procure its publication in *The Dallas News* and the Times-Herald if possible.

---

3   Handbook of Texas Online, George B. Dealey, "Belo, Alfred Horatio", Handbook of Texas Online, George B. Dealey, "Belo, Alfred Horatio," accessed, January 17, 2017, http://www.tshaonline.org/handbook/online/articles/fbe44. Alfred Horatio (A. H.) Bello (May 1839 – April 19, 1901) was born in Salem, North Carolina. In 1861, he joined the 55th Carolina Infantry Regiment and rose in rank to colonel of the regiment. He was wounded at the Battle of Gettysburg and at Cold Harbor. After the war, he moved to Houston, Texas and became a partner with Willard Richardson and published the *Galveston Daily News* and the *Texas Almanac*. They founded the company *Richardson, Belo and Co.*, and after Richardson's death, Belo became the sole owner and renamed the company, *A. H. Belo & Co.*
   In 1885, Belo founded the *Dallas Morning Newspaper,* which was the first newspaper of an eventual newspaper chain he would own. He married Nettie Ennis, and they had one son. Colonel Belo died on April 19, 1901 in his family's summer home in Ashville North Carolina. Belo had never fully recovered from his battle wounds and sought comfort and relief many months out of the year outside of Texas.

Thanks of the camp were also tendered Col Belo for his valuable contribution.

Sterling Price Camp, U.C.V. Dallas, Tex. – Comrades: In response to your request, so graciously presented by Judge Watts, I will give you some reminiscences of the Battle of Gettysburg.

After the battle of Chancellorsville, Gen Lee spent some time in reorganizing the army into three corps, commanded respectively by Gen. Longstreet, A. P. Hill and Ewell, and sometime in June Ewell's column, taking the left of the line, we advanced into Maryland.

It was an army of veterans – an army that had in two years' time made a record second to none for successful fighting and hard marching. What a contrast between the enthusiastic volunteers who fought at Bull Run in 1861 and his army of trained veterans marching into the enemy's country. As a writer describing the second crusade said: "It was a goodly sight and every man's heart was lightened and his courage strengthened as he felt that he himself had his share and part of the glorious whole." Gen. Alexander, in the Century War Book, writes: "Except in equipment, a better army nerved up to its work, never marched to a battlefield."

Gen. Ewell proceeded to within a few miles of Harrisburg, Pa., and had that city within his grasp when he was recalled to join Lee at Gettysburg. Gen. A. P. Hill's corps, to which I belonged, passed through Hagerstown, Md., and Gen Heth's division camped at Cashtown on June 29.

Gen. Lee's headquarters were near us and Gen. Henry Heth asked permission to send one brigade into Gettysburg on the morning of June 30 to get a supply of shoes. He sent Pettigrew's North Carolina brigade, but they found the town occupied by what they thought was militia, and having instructions not to precipitate a fight, withdrew. Gen. Heth then asked permission from Gen. Lee to send two brigades the next day,, which was granted, but he has told me several times after the war that Gen. Lee felt very solicitous about the movements of the enemy, as Gen. Stuart, commanding the cavalry, had gone on a raid near Washington and left Gen. Lee, as he remarked, "without my eyes." Heretofore his cavalry had not only partially veiled his own movements, but had afforded valuable information as to the movements of the enemy.

However, on the morning of July 1, Gen. Heth ordered Davis' and Archer's brigades to advance upon the town, and about 9 o'clock we passed Pettigrew's brigade. In conversation some of the officers said we would find militia in town. We had not advance very far before we were ordered to throw out a line of skirmishers and immediately after that the first gun was fired by Marye's battery and was responded to by Hall's battery on the Federal side.

The Fifty-fifth North Carolina was to the left of the line and as the cavalry was threatening them, a company was thrown out to protect our left flank. In this way we advanced with continual skirmishing line of battle following closely afterward. After crossing Willoughby Run the firing became very heavy and the order to charge with bayonets was given, and we started with a yell. Col. Connolly commanding the regiment, fell seriously wounded, and I went to him and asked him if he was badly hurt. He said, "Yes but the liter-bearers are here; go on and don't let the Mississippians ahead of you."

We soon broke the Federal line, which was well marked by their dead and wounded. The first wounded man I asked replied, "We are Joe Hooker's men and have marched five miles this morning," so I told one of my officers that we had struck the regular army and not the militia. This Federal force was Cutler's brigade and it was completely routed. In the meantime Archer's brigade on our right had met the "Iron Brigade," commanded by Gen. Reynolds who was killed in that first engagement.

After the repulse of Cutler's brigade we continued our advance and soon saw another Federal force coming on the battlefield, one regiment which proved to be the Sixth Wisconsin, marching at right angles with us. They formed a line of battle and changed front to meet us. They formed a line of battle and changed front to meet us and at the same time were joined by the Ninety-Fifth New York and the Fourteenth Brooklyn.

I was so impressed with the fact that the side charging first would hold the field that I suggested to Major Blair, commanding the Second Mississippi on my right, that we should charge them before they had their formation completed. He agreed to this, but just at that time we received orders to form a new alignment. At the same time the Federals, taking advantage of this, were advancing and before our new alignment could be completed, charged up to the railroad cut. One officer, seeing me, threw his sword at me and said, "Kill that officer and we will capture that command." One of my men, however, picked him off and we were able to get out of the railroad cut after a severe struggle.

The following extract from the report of Col. Rufus R. Dawes will show the loss he sustained in that short time, and strange to say, he and Major Pye had the same conversation as Major Blair and myself about the successful charge.

Extract from report of Col. Rufus R. Dawes, commanding Sixth Wisconsin regiment:

"I was not aware of the existence of the railroad cut and at first mistook the maneuver of the enemy for retreat, but was undeceived by the heavy fire, which they at once began to pour upon us from their cover in the cut. Capt. John Parkham, always a dashing leader, fell dead while climbing the second fence, and many were struck on the fences, but the line pushed on. When over the fences and in the field, subjected to an infernal fire. I first saw they Ninety-Fifth New York regiment coming gallantly into line upon our left. I did not then know or care where they came from, but was rejoiced to see them. Farther to the left was the Fourteenth Brooklyn regiment, but I was then ignorant of the fact. Major Edward Pye appeared to be in command of the Ninety-Fifth New York. Running to the major I said, "We must charge." The gallant Major replied: 'Charge it is.' 'Forward charge!' was the order I gave, and Major Pye gave the same command. We were receiving a fearfully destructive fire from the hidden enemy. Men who had been shot were leaving the ranks in crowds. With the colors at the advance point, the regiment firmly and hurriedly moved forward, while the whole field behind streamed with men who had been shot, and who were struggling to the rear or sinking in death upon the ground. The only commands I gave as we advanced were: 'Align on the colors!' 'Close up on the colors.' The regiment as being so broken up that this order alone could hold the body together. Meanwhile, the colors fell upon the ground several times, but were raised again by the heroes of the color guard. Four hundred and twenty men started in the regiment from the turnpike fence, of whom about 210 reached the railroad cut. Years afterward I found the distance passed over to be 175 paces.

The Federals did not advance beyond the railroad cut, and our new alignment complete, there was a comparative lull in the fighting until Ewell's corps, coming in to our left, formed a junction with us. The fighting was then resumed and kept on during the whole afternoon, resulting in our complete defeat of the First and Eleventh corps of the Federal army, and our capturing 4,000 or 5,000 prisoners.

During the night both sides were occupied in bringing up reinforcements. Gen. Pendleton, commanding the artillery, told me in Galveston since the war that on the evening of the second day he was on the advance line and sent courier after courier back to Gen. Lee, with information as to the Federal troops coming up and urging immediate attack on our part. He says Gen. Lee gave these orders, but for some reason they were not carried out.

So, the morning of the 2d of July past, the Confederates occupied Seminary Ridge and the Federals Cemetery Ridge. In the afternoon heavy fighting at different points, without much connection, continued all around the base from Culp's Hill to Little Round Top. Gen. Lee stated the results. "We attempted to dislodge the enemy and gained some ground. We were unable to get possession of their position." Gen. Meade's report to Gen. Halleck that night said: "The enemy attacked me about 4 p.m., this day, and after one of the fiercest contests of the war, was repulsed at all points. We have suffered considerably in killed and wounded." In the fourth volume of Roade's history of the United States, just published, he states: "The feeling among the officers in Meade's camp that night was one of gloom. On the first day of the battle the First and Eleventh corps had almost been annihilated. On the second day the fifth and part of the Second had been shattered, and the Third, in language of its commander, who succeeded Sickles, was "used up," and not in condition to fight. The loss of the army had been 20,000 men, only the Sixth and Twelfth corps were fresh."

The Attack of Johnson's Division, C.S.A., on Culp's Hill. Edwin Forbes. *Library of Congress.*

The morning of July 3 opened with an attack on the right of the Federal line and then there was a lull until about 10 o'clock, when the artillery duel began, in which over 200 cannon participated, and, as a celebrated general said, "It was a terrific and appalling cannonade." The lines of battle were about a mile apart, and the infantry felt that they would have to charge across that space.

You have doubtless read of the famous charge in which 30,000 men from Longstreet's and Hill's corps marched steadily and coolly against the storm of canister shot, shell and the enemy's bullets, and in the final assault, remember the words of the immortal Armistead as he leaped the stone wall, waved his sword with his hat on it, and said: "Give them the cold steel boys," before he fell, mortally wounded.

Gen. Hancock, who was said to be the best tactician of the Federal army, was in command at that immediate point, and in his report to General Meade said: "I have never seen a more formidable attack. The enemy must be out of ammunition, as I was shot with a ten-penny nail."

And here I will state that my regiment, though it had suffered severely from the two days fighting, was in the final charge and three members of it, namely Capt. Whitehead, Lieut. Falls and Sergt. Whittlesey, reached the extreme point of the Confederate advance on that fatal day. Capt. Whitehead was killed by a shell from our own batteries striking him in the breast, but the other two are still living. A few years ago Lieut. Falls and Sergt. Whittlesey visited the battlefield with Major W. M. Robbins of the commission and located the exact spot which they reached, which is about eighty yards to the left and beyond the point where Armistead fell. By a strange coincidence on that very day some survivors of the Federal regiment stationed at that point on July 3 were visiting the battle- field and confirmed the statements of Lieut. Falls and Sergt. Whittlesey, stating that they saw three men, and pointing at the spot where Capt. Whitehead fell. With this evidence, which was conclusive, the Commission has placed three stakes to mark the point, and to the Fifty-fifth North Carolina reg- iment belongs the credit not only having opened the fight on the first day, but of having reached the farthest point of advance on the first.

After the repulse of the charge those who could fall back to our original line on Seminary Ridge. Lt. Col. Freemantle, an English officer, in his diary says: "Gen. Lee rode up to encourage and rally his troops and said to me, "this has been a sad day for us, Colonel – a sad day; but we can- not always expect to gain victories." An officer reported the state of his brigade and Gen. Lee immediately shook hands with him and said, "Never mind General, all this has been my fault, and you must help me out of it the best you can." However, after the war Gen. Lee declared, "Had I had Stonewall Jackson at Gettysburg, I would have won a great victory."

The respective forces engaged in this battle were: Confederate 70,0000, Federal 92,000. The losses, according to the official returns published in the Century War Book, were: Confederate killed, wounded, captured and missing: 20,451: Federal killed, wounded, captured and missing 23,892.

Twenty-five years after the battle, I visited the field at the request of Col. Bacheler and Major W. M. Robbins of the Commission. Col. Bacheler was a graduate of West Point, in the summer of 1863, he went to Gettysburg and had spent a great deal of time in getting up statistics relative to the three days' battle. He told me that he did not know of any other battlefield that afforded so much food for thought and study in a military man as the Battle of Gettysburg.

We deviled two days to visiting all parts of the field. On the morning of the first day we stated where my regiment first field off to the left of the Cashtown rad and formed its line of battle. We then walked over the ground where Cutler's brigade was shattered to the fatal railroad cut and went over all the details of that fierce struggle, and then took up the line where Ewell joined us and where the battle raged so fiercely all the day, finally winding up in Gettysburg, where Gen. Lee had his headquarters on the night of July 1.

The following morning bright and early we drove out to the extreme left of the Confederate line and looked over the ground fought over on the afternoon of that day, from Culp's Hill to Gettysburg. After dinner we followed the line of the extreme Confederate right and heard Major Robbins' description of the gallant action of Hood's division at little Round Top. Finally we walked over the ground of the charge of the last day and on reaching that point we found a large bronze book containing all the regiments and brigades participating in that dreadful contest. How peaceful this was, compared to the same time so many years ago.

That night at supper, after having discussed so many details of the battle I said to Major Robbins: "What are your conclusions after your investigations?" he said, "We were very near victory several times, but I have concluded that God Almighty did not intend it."

Within the past few days I have received a letter from the gallant Major, who has since the war has been a member of Congress from North Carolina, and is now a member of the Commission. As it gives the latest information concerning what is being done at Gettysburg. I will, in conclusion, read you his letter:

"Statesville, N. C., Jan. 10, 1900. – Col. A. H. Belo: My Dear Colonel – your favor of the instant is just received – forwarded from Gettysburg to my name here, where I am on a visit. In mid-winter we can do little outdoor work on the battlefield, and office work, such as preparing inscriptions, etc., with the war records before me, can be as well done here.

"We have not yet published any map of the Gettysburg Park and battlefield. We have been much delayed at our work by the difficulty of procuring of the Government, from some of the land owners, the title of lands embracing very important parts of the battlefield, having been compelled to resort to condemnation proceedings in the courts, wherein every possible quibble is interjected in or to plan out the cases, and swindle Uncle Sam. The Georgians and Tennesseans freely donate the lands needed for avenues, etc., at Chickamauga and Chattanooga, so Gen. Boynton informs us, but we are far from making it so at Gettysburg.

"The lines and positions of the Union volunteers have nearly all been marked by the states of the North. The main purpose of the United States Government is taking charge of this field was to have something done for the Confederates and the Union regulars, and also to have common roads and avenues constructed so as to make all parts of the field easily accessible. We are making good progress with this work, but have not yet felt prepared to publish any official map of the field or history of the great conflict that made it memorable. We have in course of preparation a map showing it fully down to the smallest details and with all possible accuracy.

"You express a wish to have an account of my personal experiences on the battlefield, etc. Well, all old soldiers, I believe, are fond of fighting their battles over again, and I should prefer to do so by word of mouth. If only I could have the great pleasure of being with you face to face. I enjoyed very much your visit to Gettysburg and should be delighted to have you come again and go over the field with me. You should find many improvements made since you were here: excellent Telford avenue battle lines, one running right along where your Mississippi and North Carolina have encountered and beat Cutler's New York and Pennsylvania brigade: many maintained tablets showing the positions and recounting in brief and terse terms the movements and achievements of Confederate commands in the battle. A great many guns on iron gun carriages, showing the positions of Confederate batteries, the guns being of the same class and caliber of those which the comparable batteries were contained, five iron tablets, 15 feet high, one at the northwest corner of the field overlooking the ground where you fought one on the Confederate line towards its right flank, one on Culp's Hill, one on Big Round Top and one in the center of the field, near where the final assault of the third day was so gallantly made and so tragically ended. Do come and see us again and let me show you over the field, and ring with you some of those heroic Texans of Robertson's brigade, by whose side we Alabamians fought against Round Top and Devil's Den, but Round Top ran up too much toward Heaven, and we didn't seem to make quite as good progress in that direction.

"As to my own part in the battle, I was acting Major of the Fourth Alabama regiment of Law's brigade, Hood's division. On the 1st day of July the rest of the division marched to the vicinity of Gettysburg, but our brigade was left on outpost duty at New Guilford, in Franklin County, twenty-five miles from Gettysburg. At 3 o'clock a. m. July 2 we were informed that a battle was raging there and were ordered to hasten to it on a forced march. We joined our division there, formed battle line on the extreme right of the Confederate army at 4 p. m., one mile west of Round Top, and were ordered forward at once to attack that strong position. Two of our regiments, the Forty-Fourth and Forty-Eighth Alabama, were obliqued to their left and assisted the First Texas and Third Arkansas in capturing Devil's Den and the adjacent rocky ridge. The other three regiments, Fourth Fifteenth and Forty-seventh Alabama, together with the Fourth and Fifth Texas moved against Little Round Top. I have always believed we would have taken it if we had not been so fagged out by our long, forced march on that broiling July day; and moreover, we had to climb over the steep and ragged spur of Little Round Top before reaching the foot of Little Round Top, on the summit of which was the enemy's main line. When we arrived there many of our poor fellows were fainting and falling, overcome with heat and weariness, and in spite of exhortations from their officers, the men in line felt that they must lie down and rest awhile before making that second climb and storming the enemy's position on the crest. Thus our line stopped its advance, lay down among the rocks and boulders and simply returned the fire of the enemy. Momentum was gone, and, though they kept up the conflict till nightfall, they never went much beyond the point reached in their first effort. You know about where that was, for I showed you in the boulder near where I stood, at the right flank of the Fourth Alabama, while the leaden hail-storm poured down upon us and filled my eyes with grit and gravel, knocked off the big rocks about me.

"Fate was against us there, if the attack on Little Round Top had been made twenty minutes earlier it would have been taken without opposition. I spent two hours last summer with ex-Gov. Chamberlain of Maine, going over the ground of our fight there at Little Round Top. He commanded the Twentieth Maine regiment of Vincent's brigade in that fight and the position of his regiment was partly in front of the Fourth Alabama. He and I remembered the conflict and its various features and incidents precisely alike, and the point where he himself stood in the heat of the battle is about fifty yards only from my own position. He assured me that his regiment and its brigade had not been there more than fifteen minutes before our fire opened and that if our attack had been twenty minutes earlier we should have found Little Round Top undefended. Anyone can see now that this little mountain, on the extreme left of the Union line, was the key to the battlefield, and if the Confederates had seized it and dragged some of their artillery up there, as they easily could have done, they would have enfiladed Meade's entire line and made it too unhealthy for him to remain there, but it was not so deemed by the All-wise.

"We Alabamians and our Texas comrades lay on the western slope of Big Round Top all day July 3, and the breastwork of stone which the boys with their own hands threw up there is standing yet just as they left it. You may know it makes an "old reb" like me feel his heart swell and his eyes moisten somewhat as he walks about there now and then all alone. We were idle all that day, except some encounters with the Federal cavalry hanging on the right flank of our army. Gen. Farnsworth with some regiments broke through the picket line and galloped up into Plum Run Valley in our rear that afternoon. The Fourth and Fifteenth Alabama were ordered to face about and charge down the lower slopes of Big Round Top to repel this cavalry, which we did without difficulty in a few minutes. A volley was fired which killed Gen. Farnsworth's horse and brought him down mortally wounded, and as a squad of Alabamians approached him he pulled a pistol and fired it into his own bosom, killing himself instantly, it is known that he had an altercation with Kilpatrick immediately before that charge in which he urged its futility, and that Kilpatrick spoke to him offensively, saying that if Farnsworth did not wish to lead it, he would lead it himself or find some officer who would, where-upon Farnsworth , with an indignant remark, dashed away at the head of his cavalry, and it has been suggested that the sting of Kilpatrick's remarks may have prompted that final act of suicide. But, as he had five desperate wounds in the breast, it is probable that the agony he suffered from them made him seek immediate death as a relief. As this suicidal act of Gen. Farnsworth has been disputed by some, I deem it proper to say that, while I did not see it myself, I was informed of it in less than an hour afterward by Lieut. Adrian of the Fifteenth Alabama and other men of the highest character who said they did see it and who had no possible motive to fabricate such a story if it were false.

"You know we all resumed our original battle line on Friday night, July 4, and lay there all day Saturday, the 4th waiting for Meade to attack us and give us a chance to pay him back in the same card which he dealt us, to-wit, a repulse. He had stood all the while on the defensive to a position well-nigh impregnatable and with superior numbers, while all the assaults were made by the Con-federates. We wished to turn the board around and try the game that way, but Meade ignored our challenge. Therefore, on Sunday morning, July 5, we turned towards Virginia and after another banter of several days at Hagerstown, which we did not accept, we crossed the pontoon at Falling Waters on July 14 and the Pennsylvania campaign was ended."

A BRAVE COLONEL'S OBITUARY

A. H. BELO
55TH NORTH CAROLINA INFANTRY
Galveston, Texas
Honey Grove Signal
April 26, 1901

Last Stand of the Army of Northern Virginia, commanded by General Lee. Edwin Forbes. *Library of Congress.*

Col A. H. Belo, principal owner of the Galveston-Dallas News, died at Asheville, N. C., last Friday. Of this distinguished man much can be said in praise. He was a brave soldier and at Gettysburg received wounds which rendered practical-ly an invalid during life and finally caused his death. He embarked in the newspaper business at Galves-ton many years ago and two of the greatest dallies in the south are the monuments that speak of his success. He was not a writer, but a manager; a far-seeing, progressive business man. He surrounded himself with the best talent he had and made a paper the people could not want to do without. Texas never had a true friend and his death is mourned throughout the great state for which his papers have labored unceasingly.

Attack of the Louisiana Tigers on a battery of the 11th Corps. Alfred R. Waud. *Library of Congress.*

AN ANGEL OF MERCY

NANNIE H. RIGGS-BLEDSOE
CIVILIAN
Independence, Texas
Daily Eagle
September 6, 1918

A Romantic Reminiscence Of The Civil War

On the first day of July, about 3 o'clock p. m., 1863 there was found on the battlefield of Gettysburg a soldier paralyzed by the passing of a minnie ball through his body and lodging on his spine. Robert August Smith, Company G, Eight Louisiana regiment of infantry, was carried to the improvised field hospital about sundown and the ball was removed from his body. On the third day of July he was removed to an old barn near Emmitsburg, Md., where a temporary hospital was erected for the Louisiana wounded soldiers. On the morning of the fourth of July the Confederate army retreated across the Potomac into Virginia, leaving the wounded soldiers as well provided for as could be under the circumstances.

General Harry T. Hayes, commander of the First Louisiana (Tiger) brigade, passed through the old barn and bid every wounded soldier of his command goodbye. Coming to Smith he was shocked to find that he had been neglected and his wound was not dressed. The general reprimanded the surgeon in charge and ordered him to attend to Smith at once, which he did, very much to Smith's relief and comfort.

About 8 o'clock on the morning of the retreat of the cavalry had a skirmish around the barn and the building was pretty well riddled by the balls but causing no injury done into the inmates.

Pretty soon after, the passing of the cavalry many struggling Yanks passed through the barn, guying and cheering as soldiers do. Mr. Sokoloski, the old German who owned the barn, came in and said to the soldiers the fall of Vicksburg that day; exulting in the failure of the rebels, as he called them.

On the morning of the fifth of July, Miss Annie McBride visited the hospital with Dr. Strickland, who was left with the wounded, to ascertain the needs of the wounded prisoners. When they came to Smith, lying on a bed of straw paralyzed, Dr. Strickland, expressed his surprise at the tenacity with which Smith clung to life. Miss McBride, stooping down and passing her fingers through the bushy locks of the wounded man, remarked, "I will bring you a little Louisiana friend to nurse you tomorrow."

The next day she brought an angel of mercy, Miss Nannie H. Riggs, saying, "Here is your Louisiana friend. She is the daughter of Dr. Jas. R. Riggs, deceased of Millikin Bend, La."

Now when General Grant was besieging Vicksburg he occupied the home of Mrs. Bledsoe a pass to Emmitsburg to be with her children and out of danger till the war was over.

This angel of mercy at once went to work to make her patient as comfortable and as well as possible. The first thing was to clean up, provide clothing and bedding and suitable food.

After being made comfortable, the wounded soldier slept a sweet sleep and dreamed of his widowed mother and little brothers and sisters in the far-off land of the pelican and the magnolia. When he awoke he spoke of mother and home. Then Miss Nannie proposed that he write to his mother and she would see that the letters would pass through the lines to dear mother. She provided the material and held it so he might write the message with his own hand that he was yet alive and under the care of a kind providence and being nursed back to life. That letter did reach the distressed mother and family and was the only word from the boy till he reached home Rienville Parish, La., August 13, 1864, about a year after.

Attending almost daily, bringing suitable nourishment and encouraging cheer, Miss Nannie continued her ministrations till the 20th of July, when those soldiers could be transported were sent to hospitals where they might be provided far more conveniently in the north.

Miss Riggs brought her album and requested Sergeant Smith to write a memento and she gave him her address as Independence, Washington County, Texas, as her future home when the Civil War was over. She gave as a keepsake a talisman, a pearl case, containing a gold pencil, knife, a small cushion and a strand of pearls and a rosary. And when they clasped hands and said the last goodbye there passed to his hand a roll of "greenbacks" to supply his future wants.

Sergeant Smith was carried to the hospital, Devil's Island in New York Bay, where he remained until November 21, 1863.

During the time he corresponded with Miss Riggs and received from her and her mother financial aid. A few days after he was able to walk again he was sent by ship via Fortress Monroe to City Point, Va., thence to Macon, Ga. There he remained visiting relatives and friends until August 3, 1864. He was exchanged in February 1865. During his stay in Georgia he met Miss Annie Gertrude Dunham to whom he married November 22, 1866.

In February, 1867, while they were walking about the yard, they read in a scrap of the New Orleans Current the marriage of Miss Nannie H. Riggs to D. L. Bledsoe.

Mr. Smith "Independence, Washington County, Texas," he at once addressed Mrs. Nannie Riggs-Bledsoe there, requesting the answer from Mrs. Nannie R. Bledsoe, claiming to be the identical lady. In reply to this letter Mr. Smith asked for a copy of the lines written in her album at the barn in Pennsylvania. When it became the identity was complete.

Then came years of correspondence till the Confederate reunion at Dallas when Prof. R. A. Smith visited Mrs. Bledsoe at the home of Mrs. Sarah R. Moore in Bryan. This visit quickened the correspondence and there was an exchange of photos and visits by the children.

Professor Smith and his wife, a charming old lady with snowy locks, are visiting Mrs. Bledsoe and her sister Mrs. Moore.

Verily our good deeds bloom and their fragrance is wafted along the shores of our declining years. True gratitude is the first true love and this is eternal.

FORMER ENEMIES AT GETTYSBURG,
LATER BROTHERS OF THE CLOTH

P. F. BRANNON
15TH ALABAMA INFANTRY
E. J. NEWS
13TH NEW YORK INFANTRY
Galveston, Texas
Galveston Daily News
July 22, 1894

Camp To Sanctuary.
Peculiar Meeting of Soldiers Who Are Now Priests.
Baltimore Sun.

A peculiar meeting of former wearers of the blue and the gray took place yesterday at the Church of the Immaculate Conception, Mosher street, near Druid Hill avenue.

Rev. E. J. News, a former Union soldier, celebrated mass at the church. At the same service the sermon was preached by Rev. P. F. Brannon, a former Confederate drummer boy.

They had been in the opposing armies at Gettysburg and other battles but had never met until Saturday.

Both went from an army of conflict to the army of the church and abandoned their uniforms of blue and gray for the cassocks and stole.

Rev. P. F. Brannon is a native of Alabama, and enlisted in the Fifteenth Alabama Confederate regiment as drummer boy. He was just 13 years old at the time of his enlistment and continued in the service throughout the war. After the war he began his clerical studies and was ordained a priest. He is now in charge of the parish of Weatherford, Parker County, Texas. Early in the summer he came north and has been visiting at Emmitsburg, Md. On his way south he stopped in Baltimore, and on Saturday visited the priest house of the Immaculate Conception church meeting Father News there.

Rev. E. J. News was born in Ireland, but came to the United States when he was 8 years old. He enlisted in company H of the thirteenth New York volunteer regiment in 1862, and served three years. He was a Corporal when mustered out. Although an active participant in nineteen general engagements, Father News was never wounded. His record as a soldier was so good that a warrant as corporal in the regular army was sent for him after he had begun his studies for the priesthood, but he declined the appointment.

Father News studied at Niagara University, New York, and at Germantown Seminary, Pennsylvania, where he was ordained in 1872. After twelve years mission work in Missouri he came to Baltimore and here spent six more years in mission work. One year ago he went to the Immaculate Conception Church, after a year at Germantown in parish work.

The priests found much food for talk in the coincidence of their meeting and former occupation.

PARTICIPATED IN EVERY BATTLE

WILLIAM M. BROWN
1ST ROCKBRIDGE LIGHT ARTILLERY BATTERY
Marlin, Texas
Austin American-Statesman
August 10, 1902

Comrade W. M. Brown was a brave and efficient solder and officer of that grand Army of Northern Virginia, commanded by the peerless Lee. As the first alarm of northern invasion of his native state rang through our land he dropped his collegiate text books and responded to the call of arms. He was one of the first of that bright and brave body of men who organized the Rockbridge artillery, a battery composed of the best blood of Virginia youth and a battery that won renown in every field of battle fought by the Army of Northern Virginia. This battery was commanded by Captain Pendleton, a graduate of West Point, and an Episcopal minister, who became a brigadier general and chief of artillery of the Army of Northern Virginia. This battery, had the honor of firing the first gun in the opening campaign. General Patterson was moving up the battery of Virginia with a splendidly equipped Federal army when his advance was met at the Falling Waters by the Confederate forces and the Rockbridge Artillery opened the fight, Comrade Brown himself firing the first shot.

Comrade Brown was a member of this battery, was in all the engagements of the Army of Northern Virginia, having been wounded at Sharpsburg, but recovering and returning to the army in time to serve his gun at Fredericksburg. Comrade Brown was again wounded at Gettysburg and was captured by the enemy's cavalry, who charged into our unprotected ambulances returning to Virginia filled with wounded soldiers, and he was then a prisoner of war at Johnson's Island until after the close of the war. After his release he returned to his old home in Virginia, but very soon came to Texas and settled in Marlin.

CAPTURED WITH TWENTY MEN AND SIX WAGONS

M. T. BRUCE
18TH VIRGINIA CAVALRY
Dallas, Texas

Enlisted in the Confederate Army June 17, 1863, on the march to Gettysburg, as private in Company E, Eighteenth Virginia Cavalry, Gen. Imboden's Brigade, independent, Army of Northern Virginia. My first Captain was Scott and my first Colonel was George Imboden. Was attached to Capt. John M. NcNeil's company. Was wounded in the face near Clear Spring, Md., on returning from Gettysburg with a foraging party of twenty men and six wagons. Nineteen out of the twenty were wounded. Was taken prison near Cumberland Md., in 1864, and again at Moorefield in 1865, escaping both times. Was made an orderly to Col. Geo. Imboden in 1863. My principal work was in skirmishing and supporting supply trains in surprise attacks and defenses. In these we got many prisoners and horses and other plunder of war.[4]

IN THE HOSPITAL DURING THE BATTLE

ANDREW JACKSON BRUMLEY
44TH ALABAMA INFANTRY
Brownwood, Texas

I was in the hospital during the Battle of Gettysburg. Our company and regiment was in that battle and we lost our Captain John Teague. I tried to do my duty as a soldier.[5]

---

4   Yeary, *boys in gray*, p. 91.
5   Ibid., p. 95.

LONE STAR VALOR

KERR COUNTY'S LAST CONFEDERATE

THOMAS W. BURGE
27TH TEXAS CAVALRY
Albany, Texas
Kerrville Times
November 6, 1941

Kerr's Last Confederate Vet Succumbs
Thomas W. Burge, 99, Who Saw Service in Battle Gettysburg, Buried at Albany

Thomas W. Burge, 99, declared to be Kerr County's last Confederate veteran and a survivor the Battle of Gettysburg, was buried Sunday in Albany, the home of two of his three surviving sons. He was the father of Mrs. R. T. Lee of Kerrville, with whom he made his home the past seven years. His death occurred Thursday of last week in the Confederate Home in Austin, which he entered two months ago.

The venerable Confederate veteran lived to within half a year of the century mark. He was born in the spring of 1842 in Fayette County. During the past seven years he was a familiar figure on the courthouse plaza and at other gathering places of need men. Among his favorite pastime was the relating of tales of Civil War days.

Rites in Albany were held from the Baptist Church and were joined by an American Legion escort of honor. The survivors especially the appreciated the honor paid by World War veterans to a Texas volunteer for the cause of the Old South, one of the rapidly thinning ranks of Civil War soldiers.

The aged man had outlived four of his eight children. The survivors include, in addition to the Kerrville daughter, three sons, Sam and Tom of Albany, and Joe of Odessa; 34 grandchildren and 37 great-grandchildren.[6]

PISTOL READY FOR ACTION YEARS LATER

L. H. BURT
7TH SOUTH CAROLINA INFANTRY
Temple Weekly Times
May 26, 1892

A pistol that was loaded by R H Burt the day before the Battle of Gettysburg was taken out the other day if it would shoot: every chamber fired clear. It was an old cup and ball.

CAPTURED IN THE WAGON TRAIN

JAMES J. CARNES
2ND GEORGIA INFANTRY
Dallas, Texas

Born near Columbus, Ga., where I enlisted in the Confederate Army on April 16, 1861, as private in Company A, Second Georgia Battalion, Wright's Brigade, Mahone's Division, Army of Northern Virginia. I received a slight wound in the right hand at Gettysburg. As the term of our enlistment had expired (we enlisted for twelve months), we went home in April and re-enlisted with the under-

---

6   Thomas H. Burge's service record indicates that he was in the 27th Texas Cavalry regiment was never a regiment in the Army of Northern Virginia or served east of the Mississippi.

standing that we were to still keep our four companies as the Second Georgia Battalion. Our second trip was to Richmond in time for the battle of Seven Pines, then to Fredericksburg, where we met Burnsides on Dec. 12th, where we lost our first man E. A. O'Neal; then to the Wilderness and then to Gettysburg arriving on the 30th of June and began the great fight next morning., the 1st of July 1863. Here I was wounded and captured with the wagon train about the 5th of July, and sent to Fort Delaware. After four months imprisonment I returned in time to be in front of Petersburg on the 7th of February, 1865, and was under fire till the surrender at Appomattox on April 9, 1865.[7]

HARSH LIFE IN A PRISONER-OF-WAR CAMP

C. N. CARPENTER
15TH ALABAMA INFANTRY
Copperas Cove, Texas
Fort Worth Daily Gazette
May 10, 1891

Extract of letter from C. N. Carpenter. Copperas Cove, Tex., "I saw men freeze to death in the winter of '63-64. My feet are yet frost-bitten. I was captured at Gettysburg in '63, weighed in Baltimore on my way to prison 212 pounds, was let loose of the 14th of June, 1864, weighted in Philadelphia eighty seven pounds, not sick but starvation. I never ate rat or dog, but it was because I could not get the article. I saw men die of starvation and cold, freeze to death begging for something to eat as long as they had breath to talk. Can give address of others who will corroborate all this." Mr. C., belonged to Company I, Fifteenth Alabama Volunteer's, Stonewall's corps, and states further that "the half has not been told."

ONLY ONE BLANKET

LEWIS CASH
1ST TENNESSEE
INFANTRY
Forney, Texas

I was wounded at Gettysburg by a shell and was hit by a minie ball in the thigh. Was taken prisoner at Gettysburg. Was not promoted. Was twenty-one months in prison at Fort Delaware and had two hardtacks at a meal. The weather was cold and I suffered all the time I was there, as we had only one blanket to the man.[8]

Tennessee Monument, Gettysburg National Military Park. *Joe Owen.*

---

7   Yeary, *boys in gray*, p. 120.
8   Ibid., p. 128.

CONFEDERATE ESCAPES TO GETTYSBURG

R. D. CHAPMAN
55ᵀᴴ GEORGIA INFANTRY

Houston, TX
Houston, Post
May 7, 1922

At the age of 83, after 20 years intermittent effort, a Houston veteran of the Confederate army is preparing to publish a book, telling his own story of the War Between the States.

Captain R. D. Chapman, well known Houstonian and veteran of the war of '61, has written this book, which is chiefly a vivid account of the old soldier's experiences while fighting in a Georgia regiment against the Union forces during those stirring days.

His days as a soldier on the line, his capture, imprisonment, subsequent escape and service with the Southern army until the surrender are graphically told in Captain Chapman's narrative.

The veteran has an interesting story. Born in Houston County, Ga., on the 8ᵗʰ of December, 1839, the gallant soldier was barely 20 years of age when the war broke out. Casting his lot with the Confederacy, Captain then Lieutenant, Chapman joined company E, 55ᵗʰ Georgia regiment, Confederate States army, under command of the illustrious General Bragg, moving into action against the Federal troops in the early fall of 1862.

The veteran remained with General Bragg's command on the many raiding expeditions this army participated in, being promoted to the rank of captain on the field during one of these raids.

In the late fall of 1862, Captain Chapman, together with the balance of General Bragg's command, retreated to winter quarters at Cumberland Gap, remaining there until taken prisoner when Bragg surrendered to General Burnside of the Union forces after a terrific battle in the early months of 1863.

Captain Chapman was sent to the Union prison on Johnson Island, Lake Erie, where he remained five months, finally being sent from the island to Point Lookout. During the transfer the veteran eluded the vigilance of his captors, escaping through a car window at York, Pa.

Captain Chapman succeeded in remaining at liberty for ten days, during which he worked his way South until he reached the outline of the Southern army.

He returned to active service under General Joseph E. Johnston when that leader was situated in the path of General Sherman's march through Georgia. He was present at the fall of Savannah, engaging in skirmishes against the Federal troops throughout the Carolinas.

The veteran's last battle against the Union forces was at Bentonville, N. C., just before the final surrender of the Confederacy to the Federal army in April, 1865.

Another particularly exciting and interesting chapter in the veteran's book is given to his experiences in the federal prison on Johnson's island and his escape while in transit from the island to Point Lookout. An extract from the book follows.

In Prison.

"We arrived at Johnson's Island September 30, 1863, and were located in block No. 9, among strangers. Prisoners were located according to their date of arrival, hence we were separated from the officers of our regiment who had preceded us. Our prison comrades were mostly Missourians who were captured at Island No. 10. They were very agreeable companions, and some were men of distinction in the persons of Breckenridge and Wooley of Kentucky. Choctaw and others from Indian Territory.

"Johnson's Island was in the southwest part of Lake Erie, between Ohio and Canada, near Sandusky City. The prison enclosure contained seven or eight acres and 2500 or 2600 officers were held as prisoners of war, who were composed of the best talent of the South; the professions of law, physic, theology, mechanism and agriculture were all represented. The prison walls were about 18 feet high, with an elevated parapet on the outside for the sentinel's beat. The walls were made of plank of considerable thickness and strength, the prison quarters were of rough plank on the box house style, about 80 feet by 25 feet, with a partition across the center, a door on each side of the partition and a 10 foot cook room at each end of the building. These buildings were two story; the upper story of the same dimensions and capacity of the lower story; each room accommodated 30 men. A large stove was used for heating each room, and a large cook stove in each cook room. The allowance of the wood in cold weather would last generally until 9 o'clock at night. The sleeping bunks were made out of rough plank, three by six feet, one above from floor to ceiling; a sack of straw in the bunk and two blankets were furnished for each man, and two men slept in one bunk. Our rations were reasonably good for a prison fare, and in sufficient quantity except when the lake would freeze over and the ice began to thaw, so that neither wagons nor boats could travel. At short intervals our rations ran short, our clothing was very insufficient for that climate, and we suffered extremely of cold, some becoming frostbit and many contacting disease, resulting in death. During my stay on the island from September 20 to February 9, 1864, was said to be a period of the coldest weather that had been experienced in many years. The dead house was an awful sight, 20 or 30 men laid out in a frozen state for a week or 10 days and often buried in a watery grave.

R. D. Chapman. 55th Georgia Infantry. *L. E. Basile.*

The escape. "To make my escape more possible, I sought to secure a small saw kept and used in the curiosity shop by an ingenious workman who had collected quite a variety of Tinker's tools; he had two small saws on his work bench, and relying upon his patriotic generosity, I applied to him for one of his saws. My request was promptly met by an insulting denial. I left him in disgust. Soon the federal officer appeared on the parapet over the gate, and commenced calling the roll in alphabetical order, commencing with A. All the prisoners, to whom the order of exit applied, had assembled at the gate, ready, waiting to step out when their names were called. As the roll progressed to bid their departing comrades an affectionate farewell. The Tinker who had refused me the use of one of his saws left his work bench, and went out to see his friends off; taking the advantage of his absence I stepped back to the prison house and swiped both of his saw, placing the saw blade in my shoe quarter and the handle up my pants leg.

"Thus with a Tinker's saw in each pants leg, I bid my friends goodbye, and when my name was called I stepped out with a clear conscience, and should the Tinker every charge me with the theft of his two little saws, I would plead limitation, deny the allegation and demand the proof.

"This was the 9th day of February, 1864. We were marched to the ferry boat, crossed Lake Erie and landed at Sandusky City, under a strong guard and I saw no way of escape.

"Late in the evening we stopped at Harrisburg, Pa., and drew one day's rations. As usual, this day's ration was consumed the first meal. "All plans and efforts to escape had failed, and this was the last night before reaching Point Lookout prison from which there was no chance of escape.

"My determination to escape had not abated; I had learned that 'Eternal vigilance is the price of liberty.'

"Though the night was dark' and cold, and life itself poised upon the perilous venture, yet the light in the window of hope had not grown dim; the irrevocable decree had gone forth and from it there was no appeal. This night must settle the issues of liberty or death.

"I made my intentions known to a few friends. Captain T. I. Ball of Cuthbert, Ga., gave me five dollars in gold; Lieutenant Bowling gave me valuable information as to the geography of the country. He was wounded in the Battle of Gettysburg, and while in the hospital, a party of charitable ladies of Emmetsburg, Md., visited the sick and wounded soldiers at Gettysburg, Pa. Miss Annie McBride, one of the ladies, and Lieutenant Bowling became confidential friends. He gave me her name and informed me that her father was an old Roman Catholic and a true Southern man.

Emmetsburg was about 35 miles from the railroad in a westerly direction, and York, on the Pennsylvania Central, was the place where I expected to escape from the train.

My escape had to be made through the window of the car while in motion. At every stop the guards on the platform would step down and form a line of guard on each side of the train, and when the train started they resumed their places on the platforms. This rendered my escape more perilous, as I could have no choice where or how I would land. It was 1 o'clock at night; most of the prisoners were asleep, but those who were advised of my intention, were wide awake, and it was understood so that they might fix for rest and sleep; and when the whistle blew for York, every fellow commenced spreading down his blanket, and if he didn't have a blanket of his own he got somebody's blanket or overcoat, and joined the blanket brigade. As the train pulled out amid the blanket confusion I slipped out, my left leg and body, holding firmly to the window sill, and in the struggle to keep my head from going first, my right foot refused to clear the window. Thus climbing to the side of the car, head in one side of the window and one foot in the other side, I extended by arms, lowered my body; my foot cleared the window and I turned loose; and the, thunder and lightning, earthquake, dirt, dust and blood – all were in evidence, but my mind was clear and no bones broken. I remained as I had fallen until all the train cars had passed; the fall did not hurt me much as striking the ground, my feet first, then my head, shoulder and arms; they were badly lacerated.

"The excitement of my friends and the guard with uplifted gun glittering in the light, pressing forward, presenting a scene that time can never erase. The train had passed a short distance, the guard reported my escape and the train stopped; another train came approaching me from the rear, reflecting its headlight toward me; I realized my perilous position, arose and retreated rapidly at right angles from the railroad.

"Dazed, dusty and bleeding, the headlight from the approaching train so confused my vision that my progress was quite difficult in the dark. I soon found myself upon the slope of a mountain, overlooking the town. The federal guards came back looking for the escaped prisoner while I was resting securely and watching the movements of their signal lights. They gave up the search, returned to their train and pursued their journey, carrying my comrades to a prison of hopeless despair, where they remained until the end of the war. Truly, I felt, friendless and forsaken. It was the lonely hour of a dark, cold night, February 11, 1864, a lone Confederate soldier had invaded Pennsylvania, flanked the enemy and gained an eminence overlooking the city of York.

A STOUT SOLDIER

JAMES B. CLARK
18ᵀᴴ MISSISSIPPI INFANTRY
Austin, Texas
Daily Texan
January 9, 1909

Enlisting in the 18th Mississippi Regiment, General Barksdale's brigade, he proved himself a stout soldier and served through the entire war. He was present in the battles of Drury's Bluff, Winchester,

Fredericksburg, Antietam and Malvern Hill. When Pickett's Division broke through our center at Gettysburg in the great Friday's fight, Clark was captured but, fortunately unwounded. He spent the next nineteen months as a prisoner of war on Johnson's Island, in Lake Erie, where Tileton and other classmates did what they could to relieve the imprisonment, and he cherished warm remembrance of their kindness. When he was at last exchanged he rejoined General Lee's army in Richmond about a month before the close of the war.

A COMPASSIONATE JUDGE

JAMES B. CLARK
18ᵀᴴ MISSISSIPPI INFANTRY
Austin, Texas
Houston Post-Dispatch
December 28, 1924

Austin, Texas. Dec. 27. – A unique monument to the memory of a man, a memorial in the form of a dinner, is given here every year at the University of Texas by the university Y. M. C. A.

The Judge Clark Christmas dinner as it is known, was originated by Judge James B. Clark, dean of students at the university from its founding in 1883 to the time of his death, some 10 years ago. Since 1913, shortly after Judge Clark's death, the university Y. M. C. A. has had charge of the project, which it has continued each year as a memorial to the originator of the practice.

For many years Judge Clark at his own expense held the banquet in the basement of Breckenridge hall, dormitory for men. When the B. Hall lunch room was closed he transferred the banquet to the Y. M. C. A. building, and this renovation took up the project at his death.

Judge Clark's chief reason for inaugurating the Christmas dinner, outside of his love for the student body, is said to have grown out of an experience during the Civil War. He was captured while serving in the Confederate army, at Gettysburg, in 1863. Nineteen months' imprisonment in a camp at Johnson's Island followed. For five months of that time, Judge Clark later said, he did not know what it was to have his hunger appeased. Putrid meat, and hard, moldy bread were said to be his only rations. He resolved, while in prison, that he would never allow anyone to go hungry if he could prevent it. The Christmas dinner was inaugurated as an expression of his feeling.

TWO GREAT ARMIES

JAMES R. COLE
22ᴺᴰ NORTH CAROLINA INFANTRY
Dallas, Texas
Galveston Daily News
January 13, 1907

On the first day of July 1863, two great armies the best and bravest this world ever saw, commanded by two great Generals were about to grapple in deadly battle on the heights of Gettysburg in Pennsylvania. Each was fighting for the existence of a nation, and the destiny of two great peoples hung upon the bright bayonets of the contending hosts.

Seventy thousand Southern soldiers under Lee and Longstreet and Ewell and Hill and Stuart with Pender, Pettigrew, Hood and Gordon and Pickett were about to seize by the

James R. Cole. *Texas Preservation Board.*

throat 100,000 veterans, from the North commanded by Meade, Hancock, Reynolds, Sedgwick, Slowcum and Sickles. In that Northern army was a brigade called the Iron Brigade of 3,000 men from the great Northwest, brave, bold, strong, powerful who boasted that they had never met their match. They were placed by their General in a very important position, and to hold it at all hazards. They threw back the stern reply: "If we can't do it, who can?" Opposed to this powerful brigade in a long line of battle were four regiments of boys and young men from the farms and hills of North Carolina, 3,000 strong, commanded by one of the finest and most loveable of men, Gen. J Johnston Pettigrew. And now occurred the greatest and most terrible dual that was ever fought in all the ages. One of these regiments from the South of 800 men was commanded by a dark eyed, rosy-cheeked, beardless boy of twenty-one years – Henry Burgynne. Another was commanded by a tall, straight, graceful, polished British nobleman, Col. Leaventhorpe, who had fallen in love with a beautiful girl among the mountains and married her and made his home in the midst of the lovely scenery in Western North Carolina.

Forward went the North Carolinians beautifully uniformed, splendidly disciplined, keeping steps like cadets on parade. Soon the fire began to flash, soon the canons began to roar; soon the rifles began to crack, soon the rebel yell rose in the air. Sternly stood the Iron Brigade like a Gibraltar and the storm of death flashed like lightening from their rifles. Death now rose upon every breeze, heroes fell every second, thunder answered thunder, bullets meet in mid-air and whistled brilliantly dyeing the plain with blood. Onward swept the Carolinians led by Pettigrew and Burgynne and Leaventhorpe. Closer and closer until the red eyes of the North glared into the red eyes of the South and sword clashed against sword and bayonet crossed bayonet and pistol answered pistol. Within thirty paces these lines stood with leveled guns and poured death into each other's faces. Down went the flag of the Twenty-Sixth North Carolina – another man raised it, a bullet went crashing through him; another man seized it; down it went again, down, down, until eleven men had fallen bearing it forward, and Pettigrew's adjutant seized it and immediately fell dead. Then the boy hero, Col Burgynne seized it and waved it aloft and rolled down instantly with the flag winding itself around his dying form; forward rushed the Lieutenant-Colonel to lift the flag from the ground when a Lieutenant cried: "Don't touch that flag, it is death," but he waved it over his head, saying, "it is my time now!"

Will the Iron Brigade never yield – will it? Yes, they gave way, they retreated, the Iron Brigade is broken at last, and a brave Sergeant, as he retreats looks back and sees the towering form of Lieutenant-Colonel Johnson bearing the flag, and taking aim across the limb of a tree sends a bullet crashing through the neck of the Southern officer and he falls in the earth, the fourteenth man that fell carrying the flag of the Twenty-Sixth North Carolina Regiment. Five hundred and eighty-eight men out of 850 in that regiment fell on that battlefield in that frightful duel – but they broke that Iron Brigade. Ah, what a sight was that!, enough to make the angels weep.

The first day of this great battle closed with a great victory of half of the Southern army over half of the Northern army, and thousands of Americans lay dead upon the field around that Pennsylvania village.

A heroic picture rises to my eyes as I gaze upon a long line of noble forms lying in regular battalion formation with a fair-haired boy in their midst so still as though dreaming of his loved ones in Randolph county. Surely they will rise at the sound of the bugle at reveille and charge again upon the countless enemy. No, no! like the old guard of Napoleon, "They sleep their last sleep, they have fought their last battle, no sound can awaken them to glory again."

Two hundred and forty North Carolinians, the second battalion under their boyish Lieutenant Colonel, Lee Andrews, my classmate and college, was placed in line of battle and at nightfall they had met the enemy and held their ground, but oh, pitiful sight, while forty of them were standing with their rifles firmly grasped and their pale faces set, two hundred of them were stretched upon the field bleeding or dead and the boy commander in his bright uniform, with his sword by his side, had given up his life for his country. The shades of night occupied the landscape. Armies from the South and West and North were hurrying the fate of millions of people. As the sun rose over the eastern hills on July 3, 1863, the thunder of cannon echoed along the valleys and ridges as lee hurled his legions against Meade's entrenched hosts and the great Gen. W. D. Pender, young and gallant, was hurled from his horse by a cannon ball as he galloped over the field.

Away to the right, Longstreet was leading his men against Sickles and the hosts occupying the hills and the cannons and the muskets and the rifles were covering the ground with the dead, while the sound of the conflict resembled a battle of contending clouds as lightening flashed and crossed and recrossed and pierced the opposing clouds and thunder answered thunder. Farther to the right Hood the immortal, at the head of his Texans, was charging Little Round Top and was making the century to reel as bayonets crossed bayonets and the rebel yell answered the hoarse thunder of the cannon. But Hood fell and the Texans lost their great leader.

Again the curtain of night came down over the earth and darkness hid the ten thousand heroes, while the air was charged with the shrieks and moans of organized warriors bleeding in the valleys and on the hillsides of Gettysburg.

Call the roll of the Twenty-Sixth North Carolina Regiment. Harry Burgynne's regiment that fought the duel with the Iron Brigade. Eight Hundred and fifty names were called, eighty-six answered. The rest are killed or wounded. Call the roll of Company F. Ninety-one names are called; not a man answered, every one killed or wounded. Who calls the roll? The First Sergeant who sits against a tree with his arm broken. In one company are three sets of twins – at nightfall five of them are dead.

At midnight after that woeful day, two solitary horsemen sat on their steeds in the midst of that great battle strain. Only the dead and wounded were there – the moans and the cries of 30,000 men pierced the air while many thousands lay still in death. One of those horsemen was the leader of the Southern army. His plans had failed; his tremendous efforts were unsuccessful; more than 20,000 of his Southern soldiers had gone down on the bloody battlefield to obey his orders. He saw empire slipping from his grasp. He saw a million of ghosts from a thousand battlefields and a lost cause sinking behind the mountains at Appomattox. Then his head sunk upon his breast and from the depth of a broken heart he cries, "Too bad! too bad! too bad!"

Turning to General Imboden, the other horseman he said, "Gather up the wounded, collect the wagons and ambulances and start them for the Potomac. I place them under your charge," and the next night at the close of the 4th of July, the saddest anniversary of American Independence since 1776, the army of Northern Virginia, under Lee commenced its retreat, preceded by 10,000 wounded.

By day and by night without halting they marched Southward toward the Potomac and over un-availing heroism and sacrifices, but defiant with unabated courage. The rain poured down from the gloomy clouds as though weeping over misfortune. Large stretching miles were crowded with ambulances filled with the wounded, every jolt, every rock producing agony and causing groans and shrieks and cries. In one ambulance side by side lie Pender and Scales, my Major General and Brigadier General, the one mortally wounded and soon to die, and the other to rise again to face the enemy and became Governor of his state. Farther on, tossed from side to side, is the heroic form of Hampton, the great cavalry man, and the bleeding Hood, with his shattered arm; in the other are Belo and Connally, one shot through the body and the other with his arm shot off lay young North Carolinians whom I knew well; and thus the procession climbed the mountains, descended into the valleys – hungry, weary, wounded, groaning, shrieking; and the army, attacked on all sides by the enemies' cavalry and pursued by Meade's great host, bent its head to the storm, and with stern faces marched on, on, and on to the Southland. Stuart at the head of his heroes sternly covered the retreat. Wagons were overturned, dead horses and men marked the bloody route, configuration let up the darkness of the night and thus the army went with Lee, and Longstreet and hill and Ewell and Stuart reached the banks of the Potomac, after a week's dreadful suffering, and found the great river raging and there was no way of rushing and there was no way of crossing. Did they despair? Did they sur-render? They formed a line of battle, planted their artillery and faced about to meet the enemy. A few days and the water subsided, and the heroic army once more stood upon the southern banks of the Potomac. But a hero of heroes had fallen before he had crossed over. Pettigrew the brilliant scholar and warrior, standing between his retreating comrades and the charging enemy, gave up his life for the safety of Lee and his men, and thus fell the man who was victorious in the great duel with the Iron

Brigade. This was the greatest and most terrible battle fought on this side of the globe, for Lee had staked the independence of the South up on the issue and how long and fiercely he and his paladins fought to win the impossible! It is a sorrowful memory to me as I look back through the mists of the years upon those scenes, for Pettigrew was my first Colonel, Scales my Brigadier General, Pender my Major General, and Leaventhorpe my intimate friend. I commanded a regiment in his brigade.

The sun of the Confederacy had reached to meridian as Lee faced Meade at Gettysburg, and it began to descend towards the Western horizon as the steps of the Southern army were turned toward the plains of Virginia. For two years longer the matchless army fought until the guns of the enemy on a hundred more battlefields had covered the land with its dead, and starvation had made an army of skeletons – then the end came, and there was a dead nation.

ONLY THREE OF FIFTY-SIX WERE UNHARMED

W. H. COWAN
2ND MISSISSIPPI INFANTRY
Corsicana, Texas
Corsicana Daily Sun
August 12, 1921

Saw General Bee Shot.

W. H. Cowan of Corsicana was standing near General Bee when that hero uttered the now immortal words, "There stands Jackson like a stone wall." A few minutes afterwards Mr. Cowan saw General Bee shot. He was also with General Whiting when he was killed. Mr. Cowan was with Heft's brigade when Pickett was ordered to charge Hornet's Nest. Heft and his brigade covered Pickett's left. Just as they reached a stone wall ahead of them, Mr. Cowan recalls a young fellow named McGruder who was in the lead turning and calling to the others, "Boys, remember your mothers and sisters at home." Within a few minutes the young man was killed. Mr. Cowan declares that on one day during the war, twenty-two bullets went through his clothing but that he escaped without a wound. At Gettysburg there were fifty-six men in his company, he says all of them were killed, wounded or captured except three.

REMEMBERING GENERAL HOOD'S ATTACK

J. A. CRADDOCK
22ND VIRGINIA INFANTRY
Richmond, Virginia
Times Dispatch
May 14, 1916

It was about 4 P. M. on July 2 that General Longstreet's two divisions advanced to attack. General Hood's division went in first on the extreme right, General McLaw's followed a little later with his division, supported on the left by four brigades of General Anderson's division of the Third corps, under Generals Wilcox, Perry and Posey. The enemy soon was driven from his position

Mississippi Monument, Gettysburg National Military Park. *Joe Owen.*

on the Emmitsburg road to the cover of the ravine and line of stone fences at the foot of the ridge in his rear. The enemy was dislodged from these after a severe struggle, and retired up the ridge, leaving a number of his batteries on our possession. Wilcox's and Wright's brigades advanced with great gallantry, breaking successive lines of the enemy's infantry and compelling him to abandon much of his artillery. General Wilcox reached the foot and General Wright gained the crest of the ridge itself, driving the enemy down the opposite side, but, having become separated from General McLaw's, and gone beyond the other two brigades of the division, they were attacked in front and on both flanks and compelled to retire, being unable to bring up any of the captured artillery. General Hood's brigades on the right had successfully assailed the enemy's lines, and forced them through "Devil's Den," and back for shelter about "Little Round Top." The fighting here was desperate, each side availing itself of the protection of ravines and huge boulders of rock, which gave to the place its euphonious name. We had carried the wheat field and "Devil's Den," and were pressing pieces of artillery, several hundred prisoners, and two regimental flags were captured.

While in these operations the lines of the enemy were forced back on each flank, our lines having been considerably advanced as the result of General Longstreet's attack, more advantageous positions for our artillery were thereby secured, and several hundred prisoners, four pieces of artillery and six stands of colors captured. Still there was a lack of accord and cooperation in the assault of the different columns of attack and no decisive results.

Heavy Losses Among Officers Of High Rank

Our losses were very heavy, especially in officers of high rank. Major-General Hood was wounded early in the action, and Major-General Pender, Brigadier-Generals G. F. Anderson, Barksdale and Semmes, of the First Corps, and J. M. Jones, of the Second Corps, were wounded, Generals Pender, Barksdale and Semmes mortally so. At the close of the day, General Longstreet's command was so disposed as to hold the ground, gained on the right, with his left withdrawn to the first position from which the enemy had been driven, resting at the peach orchard.

A BROKEN FINGER

WALTER LOONEY CRAYTON
2ND MISSISSIPPI INFANTRY
Ennis, Texas

Born, Nov. 18, 1842, at Marietta, Miss. Enlisted in the Confederate Army at Verona, Miss., Oct. 10, 1861, as private in Company C, Second Mississippi Infantry. My first Captain was Bramley, and first Colonel was Faulkner. The middle finger of my right hand was broken at Gettysburg. My company's loss at Gettysburg was thirty-five. I was wounded in the right foot at the battle of the Wilderness. Here we met the Sixteenth Mississippi, which was put half a mile in the rear with orders to wait until they could see the Yankee's eyes and then to fire at once.[9]

SPIKED A CANNON AT LITTLE ROUND TOP

D. M. CRENSHAW
20TH GEORGIA INFANTRY
Waco, Texas

I was in thirty-seven battles, including Gettysburg – and was one of the men who spiked a gun at Little Round Top. Was never commissioned, but was in charge of camp a great many times. [10]

---

9   Ibid., p. 161.
10   Ibid., p. 162.

DIED OF A WOUND FROM GETTYSBURG FORTY FIVE YEARS LATER

CHARLES C. CROSSON
66TH PENNSYLVANIA INFANTRY
San Antonio, Texas
Bastrop Adviser
March 24, 1906

Major Charles C. Crosson, U. S. A., retired, died at San Antonio from an operation of a wound received at the Battle of Gettysburg. He enlisted as a Second Lieutenant in the Sixty Sixth Pennsylvania Infantry, Aug. 3, 1861.

EMOTIONAL MEMORIES OF GETTYSBURG

C. C. CUMMINGS
17TH MISSISSIPPI INFANTRY
Fort Worth, Texas
Fort Worth Daily Gazette
May 31, 1887

Evening Services.

The evening services were held in the opera house which, in spite of the intense heat, was filled to overflowing by the youth and beauty of our city who came to grace the occasion and by the elderly who came to join in rendering homage to the memory of the departed dead. The stage was becomingly arranged. A large cenotaph stood near the footlights over and around which was folded an American flag. This was in memory of the unknown dead who sleep in unmarked graves. A little back and to the right hung the picture of President Lincoln; beneath and to the right was a picture of General Grant, and underneath it a picture of Garfield. Directly underneath was a picture of President Arthur and to the right was that of Lee and a large steel engraving of Lee and Jackson. In the center of these pictures was a map showing the position of the troops at the Battle of Gettysburg on July 3, 1863, at 3:10 p. m. The map was planned by Judge Cummings in a few preliminary remarks. Above the map was the picture of two soldiers, one in blue and one in grey, lying, as thousands have lain, cold and dead upon the battlefield. The map was of great assistance to the audience enabling them to fully appreciate the situation. In front of the stage the Post was seated: Confederate veterans were seated at the right front of the stage; Texas and Mexican War veterans were assigned the seats of honor in the boxes; Commander Emerson, Adjutant Brown, the representatives of the press, the vocal music corps Elder Gavin and his reverend gentlemen companions, His Honor the Mayor, officers of the city government and members of the City Council, the Hon. Judge Cummings, and a volunteer platoon composed of Texas, Mexican, National and Confederate war veterans, were seated on the stage.

Judge C. C. Cummings.

The orator of the occasion, Judge Cummings, in a few preliminary remarks explained the map of the Battle of Gettysburg. There was considerable of the grim irony of fate in the Judge's remarks as he pointed out where the various generals and battalions were stationed on that eventful day. His empty sleeve hanging by his side, a relic of that dreadful conflict, gave silent evidence that the Judge knew what he was speaking about. It was a graceful act in the post to select one who had opposed them on that fateful day, and a wise act in the post to select a gentleman whose oration will add much that is splendid and valuable to the war literature of the country. Judge Cummings said:

Soldiers of the Grand Army of the Republic:

Let us glance once more at these lines when this charge was ordered. As senior sergeant of the Seventeenth regiment, Barksdale's brigade of Mississippians, I by order numbered the guns just before we started in, 417, in line. In three hours 275 went down in the storm. My little company B, had twenty-one, out of an original 100 more, not a man over twenty-five, but one married. By 7 o'clock seven were dead, seven wounded, two to death, and I and seven were alone of those left to tell how they died. They died, as in their boyish grandiloquence in camp and march they ever said they would thus.

> *"Whether the scaffold higher in battle's van.*
> *The littlest place for man to die is where he dies a man."*

When out in the wheat field you shattered our batteries with your shot and shell. These brave boys marched forward to support them and fell like grains before the scytheman's stroke. Volunteers must come and man again the wrecks of battered batteries. Then steadily they rose and went forward to certain death. Calm as a May morning were they in their "last full measure of devotion."

Prison Experience.

I will now briefly sketch my 100 days of prison life at Chester on the Delaware, the oldest town in the Keystone state, and surely the most likely remembered of any north by those who were – 2000 of us – so kindly cared for there by your good people. In the last days of June, 1863, I came down with the head of the column to the line of Mason and Dixon, at Middleburg – so called because the main street divided Maryland from Pennsylvania. I asked an old man to show me exactly where this line could be seen, about which a million had died and millions morn. He drew a mark in the center of the street and said it was just there. Then with a running bound I leaped over into Penn's woods and said: "Old man, I was something over there, but over here I am nothing but a freebooter." And so to carry out this resolve, that evening before nightfall, as we bivouacked on the Chambersburg pike I thought to sully for foraging. Soon a Dutch barn have in sight, and then a house, with its great brick oven nearby. The bar first, the brick oven next and the house last, in the order in which these thrifty people do build. I had formed a resolution most foul to charge the barnyard for fowl, but standing in the door, leaning against its facing, was a picture fair of beauty rare. It met my enchanted gaze. Imagine me repeating to her after the manner of Whittler, your Quaker poet, such a strain as this, as he has in his "Yankee Girl"

> *"O, come where no winter thy footstep can wrong.*
> *But where flowers are blossoming all the yearlong,*
> *Where the shade of the palm tree is over my home,*
> *And the lemon and orange are white in their bloom."*

> *Then could you have seen her – that pride of your girls.*
> *Arise and cast back the dark wreath of her curls,*
> *With a scorn in her eye which the gazer could feel,*
> *And a glance like the sunshine that flashes on steel.*

> *Back, haughty Southron, your sky may be brighter than ours,*
> *And greener thy landscape and fairer the flowers,*
> *But dearer the blast round our mountains which raves,*
> *Then the sweet summer zephyr which breathes over slaves."*

I went back to camp without the chickens. When the fourth day came, the fourth day of July too, I woke from a stupor of narcotics, at the field hospital near the Ridge, by the sound of the voice of the faithful black George, the friend of my childhood, boyhood, manhood, the best I ever had on earth, for he was soon to seal his devotion with his life to remain with me. All day long in the drizzling rain we trundled step by step the Chambersburg pike backward, and night found us only eight miles away, in Cashtown. The slow loss of blood all day caused me to leave the ambulance with him and seek shelter in a barn, to the left of the road, in this town. Next evening George told me that your men were coming, and I insisted that he should go and enjoy his freedom, having served me to the end. He would not go, but wanted to gain the retreating column over the mountain side in the night, so that we might meet again. Then, before they got to us I had him take my sergeant's sword and put it in the side of the barn and break it off the hilt. They could get me but not that emblem of my honor. I can yet see the stubborn steel flashing back its anger in the fading light of day, bending stoutly to its death; but it snapped, and George went weeping in the gray twilight, scaled the mountains, and next day as your pushing advance column came upon him, he ran. They saw only the gray, not the black, and called halt. He would not, they fired and he died. Such is the ending of a domestic scene of southern slave life, and among the last. Could I ever hope to find such as devoted a man and brother?

For days in that barn there, I hovered over the confines of eternity. So close to death's door was I, that I thought I could hear it creek upon its hinges, and I would have gone, too, but for a good woman. Dutch she was. One day about noon I looked over into the meadow from my crevice in the barn toward the battleground, and saw the green pastures and the silver thread of its streamlet winding through, and the blue sky above and the birds singing in the apple trees around the barn. I strained to catch once again through the opening in the barn one more glance of that heaven that bends above, as Marie Antoinette did when she died. I longed to stay, for so young and too little of life had I seen, I was curious to see too great a silken cord we were unloosing. The freedom of all men everywhere. Yet I did not fear to go, for I had naught that my conscience did not approve, and was ready for the judgment. Then it was my blinding eyes caught the dim outlines of the tawny beard of a Pennsylvania Dutchman.

He had come with his frau to see the "repels" – there were thirty of us in that barn. Then my deafening ears heard a roar as of a wild beast: "Ah, you steal my horse, my hogs, my corn, you kills my boy over dare," pointing toward the battlefield, "and now you will die, and I am glad of it." With one supreme effort I raised myself on my elbow and flung back at him: "I will not die; I will live to fight you and your sort again." Then his tender hearted wife said "Hans, Hans, let the poor repel alone; vill you haf some apple butter?" I clutched it as I would prize of gold, for bacon and hard tack had shriveled up my soul and had dried up what little blood was left me. I gulped it down; it seemed to traverse the very marrow of my bones. For days and days she came and brought me apple butter and I was saved. God bless that Dutch woman and apple butter!

One day in August, the 18th your people came and took us up the pike to Gettysburg, Baltimore and up the Delaware river to Chester. The hospital was in the high school building at the edge of town, with ample wards attached. How very elegant was all. I seemed in a land of enchantment, so sudden was the change from the barn. Patent iron bedsteads, good grub and milk punch, snowy sheets and pillows, gas jets and chandeliers, with flags overall flags, on the wall, little flags and big flags, and young flags and the old flag, with

Stars and Stripes.

Everywhere, too, were sketches from holy writ. One, especially, shall ever remain with me: "Whom He loveth He chasteneth." Surely, said I, he loves me, for now solely have I been chastened. One day in the reception room, where they had summoned me to come and met my parents from southland, I met a lady, a fair haired Saxon girl, with her father. They had a history He was a cavalier from the Palmetto state, married a lady of aristocratic art, and so Pierce Butler transferred Fannie Kemble, the renowned seductress, from the stage to his Carolina fields. This was an only child, their daughter, Fannie. Secession had divorced them. He had given up his country, She, entirely Union, wrote a book about the old flag, and the slave life she saw in the rice fields of Carolina. The daughter followed the fortunes of the father and was there with him to give his suffering people aid. It was whispered that the loyal surgeons went soft on fair Fannie. Be this as it may, certain it is she had full sway there, and did many, very glorious deeds of charity for suffering humanity, as well as done by many of your people that were not southern sympathizers. Pierce Butler, whose kinsman is now in our Senate, was gathered to his fathers. And Fannie, the fair, with the Saxon hair – what became of her? She fitted back with the little rice birds, that go north every season, to her rice fields. And when the war was at an end a titled Englishman found her wandering up and down them unmated and bore her away from us. They met by chance – the usual way. She is now over there, and ladies, I'll wager she, like Gladstone, are a good Home Ruler.

Off For Home.

Then came the happy day when we were to steam for home, down the Delaware out into the broad Atlantic via Fortress Monroe, in the good ship City of New York, Captain Chisholm – kind soul, may he live forever and never die. Like the sailor boy, I saw the ocean, wild in all its glory, and sunrise on the green, green sea – not the blue sea, but green were its waters to me, I noted too, the white track of the ship with Mother Carey's chickens fitting on in the rear, following with an intelligence, human-like, after gain from the droppings of the vessel. We passed the dark and frowning Fort Monroe, at the entrance of the James, and next, with a shudder, the shadow of that old town of the James where landed that human cargo of twenty that brought us all these incidental woes. Next arose the shore at City Point, and hastening again to the land of my sires, I stood erect with hat in hand and exclaimed:

My Name is McGregor.

And I stand upon my native hearth." Now, ladies and gentlemen and soldiers, you see I say soldiers apart from the gentle, for I doubt we be entitled to the term after all these wild works of woe and war, let us, too, have a drama with all these characters here therein. Let us call it the charlot of our new constellation, bearing therein our nation born again anew in its new birth of freedom, emblemed by Uncle Abe and Uncle Robert, as we see them here, side by side. We will have them holding the lines of the two grand forces, and we will have along Whitney and Lady Greene and Davis and Johnson and the antidote, Aunty Harriett, on whom we all done, and Uncle Tom and the faithful black George and we will traverse the world around in search of that lasting peace among ourselves and all nations, that Uncle Abe prayed on this field we might achieve. We will have, too the good master. But not the bad, but in his stead something worse. That doughty warrior who, like Job's horse of war, ever smelleth the battle from afar and paweth the valley because he was not there, and wherever fighting is to be done we will put him foremost. Then we may be assured that we will have that peace that Grant so long prayed to see, and he said he was joyed to know had come to us all before he stacked arms on the other shore. For, I venture, that if this valiant knight of the jaw-bone and wind bag but smelleth from afar a chance of war, as these honored dead here have known, he will shriek back and say that he too, has had enough.

A HAPPY CONTRAST

C. C. CUMMINGS
17ᵀᴴ MISSISSIPPI INFANTRY
Fort Worth Daily Gazette
June 20, 1891

I was captured at Gettysburg, and being among the last relay of prisoners sent forward my experience at Chester, Penn., was in happy contrast to those at Fort Delaware and Point Lookout and other points. I offered to write this for the Century magazine as a bright exception to the general rule, and in justice to my Northern brothers, but the management had not the space, so I have shown that I am at least, impartial.

MAP OF THE GETTYSBURG CYCLORAMA

C. C. CUMMINGS
17TH MISSISSIPPI INFANTRY
Fort Worth, Texas
Fort Worth Daily Gazette
August 1, 1891

**Gettysburg, Repulse of Longstreet's assault,
painted by James Walker, engraved by H. B. Hall Jr.
*Library of Congress.***

Souvenir of Gettysburg.

Judge Cummings has received from Capt. W. B. Ford of the Fort Worth Fencibles, who is on his bridal tour, a catalogue and map of the cyclorama of the Battle of Gettysburg as exhibited at Philadelphia. It is dated July 2, 1891, on margin, as sent then by Capt. Ford. It happens to be the anniversary of the day Judge Cummings was wounded there in the peach orchard, just twenty-seven years from that date. It is a souvenir that many Gettysburg veterans in this city would appreciate, which, they can see by calling at Judge Cumming's office.

SCHOOL MATES AT THE PEACH ORCHARD, DEVIL'S DEN AND LITTLE ROUND TOP

C. C. CUMMINGS
17TH MISSISSIPPI INFANTRY
Caldwell News-Chronicle
Caldwell, Texas.
January 14, 1898

The sudden death of Gen. Sul Ross was a shock to me and his other college mates here in Fort Worth – Henry Edrlegton, Oliver Kennedy and Joe Pankey. He and I were the same year and were in the same class for three years at Wesleyan University, Florence, Ala. Wes. Downs of Waco was in this class. The following Texas boys, then residents of Texas, were in the class below:

Oscar Downs, dead; Thos G. Davidson, dead; Haywood Brahan, dead; and Judge Joe Polley, living at Floresville, Texas, Brahan was for a long time identified in state politics under Goree and successor in the management of the penitentiary affairs. And I forgot to name Davis B. Gurley of Waco in the class above us all. Major Gurley and the Downs brothers were with Ross in the west, and followed him throughout all the viclasitudes of his romantic career as rough riders, and won fame eternal in asserting the right to attend to one's own affairs, and forcing others to do the same. Brahan and Polley were in Hood's brigade of Texans in Virginia, where I marched to victory with them through all these fierce fights till I left them at Gettysburg in the Peach Orchard, while they were climbing the rocky heights of Little Round Top and skulking the foe out of Devil's Den. Ask Jim Hasley, walking the streets here every day, he was there.

A DISTURBING PREMONITION

C. C. CUMMINGS
17TH MISSISSIPPI INFANTRY
Fort Worth, Texas
Dublin Progress
August 8, 1913

Gettysburg
(Mr. C.C. Cummings in the *Fort Worth Record*. Mr. Cummings has addressed the
Confederate Veterans of Dublin.)

The night of June 20th we bivouacked near Cashtown, about six miles from Gettysburg. All that day on the march I had presentiment of evil to befall me in the coming battle. Just where the clash of arms was to be we knew not, but every private was as much aware that it was going to be the decisive battle of the great war as any general. We crossed over into the enemy's country seeking to end it at a blow and Gettysburg went down in history as the field, the fatal Flodden field. All the day of the 30th I was obsessed with this presentiment of evil and I confided my forecast to Lieutenant Colonel Fizer, saying I preferred a wound in the arm that I might escape being shot again after being down, which frequently happened when wounded in the locomotive powers. Fizer was a dressy comrade and preferred a wound in the leg, as he did not wish to mar his shape. We both got our preference on the second day in the peach orchard where we went up against Sickles' corps in that valley of death. That night of the second, there was gathered in a tent in a field hospital on the grounds all the field and staff of our regiment, the seventeenth Mississippi, except Dick Jones, the adjutant killed on the field. Colonel Holder was there with a wound in the groin; Fizer with a wound in the leg, as he preferred, and the writer, sergeant major, in the hand, as I preferred; Major Pulliam also in the hand, and Brown Jones, the Colonel's orderly, about fifteen in the body. We bivouacked at Willoughby Run on July 1st, where was opened the first day's battle and where a monument has been erected to the memory of the Federal General Reynolds, killed there that day. I claim to be the original reunionist, of the Gray and Blue. For when I was shot in the hand and while the blood was filling my buck gauntlet (I put on my best to die like a soldier,) two New York Zouaves running my way to avoid capture by our gray boys, who had broken through a barn on my left, and who would have served them roughly for the resistance they made. I beckoned them to come to me and I flung my arm around the neck of each, making a wounded squad, which our long experience told us would save us from being fired upon, and so I came off the field with my two prisoners. Wouldn't it be passing strange if I should meet one or both after fifty years at Gettysburg? Sickles will be there and they were Sickles men. Sickles and I exchanged compliments that day. I gave him my hand and pulled his leg. All the third day of July, 1863, we lay prone of our wounds in the hospital tent on the field of Gettysburg and heard the thunder of this legions or guns – big guns – from both sides, such guns as were never heard on the American continent. It was what has gone into history as "Pickett's charge" and while there were others, who crossed the deadline with Pickett to the high water mark, yet old Virginia our dear old mother, bore on her sacred bosom the bosom of war for us all. So let her son Pickett go down in history as the hero of us all.

RANKING OF THE BATTLE

C. C. CUMMINGS
17TH MISSISSIPPI INFANTRY
Fort Worth, Texas
Denton Record-Chronicle
October 13, 1913

Judge Cummings Spoke At Church "Gettysburg," Sixteenth Decisive Battle of World's History." Interesting Subject Of Gettysburg Veteran's Address Here Sunday.

The address of Judge C. C. Cummings of Fort Worth, Confederate historian for the U. C. V.'s was delivered to an audience which fairly well crowded the First Christian Church on Hickory Street, Sunday afternoon. Subject of the talk "Gettysburg, the Sixteenth Decisive Battle of the World," made it one doubly interesting to the veterans, recalling to many of them who had been with Lee in the struggle between the "two ridges" of the little Dutch town all the fierce hope of victory with which the first three days fifty years ago had begun, and the bitter certainty of defeat which followed the second day's battle. The church well filled after the Confederate veterans marched in, after the flag, to places reserved for them and the young men of the Reagan and Lee societies of the North Texas State Normal followed.

After announcing his subject, and a short explanation of it, Judge Cummings spied Dr. J. R. Edwards in the audience and asked him to come up to the platform, laughingly desiring him to act as "witness" to the story of the Battle of Gettysburg, where he and the speaker were comrades. It was a rule made in Lee camp, he said, never to tell a theory unless you had provided yourself with a witness, after which statement he extracted a promise of unrestrained endorsement from Dr. Edwards.

Tells of 1913 Re-Union

A short delineation of the pleasures of the recent Gettysburg celebration, which Pennsylvania as hostess to the boys in blue and gray, was a great pleasure to many of the local veterans who were unable to attend the "peace" reunion. Their greeting at Gettysburg, he declared, was as warm as it had been on a memorable day fifty years ago, though of a deferent sort. Beginning with his story of the great battle in which 72,000 Confederates and 83,000 Federals were engaged, the speaker introduced a map of the city of Gettysburg, pointing out the places concerned as he told them. He followed the movements of Lee's Army of Northern Virginia from Chancellorsville, where Jackson, "the right hand of Lee," was mortally wounded and died, to the assembling of the army at Culpepper's Heights on the eighth of June, with Gen. Hooker just across the creek.. On June 25 Lee crossed the Potomac, Hooker having crossed at Edward's Ferry previously. Lee, whose plan was to move up into the enemy's country, came on to Chambersburg, and sent Gen. Gordon on ahead to threaten Washington. Lee halted, and he learned at Chambersburg that Hooker was in the neighborhood on the line above. Stewart was not successful in crossing the Potomac to get news of the movement of Hooker's army. The speaker digressed a little to compare the Battle of Gettysburg with the fifteen other decisive battles of the world, saying that while at Waterloo, where Napoleon met his defeat, there were about the same numbers engaged and last in the battles that the great emperor was effectively crushed with the defeat on the battleground of Waterloo, while after the Battle of Gettysburg, Lee calmly turned and stood ready to meet Meade, should an attack be made.

Compliments Gen. Meade

The speaker complimented the command of Gen. Meade, who was in the charge of the army three days, following the removal of Gen. Hooker. He told of Lee's orders to his troops to assemble at Cashtown, meaning to form the base of his operations at the foot of the Blue Ridge mountains, Rhode's division developed fight, and Lee ordered the Cashtown troops forward to Gettysburg and Gordon's troops, far in advance, back to the small city.

Then followed an intensely interesting description of the three days' battle itself, with a description of "the most beautiful battleground in the world," then the speaker pointing out each place and movement on the map of Gettysburg.

The speaker made himself very clear on the point of his right to the title of "Confederate" soldier, declaring that the surviving men in the old ranks of gray were Confederates still, and only "ex-soldiers. That they had fought for what they "believed" to be right was his emphatic statement, without bitterness. That the great rebellion was as necessary to the future cementing of the Union as any other agent, he believed, and blood, he said, was the only cement that would answer.

Giving the definition of history from a modern encyclopedia, he amended it by an edition. "History is the science of the progressive development of the human race," "under the guidance," he amended, "of a Supreme Power."

The speaker spoke for a short time of his personal experience in the war, the loss of his right hand, which came about when he "exchanged courtesies" with a Federal soldier, giving him a right hand for left leg. His capture at Cashtown and three or four months imprisonment, and other incidents of his personal experience made interesting telling.

A Faithful Slave

C. C. Cummings
17ᵀᴴ Mississippi Infantry

Fort Worth, Texas
Fort Worth Daily Gazette
June 16, 1894

A Faithful Slave Who Followed His Master Unto Death
Editor Gazette,

Col. J. W. Friend's article, "Old Sol," about the good old darkey of his mess "endurin ob de wah" is a timely remembrance of the faithful man in black, who followed our fortunes in the "storm cradled nation that fell" as little children, and whose kind, simple, humble souls will never be equaled by another such race in another such patriarchal age. I too would add another tribute to the memory of another such who was with me from the first battle of Manassas till the Battle of Gettysburg, where he lost his life for his friends. The Mater of the human heart says greater love hath no man than this. My father – Kentucky born – brought him from Kentucky and we called him Kentucky George to distinguish him from another on the place of that name. Early in April, 1861, I enlisted when the tocsin sounded for home defense and George was my constant companion till his death. We were about the same age and never in my life have I met a character, white or black, whose gentle humility of spirit came so near the standard as set up by Christ as this poor, kind, sable-skinned son of Africa. He was not afraid to fight either. At the battle of Leesburg in October, 1861, noted for being the death of General Baker, Lincoln's friend and for whose Lincoln mourned so sincerely, when my regiment (Seventeenth Mississippi) rushed in about sun down and decided the fight, we ran over two howitzers which George assisted to carry in triumph from the field. But he was more valuable to us as a cook and forager than a fighter, so we were careful to keep him in rear. When wounded at Gettysburg I had orders from our surgeon to remain and be captured or a move would disrupt the artery just taken up. But when the army began to move back on that morning of the 4ᵗʰ of July, 1863, I called to George to get me an ambulance which he did and all day we moved back on the pike in that slow drizzling rain and when night came we had only got eight miles at Cashtown. Sure enough, the artery broke and I had to stop or bleed to death. That night we slept under the same blanket – George and I – on the porch of a Pennsylvania Dutchman and in the morning repaired to a barn in an apple orchard opposite. About sundown George told me the Yankees were coming and had begun to separate all the black folks from their masters. I told him his freedom he had and earned and was his, but he did not want it that way, and would not have it so. He determined to go back over the mountains that night and join the regiment and wait for me to be exchanged.

I told him then to go as he desired, but to first break my sword so the Yankees could not get it.

I was sergeant major of the regiment. Its gleam and glint in the dying sunlight of that woeful day as it broke in twain to the crack of that barn is yet as vivid as yesterday. I was in prison and never joined my regiment after being exchanged and never knew the fate of poor faithful George till about a year after poor faithful George till about a year after the end of the war. He had made it safely over the mountains and was nearly of our forces when he was stopped by a Northern lady to enquire about her son whom George happened to know in our army. He had just told her that her son was safe and a prisoner when the advance of the Yankees came up and seeing the gray jacket began firing on, it and George was killed. The lady saw him buried and brought the story over the lines.
C. C. Cummings

REMARKABLE COINCIDENCES OF JULY 4TH

C. C. CUMMINGS
17ᵀᴴ MISSISSIPPI INFANTRY

Fort Worth, Texas
Jacksboro News
July 8, 1914

**C. C. Cummings, 17th Mississippi
Infantry Regiment.**
Confederate Veteran Magazine.

Judge Cummings Address

A small audience at the courthouse on July 4, under the auspices of the local Confederate camp here, J. C. Jones, commander, who followed by an earnest appeal for better and more efficient camp organization.

Judge Cummings main topic was the Fourth of July in History as appropriate to the day. He went back to colonial times when Geo. Washington, a youth of 21, led a party of Virginians against a force of French who were entrenched at what is now Pittsburg and on the 4th of July 1753 not far from where a battle occurred, the battle of great moment in which Washington was compelled to surrender to a superior force. Then twenty three years later after this the 4th of July 1776 came our declaration of independence. Then fifty years later this July 4th, 1826 Jefferson and Adams died, both of whom had signed the immortal document and Adams became second and Jefferson third president of the United States.

The speaker then referred to the remarkable coincidences of what occurred on the 4th of July 1863. After three days battles 1st, 2nd and 3rd of July at Gettysburg, the next day the 4th of July found Lee slowly retiring from Gettysburg, on the same day Pemberton surrendered at Vicksburg. The Confederate General Holms with 10,000 of his men was repulsed in an assault on Helena and on the 4th of July at the same time Morgan was captured in his raid in Ohio and in the same day Port Hudson was preparing to surrender and did a day or so after and there was the speaker said the bottom dropped out of the Confederacy and began slowly to settle its doom.

Then he referred to the fact that just fifty years after the Gettysburg battle 50,000 veterans of Blue and Gray met again on this bloody field as friends and four days fraternized as guest of Pennsylvania and Uncle Sam who joined in the immense expense of feeding and tending to this great host. Judge Cummings was among the visitors and reviewed the ground where his command charged down in the Peach Orchard, July 2, 1863 and where he lost his right hand.

The audience, though not large, seemed greatly entertained among whom were many young men who have come on the stage of action in a later generation. He alluded to the fact of the crus- fix-ation of the South on the Southern battle flag and aid the South, though dead and buried, had risen again with healing in its wings with a Virginian and for president, a descendent of Virginia vice president, a grandson of a Virginian as Secretary of State, a native Texan as Post Master General, a native of South Carolina as Secretary of Agriculture, a native of North Carolina, secretary of the mightiest navy of the world, a Tennessean as attorney general, a Confederate soldier at the head of the Supreme Court; the most august tribunal of the earth; a native Georgian secretary of treasury; the president lately declaring for states' rights in all cases where the issued can be managed better than the government in mass. He alluded to his attendance at the most recent reunion at Jacksonville, Florida and that De Soto's conquest of Florida in 1542 resulted in embracing the seven gulf states beginning with Florida and ending with Texas was for more than a hundred years after all called Florida. That on February 4, 1861, at Montgomery, Alabama, in the center of these seven Gulf States raised the Stars and Bars which seven states embraced these seven states and that now the canal was opened these seven states would control the commerce of the world, just as the seven stars lead the heavenly bodies in their course and that Texas was to be the lead of all the 48 stars in the galaxy of our charming circle.

Charged Through The Valley Of Death

Michael A. "M. A." Dickson
13ᵀᴴ Alabama Infantry
Lexington, Texas
Houston Daily Post
March 10, 1894

Lexington, Texas, March 9. – Mr. M. A. Dickson died this morning at 5 o'clock at the Dickson residence in this place, aged 72 years. He was for forty years a Presbyterian and a devoted Christian.

Mr. Dickson was born and reared at Spartanburg, S. C. Early in life he engaged in the mercantile business in Alabama. When the war broke out he joined the army of Virginia under General Lee. He was wounded in the foot by the explosion of a shell in the first battle of Manassas. At Gettysburg he was one of that immortal band that charged through the "valley of death" and was shot through both legs and captured there. Recovering from his wounds he was soon exchanged, and returned to his command in time to participate in the great battles around Richmond.

In the battle of the Wilderness he was shot down again by a bullet which entered his side and remained in his body to the day of his death. The battle scared hero was soon in the front again and was present when the mine was sprung at Petersburg, where he fought in the deadly crater. When the battle flag he loved so well trailed in the dust and was furled forever, Mike Dickson stood with the beloved commander at Appomattox, and with his sword he surrendered all his political animosities.

Returning to his ruined home, he succeeded in rebuilding his depleted fortune by selling goods in Alabama.

In 1871 he came to Texas where he assisted his brother, the late R. M. Dickson of this place, to build up one of the best mercantile establishments in this county.

Uncle Green

G. B. Dickson
14ᵀᴴ Alabama Infantry
Sulphur Springs, Texas
Galveston Daily News
July 14, 1939

Confederate Vet of Titus County is 94 Years Old.

G. B. Dickson, better known throughout Titus County and Northeast Texas as Uncle Green, will celebrate his ninety-fourth birthday Sunday.

Mr. Dickson is one of the few Confederate veterans in Titus County. He was born near Lafayette in Chambers County, Alabama on July 16, 1845. He enlisted in the Confederate Army in 1861 and served in the Army of Northern Virginia throughout the Civil War. He was wounded on the second day of the Battle of Gettysburg and on the next day he was taken prisoner. He was later released in exchange of prisoners. He was captured again and was a prisoner at Point Lookout, Maryland, when General Lee surrendered at Appomattox.

Mr. Dickson moved to Titus County in January, 1877. In 1880 he was chosen deputy sheriff for the county. He voluntarily retired from public office in 1932.

SABER WOUND

ELIAS DIE
1ST LOUISIANA INFANTRY

Fuqua, Texas
Houston Post
July 5, 1910

Die. – Fuqua, Texas, July 2. – Elias Die, a venerable and respected citizen of this place, died this afternoon. Mr. Die was over 70 years of age, a Confederate veteran and a survivor of the Battle of Gettysburg. In Lee's retreat after the battle Mr. Die was wounded on the head with a saber and captured by the Federals.

INJURED ON JULY 1ST

MOSES DILLON
97TH NEW YORK INFANTRY

El Paso, Texas
El Paso Herald
February 10, 1897

He enlisted from Utica, N. Y. on April 12, 1862, in the 9th New York infantry in the "Conkling Rifles," known also as the Third Oneida, being composed almost wholly of men from Oneida and Herkiner counties. In April 1862, it was assigned to Durgee's brigade and in May took the field with Prickett's division of McDowell's corps of the army of the Potomac. He participated in the battles of Cedar Mountain, Rappahannock, South Mountain, Antietam, Fredericksburg, (being wounded in the last two fights) Wilderness and Gettysburg, where July 1, he was badly wounded in the left arm, which has been nearly useless to him ever since. At Gettysburg he was highly commended by the colonel of his regiment and by commanding General Robinson for his valor in that days battle. He was discharged December 31, 1863. After leaving the service in 1864, he contracted in Nashville, Tenn., and was there when Hood made his famous raid on Nashville,

97th New York Infnatry Regiment Monument.
Boy Scout Troop #14.Utica, NY.

when he again took the field as captain of a volunteer force under Major Irvin, then U. S. Marshall of Nashville.

BROTHERS REUNITED AFTER FORTY YEARS

HOWARD DIVEN
6ᵀᴴ NEW YORK HEAVY ARTILLERY REGIMENT
WALTER C. DIVEN
UNKNOWN CONFEDERATE REGIMENT
Cameron, Texas
Dublin Progress
January 24, 1913

Brothers Meet after Forty Years' Separation.
   After being separated for more than forty years, two brothers, Walter C. Diven of Baltimore, Md., and Howard Diven of Cameron, Texas, Confederate veterans, both of whom have long passed their 76ᵗʰ milestone, were reunited when Howard paid the elder brother a visit. The two sons of the late Jeremiah Davis of Pennsylvania, separated at the outbreak of the Civil War. The younger brother joined the Confederate forces under Gen. Lee and served as a spy in several skirmishes preceding the Battle of Gettysburg. Later he came to Texas. The Texan planned to surprise his brother, so he went to the house and asked for food. His brother's wife gave it to him. He then asked to be allowed to eat in the kitchen. Mrs. Diven then became suspicious and called to her husband. The latter came in and threatened to punish the beggar. Just then he recognized the man as his brother, and the scene that followed was a joyous one.[11]

HARSH CRITICISM OF GENERAL LONGSTREET

Austin Weekly-Statesman
September 24, 1874

   Eighteen months ago General Pendleton formerly of General Lee's staff, announced in a public lecture in the city of Mobile that the Battle of Gettysburg was lost to the South through the treachery of General James Longstreet. We did not believe the statement when we read it, even though it came from the lips of a soldier that whom the South had none purer nor brave in the day of his sorest need. But since developments of Monday last, since the appearance of Longstreet at the head of the Metropolitan police, prepared to hurl his messages of death upon the citizens of New Orleans, who were assembled to demand relief from the infamous tyranny under which they were living, we withdrew our incredulity and are prepared now to believe that no deed of infamy could be named or conceived of that he would not gladly be a party to. – ***Dallas Herald.***

IN DEFENSE OF GENERAL LONGSTREET

R. W. DOUTHAT
11ᵀᴴ VIRGINIA INFANTRY
Waxahachie, Texas
Waxahachie Daily Light
July 21, 1909

Opening Of The Chautauqua.
   Secretary Parker then made the usual announcements and introductions the speaker of the eve-

---

11   Walter C. Diven is not listed in any database or Civil War service records.

ning, Dr. R. W. Douthat, professor of Latin in the University of West Virginia. Dr. Douthat spoke on the subject of "Gettysburg." Special seats were reserved for the old soldiers and many of them were present to hear the lecture.

The speaker defended Gen. Longstreet from the charges that were made against him, charging that the battle was lost because of him. Dr. Douthat, who served under Longstreet, during the four years of the war, said he was not as popular with his troops as Jackson, nor was he a strategist, but that he was loyal and did his duty. At the Battle of Gettysburg, said the speaker, Longstreet was not needed on the first day of the three days' contest, for on that day the Confederates greatly outnumbered the Federals. Besides, said the speaker, Gen. Longstreet was detained on the first day for the reason that the infantry column had gotten in ahead of him and impeded his corps. At Gettysburg, said Dr. Douthat, Gen. Longstreet bore the brunt of battle, and did what few corps generals did – placed himself in front of the battle, waved his hat and led the fight on the second day, when the fiercest fighting on the entire day was done; which as the speaker said, the wheat field in which the second day's fighting was done was mowed clean by bullets and trampling men, when every depression was a pool of blood and dead and dying men covered nearly every foot of ground.

The Confederates first great mistake of the battle, said Dr. Douthat, was on the first day, when they stampeded the Federals, had them in precipitate defeat three hours before the sun sank, and then failed to press the rout. Had that rout been pressed, said the speaker, there would have been no Gettysburg, and the Confederacy would have occupied Washington. The further advance was not made, it was stated, because the generals in command believed it was the will of Lee that a general action, should not be brought on then.

The six other mistakes were listed as failures of various generals to give support when needed on the second day's fighting, when the Confederate line of battle resembled a fish hook in outline, and when the great mass of the federal army was engaged with Longstreet. At that time, said the speaker, the federal center was pierced and artillery captured. The speaker said that the federal army could have been cut in two then. At another time, he said, the Federal line where weakened by the withdrawal of troops to oppose Longstreet, was broken, and the throw of the enemy's ammunition. Confederates were within a stone's and could have seized it had they hurried on, but they withdrew fearing a trap. Other instances of a like nature were mention.

Speaking of ordering of the charge of the third day, when 14,000 men charged seven-eighths of a mile across an open field, under the fire of cannon and musket, the speaker said that the cessation of the enemy's artillery fire was misinterpreted by the Confederate corps leaders; that it was believed the enemy was withdrawing, and the time to charge had come, when the enemy was only cooling the overheated guns – that Pickett declared he would charge; that Longstreet was silent to the suggestion, knowing as he did the fearful odds against such a charge; that Pickett reiterated his determination to charge, and Longstreet, by silence, gave consent.

The fearful ordeal, Dr. Douthat said, was in awaiting the charge, exposed to the fire of the Federal cannon. Three hundred cannon had fired, and shells exploded everywhere.

"You might think that I would say," said the speaker, "that 14,000 heroes were assembled in that gray line of battle, but I will not say that. You can never get together that many heroes in one line of battle at one time. You old soldiers will understand that. A man may be ever so brave today, but tomorrow some unfavorable condition of the body or mind may make him a coward. This week he may be perfectly well and a brave man, the next he may be downhearted and afraid to go into the fight."

The speaker told of the demoralization of good soldiers under the heavy fire, a demoralization that was not confined to the Confederate soldiers, for, said the speaker, when the think gray line finally reached the stone wall, with its bristling bayonets and its heated cannon, Federal soldiers threw down their

J. S. Dowell. 7th Tennessee Cavalry.
Herbert Rickards.

arms and in great fear begged, don't shoot."

The speaker's reference to both armies was kindly, and his commendation for bravery was given to the soldiers of both armies. The lecture was well received.

GRUELING AMBULANCE RIDE

J. S. DOWELL
7TH TENNESSEE CAVALRY
McKinney, Texas
McKinney Weekly Democrat-Gazette
April 28, 1927

The next important battle in which I participated was at Gettysburg where I was severely wounded. The ball entered my right breast, going through the upper part of my lung. I bled freely and while lying on the stretcher I could scarcely breathe at all but got them to raise me up to a sitting posture and breathed better. I thought it was the best breath of fresh air I ever had. They took me back to the first aid station and then sent me to the main hospital in an ambulance. The jolting of the ambulance gave me so much pain that I asked the driver to go more slowly, but he said we must hurry along. "Just listen to those shells" he said and whipped up faster. I asked a friend who was in the ambulance, taking care of me to give me my sword and pistol which were in the ambulance. I took out my pistol and told the driver if he did not go slower I would shoot him. Of course I did not intend to do so, but I had to come to the time when I had as soon been hit by a shell as bumped to death over the roads. He was kind enough to go slower as perhaps he thought he might as well be killed by a shell as for me to shoot him. The wound unfitted me for further service and besides we were made prisoners and sent to Johnson's Island where I stayed for about twenty months. Prisoners were exchanged quarterly. I got to Richmond on the 5th of March but too late for the quarter and could not be exchanged until the next quarter. In the mean-time the surrender came and I was paroled. My wound was quite troublesome and I found that I got relief when in a stooping position and have never got out of the stooping habit. I can straighten when I try, but just don't try.

RECENT UPDATE

R. W. DOWNS
21ST MISSISSIPPI INFANTRY

I was also glad to learn that the negroes did about as well as any in the neighborhood. In her letter she wished to know what had become of Bob Sims. He has been absent ever since that bloody Battle of Gettysburg in which he received a severe wound near his ankle breaking the smaller bone, his brother told me he got a furlough. I saw Robert Davis (for he has been back two or three weeks) he is well of his wound which was in his left hand, but his left finger & the one next to it is shot up & so stiff is to be useless to him. He told me he would not use his gun, his hand was yet weak & tender. I hardly think he will be able to use his gun unless his fingers get straighter & be of more use to him. I was glad to hear that your potatoes are going to turn out well. This face & truly hope you will make as many as the family will use for nothing is better than nice potatoes.

I have told Dan about the negroes running away from the neighborhood. I know he will find it out anyway so I do not try to conceal anything from him. If I did conceal such things from him other boys would make sure to say something about it & would come and ask me about it.

When Henry Harris came to the company Dan asked me if some of our negroes had run away before, if I had said anything about it. Since I told him of the negroes leaving you, he seemed at first to hate it so much his own sister had left, but since then he is as lively as any negro in this regiment & seem contented. I have no idea that he will leave me & go to the Yanks for he had a fair chance in Penn - & did not leave me. He has made enough money to take him home & back, so I think provided when he gets to the end of the railroad he takes it a foot home. Capt. Geo McGehee, our Quartermaster has now $65.00 belonging to him which I deposited with him in case he should ever come here. Mrs. (?) wished me to find out what I could about Lewis & Bill's burial and if I knew <u>where</u> they were buried & by <u>whom</u>. As far as I can learn none of our dead were buried by our men except those that are left within our lines when we fell back after the terrible charge & slaughter on Getty – heights.

After we fell back all of our dead were buried by details of our own men, that is those that were there within our lines. And it was supposed by everyone that the Yankees buried them after remaining dead on the field two or three days as they held the field. I would never write anything about their being buried because I knew it that it would distress her & do no good, you can tell her what I write to you, if you think it will not add grief to her sorrow stricken heart.

I forgot to tell you that while building our breastworks of trees, Mr. Etheridge, while cutting down a tree did not get out of the way quick enough & when it was falling, he jumped back & struck him on the ankle, knocked him down & hurt him right badly. Doubtless Ike has written to his Ma all about it. I am now messing with Jim P. & Sergt. Taylor who lived near the cold springs. I have very good messmates but often think I will leave them on account of one being so lazy about fixing up things about camp. I believe Col. Brandon has resigned at last; he came to the regiment & stayed several days & then went to Richmond. Col Moody who used to be a Major is now Col, Major Sims will be Lieut. Col. – It is quite cool here on the side of the mountains with what covering we have. We are looking for our bale of blankets found Richmond that we sent off from Fredericksburg last winter.

I believe I have written about all so I will send my love to all the family & respects to all enquiring friends I remain ever your affectionate Son, R. W. Downs.[12]

LOSS OF THE REGIMENTAL FLAG

H. C. DUMAS
26TH NORTH CAROLINA INFANTRY
Waco, Texas

I was first on the coast of North Carolina below Newburn until May, 1862. Then our brigade was transferred to Richmond, Va., and was with Gen. Lee until the surrender. I was badly wounded at the Battle of Gettysburg, July 1, 1863, and slightly wounded in the head May 12, 1864 at Petersburg, Va.

General Pettigrew was killed at Falling Waters on the retreat from Gettysburg. Gen Wm. McRae commanded us when we surrendered. My company went into the Battle of Gettysburg eighty or ninety strong. We had sixteen killed, fifty wounded and missing. The regimental flag fell fourteen times, and was finally lost the last day, while we were assisting Pickett in his famous charge.[13]

Cavalry fight near Aldie, VA, during the march to Gettysburg.
Edwin Forbes. *Library of Congress*.

12   Letter, R. W. Downs to Mother, November 1863, J. T. Downs, Sr., Collection, 1843, 1861-1929, Dolph Briscoe Center for American History, The University of Texas at Austin.
13   Yeary, *boys in gray*. p. 202.

LONE STAR VALOR

LEFT FOR DEAD

THOMAS G. DUNBAR
14TH TENNESSEE INFANTRY
St. Jo, Texas
Bryan Eagle
September 2, 1933

Taps Sounded For Aged Veteran; Fought With Lee

Another good soldier – almost the last – rejoined the personal command of Robert E. Lee. Thomas Goodrich Dunbar was one of the few remaining southern soldiers who fought directly under the great Confederate general, died yesterday at St. Jo, Texas. He was 92 years old.

Dunbar, was left for dead on the Gettysburg battlefield and twice was taken prisoner by Union soldiers. He was a native of Mayfield, Ky.

A HERO IN THE SADDLE

J. R. DUNLAP
JEFF DAVIS LEGION, MISSISSIPPI CAVALRY
Cuero, Texas
Cuero Daily Record
December 23, 1902

One of our Citizens

The following heroic achievement of Major J. R. Dunlap, now a resident of our county, taken from the *Confederate Veteran* of August this year, written by W. H. McClellan of Houston, will be read with no little interest by his many friends in DeWitt county.

The recent death of Gen. Hampton recalls one among the bravest, most gallant, and heroic acts of the late civil war by a mere youth. Maj. J. R. Dunlap, then of Kemper county, Miss., but now doorkeeper of the Texas legislature.

It was the evening of the third day of the battle that Jeff Davis Legion Cavalry Battalion from Mississippi, under command of Col. J. Fred Waring of Savannah, Ga., was ordered to charge a battery of twelve pieces of artillery that partially enfiladed Pickett's line of charge on the heights of Gettysburg. The battalion, after going through two lines of the enemies cavalry, sent to defend it, took the battery and reformed in rear of it to defend it against another approaching column sent to recapture it. This was also charged and routed, when they again rallied to the defense of the captured battery. While thus holding the battery it was discovered that Gen. Hampton had been cut out and surrounded by the enemy. Without waiting for orders, young Dunlap rushed to Hampton's rescue. Alone and unaided he killed eleven of the foe, and brought Hampton safe from the field, though he received eleven wounds in the fight and lost his leg. He still survives and is the doorkeeper of the Texas legislature. The full particulars of this daring feat can be found on page 140 of a book entitled, *Raids of Hampton's Cavalry*, also in a small pamphlet called *Hampton's Brigade at Gettysburg*.

CLOSE TO BEING HANGED

YOUNG COLVILLE "TOBE" EDMONDSON
1ST TENNESSEE INFANTRY
Forreston, Texas

Alabama Monument, Gettysburg NMP. *Joe Owen.*

I was wounded in the right arm at Gettysburg, where I was wounded and sent to Fort Delaware. For a private, I had a rollicking big time, always with something to eat and to spare; barefooted and ragged, never missed a march or a fight from Seven Pines to Gettysburg, where they got me in the right "wing" and sent me to Delaware. Not liking my fare, I jumped my board bill, ate green apples eleven days; got my back to my regiment; got a furlough home. Carried letters home for the boys and found that my mother and sisters had been badly treated, having been in prison. One sister and a neighbor woman down there. Got into a fight with "home-made" Yankees; got wounded and captured in the fight. They killed four of their own men and said that I did it. Was tried by a military commission and was condemned to be hanged. Mother got me a reprieve; was exchanged, and got home; got into Ku Klux business; got out and came to Texas.

My escape from prison at Fort Delaware. We were good swimmers, and practiced till we thought we could float. We got a plank and tied our clothes to it. It was agreed that each was to take care of himself and was to make no appeal to the others, dying if must be, without a call for help. On the night of Aug. 12, 1863. We floated on for an hour or more and felt a sensation which encouraged us to carry out our plans. Soon the wind rose and the waves ran high, and the passing of a steamer brought us great danger. The names of this crew were Tom Stewart, John McKinney, James Cashion, George Stonebreaker, John Moore and myself. John being weak, lost his hold on the board and was drifting away, but, true to his promise, uttered not a word. I saw his situation and asked him if he could regain his hold on the board, and he said: "No, I'm gone;" but I got the others to help me and we got him back. After a stay of about six hours in the water we reached Newcastle. We pulled our frail bark ashore and on untying our clothes I found that mine were missing. John, realizing that he owed me, offered me his, but the offer was declined, as I thought I would present fully as good an appearance with a limited wardrobe as he. We went four miles before we found anyone from whom we could risk asking assistance, but found a man who clothed us and gave us breakfast, dinner and supper and passed us over the Newcastle River and gave us his blessing. Without unusual incident we reached the Susquehanna River, where we appropriated a yawl; but there were no oars and the crossing was with much difficulty. John being weak, could not have held on but for my help. We crossed, however, and then the next river was the Potomac, and then there was something to eat. Then came Culpepper C. H., Orange C. H., and then the regiment. We were nothing more than skeletons, but our patriotism was just the same.[14]

---

14   Ibid., p. 208-209.

AT LITTLE ROUND TOP

WILLIAM A. EDWARDS
15TH ALABAMA INFANTRY
Fate, Texas

We waded across the Potomac to get to the Battle of Gettysburg and returning crossed on pontoons. There are some facts in this battle I have not seen in history. The 15th Alabama Regiment was the extreme right of General Lee's. Just as we began the attack Hood was wounded and Laws took command of the division. Our regiment crept over Big Round Top Mountain and fought until all our ammunition was exhausted and for want of reinforcement and ammunition was compelled to retire.

In this battle I saw General Bulger shot through the body. He fell like a dead man and after the war I met the same gentleman. He was candidate for Governor of the State of Alabama.

I saw Colonel Oats, since Governor of Alabama, mount a rock within thirty yards of the enemy and discharge the contents of a repeater in their face.

When we began the retreat back across the mountains the Federals were pressing and I was exhausted and with my third lieutenant and a private soldier, slipped into a cave in the side of the mountain and about midnight came out, located the pickets by their firing and crowded between their post which was about a hundred yards apart and reached our command in safety. I am satisfied I went as far toward Washington as any other Southern soldier.[15]

CAPTURED 200 WAGONS

D. C. EFIRD
1ST NORTH CAROLINA INFANTRY
Copperas Cove, Texas

We cross the Potomac River below Harper's Ferry and went to Rockville, a village about seven miles from Washington, where we captured about 200 wagons going from Washington to the Federal Army at Gettysburg to haul provisions for the army. We then took up the march for Gettysburg, marching five days and nights. Had several fights along the way.[16]

CLAIMED TO HAVE FIRED THE FIRST SHOT

W. J. EVANS
42ND MISSISSIPPI INFANTRY
Jackson County, Texas
Galveston Daily News
April 5, 1914

Gettysburg Battle Opened By Jackson County Veteran -- Command of Captain W. J. Evans Probably Fired First Gun in Memorable Fight in Pennsylvania. Scenes of Civil War Days Vividly Described but Much Wounded Man.

Captain W. J. Evans, now a citizen of Jackson County, was born in Morgan County, Alabama,

---

15   William A. Edwards, "Autobiography, or some incidents in my life. Reverend William A. Edwards, Fate, Texas 1847 and 1925, with epilogue by his daughter, Mrs. George C. Cochran," in *Dallas Genealogical Society, The Dallas Journal,* vol. 44, June 1998, p.3.

16   Yeary, *boys in gray*, p. 212.

more than 50 years ago. Later he made Mississippi the state of his adoption, and when the war occurred between the states, he enlisted in Company I, Forty-Second Regiment of Mississippi Volunteers of Infantry. His regiment was placed in General Joe Davis' brigade, and in the corps of General A. P. Hill. He enlisted March 4, 1861, and served one year at Pensacola, Fla, here he saw the old fortifications in which his father, Nathaniel Evans, who was a soldier in the war of 1812, had served.

Battlefields Strewn With dead.

In 1863 Captain Evans went with his regiment to Virginia, reaching there as reinforcements just as the "Seven Days Fight," around Richmond was over. The fields over which the contending armies had fought were strewn with the dead and were horrifying scenes of carnage. Captain Evans participated in many of the big battles fought in Virginia. His command, which had been besieging Suffolk, Va., about ten or twelve days, left there to join General Lee's army on its march into Pennsylvania.

"It was the grandest army," says Captain Evans, "that the sun ever shone upon. We went through Northern Virginia, wading the Potomac into Maryland. The army was in high spirits, and then struck the north bank of that historic stream, all the bands played Dixie,' and a cheer from the army went that sounded like it was sufficient to waken the dead. Crossing Maryland to Pennsylvania we passed through gap into the mountains into open ground with Gettysburg in full view. I was in command of our skirmishers, and as soon as we reached this open ground Colonel Miller, in command of the regiment, gave the order: "Captain Evans, deploy your skirmishers and locate the enemy." His order was speedily obeyed.

Began Battle of Gettysburg.

"We had hardly advanced more than 100 yards until we located the enemy, New York troops who were concealed in a wheat field, and were soon in that fight. As far as I know, this skirmish line opened the great three days' Battle of Gettysburg. Our skirmishers, being reinforced, we drove the enemy through the town to College Heights, where they took a strong position and fortified themselves. But is pulling back they stubbornly contested every inch of the ground with us. After driving them to their position on the heights, we occupied Gettysburg until the next morning.

Our command having brought on the fight the day previous, our division was withdrawn to the heights south of Gettysburg, and held under arms in reserve that day. On the third morning we were ordered to the right wing, where we were on the heights until the fearful cannonading from the 400 cannons of our armies ceased. We were then ordered to advance and drive them from their works. Then came the slaughter. We advanced in a V shape und an enfilading fire from both sides of us. We reached the works but our line had been so badly decimated that we could do nothing but surrender. Some of our men actually crossed the works I was wounded just as we reached the breastworks.

Received Seven Wounds.

Colonel Miller came near where I was lying, and seeing the blood run out of my shoes, he thought I had been killed. In all, I received seven wounds. I was shot twice after I had fallen. As I was lying helpless in this condition, exhausted and helpless, a Federal soldier came up and "was in the act of sticking his bayonet through me when a Federal lieutenant yelled at him, telling he would have him shot if he committed such a cowardly deed. The lieutenant made two soldiers carry me into a small stable, where from the loss of blood I fainted and did not know anything until the ambulance corps carried me to the field hospital on the creek the next morning.

"I remained there seven days under the shade of the trees. I laid there three or four days before my wounds were dressed. I, and a lieutenant in the Fifty-fifth Regiment, North Carolina Volunteers, were lying on the same blanket waiting to have our wounds dressed. Finally the lieutenant asked me if I was a Mason and I replied that I was not, and he said that he was and that we would soon receive attention. In a short while after that a local physician came and dressed our wounds. He did not do a first-class piece of surgery, but he brought us clothes and sent us to the hospital in Baltimore, where we were treated fairly well.

"From Baltimore we were taken to Chester, pa., on the Delaware River. We were kept here seven months and I was paroled when I got so I could go about on crutches. I was sent to City Point on the James River. From there I was sent to Petersburg, where I was relieved from service and I returned home and organized a company of cavalry to do picket service on the Mississippi River.

PERMANENT SOUVENIR

T. J. FARMER
11ᵀᴴ VIRGINIA INFANTRY
Waco, Texas

Was badly wounded in the Battle of Gettysburg in the thigh and still carry the minie ball. Was taken prisoner at Five Forks, Va., and sent to Richmond, then to Newport News and remained in prison for seven months.[17]

OTHER BRIGADES AT PICKETT'S CHARGE

LEROY FARMINGTON
11ᵀᴴ ALABAMA INFANTRY
San Antonio, Texas
San Antonio Daily Express
May 29, 1910

This morning's mail brings us a most interesting letter from Leroy Farmington of San Antonio, inclosing a clipping giving an account of the grand charge of Pickett's division at Gettysburg on July

Pickett's Charge on the Union centre at the grove of trees about 3pm. Edwin Forbes. *Library of Congress.*

3, 1863. We have not the space in this issue to publish the account but will do so later. At the close of the Civil War, both the Federals and the Virginians adopted the well-known policy of General Forrest to "get there first with the most men." In this way managing to gobble up lots of credit to which they were not entitled. They had so many advantages, especially in their near proximity to publishing houses glad to get the work and not caring a copper for the truth. Our Northern brethren not only laid claim to victories that were in fact both disgraceful and disastrous defeats in their armies, but also manufactured out of their imaginations a heroism and devotion of duty on the part of their soldiers that never was displayed, and following their lead, the Virginians appropriated to their soldiers in the Confederate armies all the honors of each and every battle in which they fought.

Tackle a Virginian today that served in Pickett's division and in telling the story of the third day at Gettysburg he will mention other comrades only incidentally. That these were on the field he cannot and will not deny, but that they took any active part in the charge or displayed any gallantry, he will only reluctantly admit. The truth is, however, that Lane's and Scales' and Pettigrew's North Carolina brigades. Archer's Tennessee brigade, as bodies, went further, fought harder and came nearer making the attack a complete success than did Pickett's division or of any part of it. That Pickett's division suffered the greatest loss of any Confederate command engaged, was due to the fact that it moved over comparatively more open ground and was the first to come within sight of the enemy. The Federals that day occupied a position behind a stone fence well up on the side of Cemetery ridge. Parallel with the general course of the stone fence and about a hundred yards in front of it, ran the Emmitsburg

17   Ibid., p. 220.

road and between the road and the stone fence – about seventy yards from the latter – was a fence built of rough slabs. From the starting point of the Confederate troops engaged to the stone fence it was about three-quarters of a mile. Pickett's men moved gallantly enough and in a well-organized body to the Emmitsburg but on arriving at that point its enthusiasm was in a great measure spent and only detachments from each of the brigade continued the charge and reached the stone fence, there to be instantly repelled and put to flight. On the left of Pickett's division advanced the brigades of Petti-grew, Lane, Archer, Scales, Davis and Brockenborough – the latter composed exclusively of Virginia regiments. The first four reached the stone fence in organized bodies, but Davis' Mississippians and Brockenbrough's Virginians went but a few steps beyond the slab fence. Archer's brigade was the last to retreat from the position they gained at retreat from the position they gained at the stone fence.

TALL TALES FOR FREE DRINKS

ANDREW J. FAULKNER
1ST ALABAMA INFANTRY
Houston, Texas

Andy Faulkner had a fine since of humor, and was one of the best talkers I ever knew. In 1883 nearly every Sunday night Tobe Mitchell, Colonel O. T. Holt, Sye Oberly and I would sit out in front of the Capital Hotel, now Rice, and listen to Captain Faulkner talk for hours. He was always full of good, clean, healthy stories and told them in the most charming manner. I remember quite a number of funny ones he told, but about the best one he used to tell on himself.

He said he was in one of the fashionable barrooms in Austin with a number of friends one evening when he noticed two rather seedy-looking fellows eyeing each other keenly. Finally one advanced to the other and said:

"Was yo at the Battle of Gettysburg?"

The other fellow said he was.

"When yo rebs drove the Pennsylvania troops back, going to Little Round Top, did you pick up a wounded Yankee boy up and put him behind some other rocks?"

The other fellow became much agitated and said he did.

"I was the boy you picked up and I knew you as soon as I saw you come in and have been trying to place you."

With that they fell into each other's arms and embraced warmly, after which they shook hands over and over. Finally each dug down in his pocket and found nothing. "If I had any money with me," said the Yankee, "we shore would have a drink over this."

The captain said it was all very touching. He had been a soldier himself and knew what such meetings as this meant, so he slipped the Confederate a dollar and told him to treat his friend. But the other gentlemen who had witnessed the scene were also touched and became deeply interested and insisted on buying an unlimited number of drinks for the two old war horses, with the result that the two got so drunk and boisterous that the saloon man had to put them out.

The captain said that a month or two later he was in Dallas and went into a saloon for the purpose of getting a drink. There was a crowd near the bar and as he entered he heard a familiar voice say:

"Was you at the Battle of Gettysburg?"

He looked and saw the two old "heroes" go through the same scene he had witnessed in Austin. Then he realized that they were two old bums, who had invented this plan for getting free whiskey from a sympathetic crowd. It worked, too, just as it had done in Austin, and as it no doubt worked in every place they visited.[18]

---

18   Story told by S. O. Young. S. O. Young, *True stories of old Houston and Houstonians: historical and personal sketches,* (Galveston, TX), 1913, p.164.

Lone Star Valor

One of Abilene's Youngest Veterans

Charles H. Foote
6ᵀᴴ South Carolina Infantry
Abilene, Texas
Abilene Daily Reporter
April 10, 1937

Abilenian One Of Youngest Living Confederates

Among the youngest living Confederate veterans is Charles H. Foote, 87 year old veteran, who joined the Southern army at the age of 15.

He is one of two veterans drawing a Confederate pension, who made application from Taylor county. The others is Robert A. Miller. Under the Confederate pension law a person, in order to receive a pension, must have been born prior to 1851.

"The Northern armies came within 12 miles of the town where we lived close to the River, but our home or land was not bothered," said the veteran. "As most southern families did, my father owned slaves, I think it was seventy."

Mr. Foote said he served under General Wade Hampton, Sixth South Carolina regiment, company D. "right after I joined, I was taken ill and stayed in Columbia for a while until I was better. I had served six months when Lee surrendered. I was at Rock Hill, North Carolina, at the time," he said.

Because he was ill much of the time before the war ended, Mr. Foote did little fighting but remembered vividly tales of Sherman's march to the sea, the Battle of Gettysburg, Lee's surrender and other battles.

Following the war the veteran attended school for a year before taking up farming as an occupation.

Born December 20, 1849, in South Carolina, Mr. Foote later moved to Alabama. With great anticipation he looks forward to a reunion of veterans of both north and south at Gettysburg in 1938. Veterans will attend the reunion with expenses paid for them and companions paid.

Rode With General Stuart

Marcellus B. Fuqua
Moorman's Battery, Stuart's "Horse Artillery"
Sulphur Springs, Texas

Was in all the engagements of Lee's Army, excepting Gettysburg in the year 1863. At the time of the Battle of Gettysburg was with General Stuart's Cavalry on their return from Carlisle, Pa. Did not reach Gettysburg until July 3. 1863.[19]

Fighting Under The Same Flag Once More

J. B. Gambrell
2ᴺᴰ Mississippi Infantry
Dallas, Texas
Houston Post
June 19, 1918

Dedication of the Enlisted Men's Club at Ellington Field

---

19   Yeary, boys in gray, p. 246.

Dr. George Green of Atlanta, Ga, director of camp activities among the soldiers for the Baptists, introduced Dr. J. B. Gambrell of Dallas, who made the principal address of the evening in the presentation address. Dr. Gambrell, whose every sentence is a terse paragraph, brought frequent shouts of laughter from the Ellington field men and from the hundreds of Houston visitors who were freely admitted into the aviation field for the first time.

In substance Dr. Gambrell said that he was at Gettysburg once making the acquaintance of some of the boys who are now men before him. He thought then it would be more agreeable to fight with these men than it was fighting against them.

He thanked God that all are now fighting on the same side in the war, under the same flag, and for the same cause.

16. J. B. Gambrell 2nd Mississippi Infantry. *Southern Baptist Archives.*

A THRILLING SIGHT

GEORGE B. GERALD
18TH MISSISSIPPI INFANTRY
Waco, Texas
Houston Post
July 13, 1913

**Charge of the Louisiana Brigade, Gettysburg.
Alfred R. Waud.** *Library of Congress.*

**Judge Gerald's Paper on Gettysburg
(From the Waco Times-Herald)**

Hugh Nugent Fitzgerald read Judge Gerald's recollections of Gettysburg, as printed in this paper, and this is his estimate as printed on the editorial page of the *Fort Worth Record:*

"Judge George B. Gerald had an interesting story of the Battle of Gettysburg in the *Waco Times-Herald* Thursday. Judge Gerald was a participant in that historic battle and his narrative is thrilling from the start to finish. Judge George Clark of Waco was another participant. He commanded a company of Alabamians and was desperately wounded. Clark witnessed the Gerald brigade as it rushed in the carnival of death, and has often said that it was the most thrilling sight that he saw during the course of the war. But let us have peace. The sun is shining and the crops are growing in Grand Old Texas."

In so far as Judge Gerald is concerned, the war period ended at Appomattox; the South fought bravely and the South lost with honor – why not have peace?

Judge Gerald has never had any bitterness toward a Union soldier; his bitterness, if any, is toward those politicians who brought on the reconstruction period, which period was hades for the South and for which there was never any justification either in law or in morals.

Had his health permitted, Judge Gerald would have been a participant in the recent exercises at Gettysburg.

A SOLDIER OF HIS WORD

J. T. GODLEY
2ND LOUISIANA INFANTRY
Corsicana, Texas
Corsicana Daily Sun
March 9, 1915

At Gettysburg.
Capt. Godley Kept Agreement Made With Comrade

The meeting of Camp Winkler Saturday has brought to mind again the terrible struggle of the sixties and some of the stirring scenes of those days. Today Capt. J. T. Godley was comfortably seated in a chair looking well and wore his usual cheerful smile. The meeting of Camp Winkler was referred to and then Capt. Godley was asked concerning an agreement made with a friend just prior to the Battle of Gettysburg. The friend was R. C. Murphy and he came here last spring from Nechees, La., to visit Capt. Godley and that is the way the story got out. Mr. Murphy and Capt. Godley entered into an agreement that if either should be wounded or killed that the other would take him off the battlefield. While the Battle of Gettysburg was raging Mr. Murphy felt a bullet having passed through one of his legs. Mr. Godley said he didn't know that his comrade had been wounded nor that his captain had overheard the agreement until that officer said to him that his friend had been wounded and that he should fill the obligation. Mr. Godley got down on his knees. Mr. Murphy crawled up on his back and was carried fully 200 yards to safety.

A PRIZED LETTER

C. H. GRAVES
MANN'S TEXAS CAVALRY
Corsicana, Texas
Corsicana Daily Sun
July 7, 1909

Mr. C. H. Graves has a letter that was written him from Fredericksburg August 8, 1863, by his cousin J. N. Graves. The letter speaks of the Battle of Gettysburg and other battles and the writer says his regiment went in the Gettysburg fight with 240 strong and came out with 150 or 160 men. It is full of news of the struggle, its hardships and perils and is replete with interest. Mr. Graves prizes it very highly.

RESCUING THE REGIMENT'S COLORS

JOSEPH HENDLEY HARRIS
3RD GEORGIA INFANTRY
Houston Heights, Texas
Houston Post
June 23, 1913

Joseph Hendley Harris was a member of Company H, Third Georgia Volunteers, enlisting April 21, 1861, and following the fortunes of the Army of Northern Virginia throughout the war, he surrendered with General Robert E. Lee at Appomattox April, 1865.

The Third Georgia was a unit of Wright's Brigade and the brigade was present throughout the memorable three day's struggle which marked the Battle of Gettysburg. Comrade Harris rescued the colors of his regiment on the third day of the battle when the color-bearer was shot down as the brigade was forced to form in a hollow square and fight its way out.

He attended the first Confederate reunion ever held by any company after the war, which was a reunion of Young's Guards at Union Point, Ga., July 1874. A tattered red silk badge for this reunion is still in the possession of Comrade Harris, who prizes it much. This reunion marked the beginning of organized reunions of the veterans who bore the Stars and Bars over many well fought fields.

Comrade Harris has resided in Houston and Houston Heights the past five years, coming here from Georgia. He is a man of family. Two brothers were with him in the Third Georgia and one was seriously wounded at Gettysburg.

A Brother Killed at Gettysburg

J. M. Hartsfield
17ᵀᴴ Mississippi Infantry
Fort Worth, Texas

Was wounded at Fredericksburg, Va., the small bone in the left forearm was broken which caused that arm to be much smaller than the other. My brother, John A. Hartsfield, and Almizi Byers, both went out with the same command which was the second company leaving our county, and both were killed in the Battle of Gettysburg, Pa. Our Captain, known as J. W. (Bud) Middleton, was also killed at Gettysburg. He was one of the finest specimens of Southern manhood I ever saw. [20]

Only Soldier Not Wounded in Company F

J. L. Hayes
26ᵀᴴ North Carolina Infantry
Celina, Texas
McKinney Weekly Gazette
October 2, 1919

We received a call yesterday from Mr. J. L. Hayes, who lives north of Celina, who subscribed for the *Weekly-Democrat Gazette* to be sent to his niece Miss. Katie Hayes, a High School teacher of Wests Mill, North Carolina. Mr. Hayes was on his way home from a visit to North Carolina his old home.

Mr. Hayes is 75 years old but does not look it. Although his hair is gray from the passing of many winters, he stands erect as a person many years younger and his walk is brisk as that of the young man. He served four years in the Confederacy. He was with Lee's Army at Gettysburg, Richmond and Wilmington. He was a member of Co. F, Zeb Vance's regiment of the 26th North Carolina brigade. R. M. Tuttle was his captain. In the Battle of Gettysburg, he was the only member of his company who came out of the battle without a wound. The remainder of his company were either killed or wounded. He participated in the battle of Wilmington, N. C., which was the last seaport of the Confederacy to fall to the Yankees.

---

20   Ibid., p. 317.

"BIGGEST COWARD" IN LEE'S ARMY

DAVID SWAIN HOOKER
1ST NORTH CAROLINA INFANTRY
Galveston, Texas

Enlisted in the Confederate Army, May 16, 1861, at Columbia, N. C., as private Company A, First North Carolina Battalion, Rhodes' Division, Jackson's Corps, Army of Northern Virginia. Was changed to the Navy at Richmond on the account of wounds received at Gettysburg where I was wounded in both legs and shoulder. Was taken prisoner July 4th, in hospital.

The first battle I was in was at South Mills, N. C., and the last was at Gettysburg. The State of North Carolina has a roster of all her troops and a history of all regiments I belonged to the regiment which won the first honor of the South. We were presented with the honor flag at Carlisle, Pa., and I won first honors of that regiment and I have a history of the matter under the seal of the State and county to prove what I say, notwithstanding I thought I was one of the biggest cowards in Lee's army, but others thought differently.[21]

UNCLE OBIE

OBEDIAH H. HOOPER
48TH ALABAMA INFANTRY
Wichita Falls, Texas
Wichita Daily Times
May 12, 1939

'Uncle Obie' Hooper, Grand Old Man Of Cotton County, Dies at Age of 95.
O. H. "Uncle Obie" Hooper, 95, Cotton county's grand old man of Civil War fame, died early Thursday evening in a Wichita Falls Hospital.

Hooper was born in 1844 in Cleburne, Ala., and moved to Clay county, Texas, in the early days. He came to Cotton county as a farmer in 1901.

"Uncle Obie" was with the 48th Alabama Infantry in the War Between the States. He believed nothing but a miracle saved him in one battle when he and three comrades ran for safety with "the bullets whistling" round his head every second. His three companions were killed. Hooper fought in General Law's brigade under General Longstreet.

Hooper attended the Gettysburg reunion last year and had a long talk with Mrs. Longstreet. "Uncle Obie" lost not time getting into the thick of Gettysburg and decided to make a speech at the historic site of the battle of Round-Top. It was such a good ones his listeners asked him to make another. Hooper was described by his friends as having an "almost incredible memory for historic facts and figures."

A TREASURED REMINDER OF PICKETT'S CHARGE

E. P. HORN
HARDAWAY'S ALABAMA ARTILLERY BATTERY
Sherman, Texas
Sherman Daily Democrat
November 14, 1916

---

21   Ibid., 334.

E. P. Horn of No. 1111 East Houston Street, this city, has a clothes brush of which he thinks a great deal. Mr. Horn was a member of Hardaway's battery during the Civil War and was in the Battle of Gettysburg. In this battle when Pickett made his historic charge the company of which Mr. Horn was a member, went to the left of Pickett's division and while making the run to gain the position, there being many dead and wounded scattered over the ground, Mr. Horn found the clothes brush, then practically new, near a dead soldier. He picked it up and has kept it since. He brought the brush downtown and it is well preserved although having been used constantly all these years.

THRICE WOUNDED

ALFRED M. HORTON
24ᵀᴴ ALABAMA INFANTRY
Murchison, Texas

Alfred M. Horton, the father of Doctor Horton, died in Murchison, Texas, in 1910 when sixty-seven years of age. He was a native of South Carolina, pioneered to Alabama, and was there married. Alfred enlisted as a private in company C, of the Twenty-fourth Alabama Regiment, of Cheatham's division of sharpshooters. Among others he fought in the Battle of Gettysburg, and in that great struggle was thrice wounded, and these wounds proved his undoing as an effective soldier and his military career came to an end.[22]

IRON BRIGADE SOLDIER

CALVIN R. HUBBARD
6ᵀᴴ WISCONSIN INFANTRY
San Antonio, Texas
San Antonio Express
May 16, 1915

Comrade Calvin R. Hubbard who passed away April 29, 1915 was born in Vermont, and emigrated to Wisconsin when very young, his service during the war of rebellion was in the Sixth Wisconsin Infantry, which was attached to the 'Iron Brigade' of the Army of the Potomac, and were glorious service at Gettysburg will never be forgotten, and will be inscribed upon the pages of history for all time to come.

By his death the State of Texas has lost an eminent and worthy citizen, the Grand Army of the Republic, a brave and patriotic member. A man who as a soldier in that justly celebrated military division known during the war as the 'Iron Brigade,' did his full duty in maintaining the integrity of our country.

DRIVING THE FEDERALS BACK

BASIL M. HUGHES
11ᵀᴴ ALABAMA INFANTRY
Luling, Texas
Lockhart Post–Register
April 10, 1930

---

22   Ibid., p. 349.

Mr. Hughes is 87 years old and is a Confederate veteran. He was mustered into service May 2, '61, and returned home May 9, '65. The editor of the *Post – Register* has known Mr. Hughes for many years and was first attracted to him by the fine horses Mr. Hughes drove in from his farm in Luling. Mr. Hughes was in many severe engagements of the Civil War, among which was the Battle of Gettysburg. He was in the charge that drove the Federal troops back from their front lines to stronger positions. Mr. Hughes has been around here a long time, has had wide and interesting experiences and can narrate a rich store of facts on almost any subject.

LEFT ON THE BATTLEFIELD

LEROY P. JENNINGS
19TH VIRGINIA INFANTRY
Mineola, Texas
The Happy Idea
July 4, 1919

L. P. Jennings was a member of the Nine-teenth Virginia Regiment. He enlisted in 1861 in Company S, 19th Virginia, Hunting Brigade, Pickett's Division, Longstreet's Corps. His company was organized at Buffalo Springs, Amherst County in the spring of 1861, with Richard Taliferro as captain. From there he went to Charlottesville and on to Centerville, and the battle of Bull Run was the first he participated in. This was his first fight of the Civil War. Next was the battle of Williamsburg, May 1862; then the Seven Pines. The next fight was the Seven Day's fight around Richmond on July 27. He was at Gaines' Mill and in that battle was wounded in the left hip. After being wounded he was sent home, where he remained for some time. As soon as he sufficiently recovered he went back into the war and his next battle was Fredericksburg, December 13, 1862.

Leroy P. Jennings, 19th Virginia Infantry Regiment.
Howell Cobb.

He was also in the battle of Chancellorsville, and the next battle he participated in was the battle everyone remembers, the bloody fight of three days at Gettysburg. In this battle Mr. Jennings was shot in the right breast. He does not remember how long he lay wounded in the field, but a long time. He was taken to the hospital, where he remained ten days, and having been taken prisoner, was carried from there to Baltimore, where he stayed three months. Mr. Jennings came near dying from the wound, the bullet having been cut out of his back.

When he recovered so he could travel, he was paroled and sent back to Richmond. Mr. Jennings should have never gone back as a prisoner of war, but he was and it was 11 months before he was exchanged. He joined his command at Gordonsville and his next fight was the Wilderness. He was there when Grant tried to blow up the Confederates at Petersburg, but instead of getting the Confederates at Petersburg, instead of getting the Confederates, he got his own men. He was in the battle of Five Forks and was wounded in the left foot and went home, and was at home just a few months when Lee surrendered.

BEGAN THE CHARGE AS A 1ST LIEUTENANT, CAME OUT AS A COLONEL

WILLIAM LOCHREN
1ST MINNESOTA INFANTRY
Minneapolis, Minnesota
San Antonio Daily Light
April 6, 1893

His service during the war was severe, culminating at Gettysburg where his regiment made the famous charge against Pickett's onslaught, Of 300 men who made the charge, only forty came out whole, and young Lochren, who started in the rush as a first lieutenant of his company, came out in command of the regiment, every officer above his grade having been killed or wounded.

Charge of Ewell's Corps on the cemetery gate and capture of Ricketts Battery. Edwin Forbes. *Library of Congress.*

BRILLIANT CHARGES

AUSTIN AMERICAN STATESMAN
SEPTEMBER 22, 1893

The *San Antonio Express* canonizes the First Minnesota regiment for the most gallant charge at Gettysburg of all history. If any of the Federal troops at Gettysburg ever came out of their works the Confederate troops did not see them. Undoubtedly the Federals fought gallantly in defense of their works against the brilliant and impetuous charges of the Confederates, but they stood on the defensive all that long, hot July day while the charging was made by Lee's army.

When Pickett's division was repulsed, it retreated under a direct and enfilading fire of Federal artillery, but every man in the division who was hit by a ball it was fired upon from behind the works at Cemetery hill. The *Express* is a little mistaken. While the Federals gallantly repulsed gallant charges of the Confederates, they were at all times under cover of their works, thrown up after the skirmish at Cashtown the day before and made formidable the night previous to the general engagement. The editor of the *Express* has evidently been misled by the oratory of the favorite son of Minnesota on Minnesota day at the World's fair.

One of the most brilliant charges ever made was by the Irish brigade commanded by General

Meyer at Fredericksburg. The brigade attempted to take Mareye's Heights, upon which was planted the celebrated Washington artillery of New Orleans, protected by a line of Mississippi riflemen in a ditch at the base of the hill. The Irish brigade came up three times in the face of the perfect hail of minie balls from the Confederate infantry and showers of grape and canister from the Washington artillery. The last time they came up they seemed to be crossing hillocks. They were, but it was hillocks of their own dead. Never was a more gallant and determined charge made than that by the Irish brigade at Fredericksburg, Va.

CHARGE OF THE 1ST MINNESOTA

WILLIAM LOCHREN
1ST MINNESOTA INFANTRY
Minneapolis, Minnesota
Austin American-Statesman
September 28, 1893

Lee's Army Charged By One Regiment.

Our highly esteemed contemporary, the *San Antonio Express,* in commenting on the speech of Representative Morse of Massachusetts in the house the other day, says he "thundered against Lochren's administration of the pension office. Morse appears to think Lochren an "unreconstructed rebel" who carries a sharp knife up his sleeve for the federal soldier. It may surprise Mr. Morse, as it did Colonel's Miller and McLemore, to learn that Judge Lochren is one of the 47 survivors of the First Minnesota, which charged Lee's entire army at Gettysburg and saved the day to the Union arms. When The Express first declared that the charge of the "Six Hundred," at Balaklava, *The Statesman* denied that any such charge was made, or if made, it was not seen by the Confederates; but as *The Express* subsequently supported its assertion by quoting a member of Mr. Cleveland's cabinet as one of the "forty-seven survivors" we concluded we *might be mistaken as we had always* recognized *The Express* as a war journal, or at least as "a brave" with his war paint always on, but when it has the temerity to declare that the First Minnesota regiment "charged Lee's entire army at Gettysburg and saved the Union arms" we must be permitted to say that we have lost faith in *The Express'* statement that such a charge was made. The fact that we now doubt whether there was a member of it and was there, we will begin to regard even Mr. Lochren as a myth – mythical as the First Minnesota. That statement about one regiment charging Lee's entire army and saving the day to the Union arms you may tell to the marines, but as we are sorter half way backing your assertions generally by injecting a little moral force into them please don't endanger our reputation for truth and veracity by telling it to any old Confederate soldier – it's too thin. Why, if one regiment composed strictly of devils, each one a duplicate of old Nick himself, had dared to charge Lee's army, and one of them would have ever gotten back home to stir up the blaze under unfortunate fellows who never had the ministrations of Sam Small's sermons, and had accidentally, as it were, dropped into that torrid zone.

Come, now, hold up, we know you are going to say that regiment whipped Lee's army. Let us whisper a secret in your ear. We can tell you what saved the day to the Union arms at Gettysburg: It was General Lee's pressing an absolute need of artillery ammunition. The day after the main battle Lee's army rested on its arms on the battlefield, while staff officers of the general commanding the artillery were inspecting the artillery ammunition wagons. A general counsel of war was in progress at General Lee's quarters near the Black Horse tavern when an officer who inspected Longstreet's artillery reported that of the 47 wagons of artillery ammunition taken into Pennsylvania by Lt. Walke, who was in charge of the train, that there were only seven wagons of odds and ends, misfits that were rejected on the field the day before. It was decided to fall back. General Lee retreated to meet Garnett's artillery ammunition train but the Federal cavalry had cut the pontoon Lee left over the Potomac and Garnett could not cross the Potomac. The last of the artillery ammunition the Confederate army had fired at Meade's army when he approached Lee's army on its line of battle, with the rear resting on a foaming and impassible stream, the Potomac. Fortunately for General Lee, Meade fell back and began to fortify, when the Confederates laid a pontoon and recrossed the Potomac safely, meeting Garnett's train on the Virginia side and there they stayed until Meade sent over a corps of his army to dislodge them. A part of the corps got back over the river; maybe that is the charge you are talking about. And now just one word more to your ear: Meade was not to blame for falling back to fortify, for whenever the Federal army confronted Lee's army the Federal general always had sense enough to await reinforcements before he undertook to tackle the Army of Northern Virginia, commanded by General Robert E. Lee, the grandest army, the braves and the truest, the noblest commander, that ever shouldered musket, unlimbered a caisson or buckled on a sword. Go to, with your one regiment charge Lee's army; why that army could whip a cyclone or suppress the eruption of a volcano.

Brigadier General William Barksdale.
Library of Congress.

DEFEAT OF JONES

GALVESTON DAILY NEWS
AUGUST 24, 1880
Defeat of Jones

Jones, a fashionable Galveston young man, is everlastingly boring people about his experiences during the war. At a little social gathering the other night he was calling about the Battle of Gettysburg. The battle had raged for about half an hour, and most of the company were praying for peace.

"Yes, it was a fearful sight. The feds rushed on us with three cheers."

"I reckon they wanted to sit down on you," interrupted Gilhooly."

The result that Jones was defeated with immense laughter.

REMEMBERING GENERAL BARKSDALE

D. G. MAGGARD
13ᵀᴴ MISSISSIPPI INFANTRY
Houston, Texas
Houston Post
June 24, 1913

One of the veterans of the Battle of Gettysburg

D. G. Maggard of 1311 Sixth Street is one of the few survivors of the Battle of Gettysburg. He joined the Confederate army when a beardless youth of 17. So determined was he to fight for the cause of the South that he ran away from the private school he was attending in Northern Mississippi and enlisted against the wishes of his father, who wanted him to wait until he arrived at the age of 18. The age at which young men were conscripted. He became a member of Company B, Thirteenth Mississippi Regiment, Longstreet's corps of the Army of Northern Virginia.

I first saw active service on the second battle of Fredericksburg, says Mr. Maggard. We had taken a position at Marie's Heights close to Fredericksburg. A large detachment of Federal forces crossed the river on pontoon bridges, and seeing that we would be cut off from the main division we were forced to retreat to the top of Marie's Heights, firing as we went. In this battle a thick army blanket I had strapped around me saved my life. The bullet passed through a letter I had received from my sweetheart, but did not quite reach my flesh. I still have the bullet and the letter.

After we had driven the Yankees out of Fredericksburg we had a long, hard march to Gettysburg arriving there on the night of the first day's fighting. We were thrown into line of battle on the following morning and remained in a lying position until 3 o'clock in the afternoon when the order was given to make the memorable charge. We went some distance before seeing the enemy. The first we encountered were a detachment of New York Zouaves, costumed in their red bloomer like trousers and decorated coats. Several of my comrades were killed in this early skirmish, but we soon compelled the soldiers from New York to retreat from behind the plank fence where they had taken their position. One of them, seeing that he had little chance of escape, crawled into a big haystack. I saw his protruding feet and yanked him out. I ordered him to the rear, and the last I saw of him he was going up the hill we had just descended from.

We soon found ourselves in the thick of battle. I saw both Northern and Southern soldiers falling around me in great numbers. The last I saw of General Barksdale he was leaning against his horse mortally wounded. He was game to the last, and I remember him calling out, 'Boys, I am a dead man, but charge 'em, damn 'em, charge 'em, and don't fall back!' Colonel Carter was also killed in the charge. I recall seeing General Longstreet riding along the lines on his beautiful horse urging his men on and issuing orders. He was a grand specimen of

D. G. Maggard.
13th Mississippi Infantry Regiment.
Houston Post.

manhood, and I saw him that day with his plumed hat and gray uniform riding his beautiful horse, I thought him the finest-looking man I had ever seen.

Those of our company followed our dying general, as we charged ahead the fight became fiercer and fiercer. Soldiers lay dying on all sides, and we were forced to trample upon scores. Our company was soon cut off from the others, and my comrades were falling fast. Before long I discovered myself surrounded by Northern soldiers and was disarmed. It is the wonder of my life to this day how I escaped uninjured. I was taken with many other Confederates who were captured to a 'bullpen,' where we were kept under guard. The next morning we were forced to march to Westminster. I was barefooted and before long I was so footsore that I could hardly walk It sure made me 'hot' to have a big Yankee behind me on a horse prodding me on with his bayonet when my feet were nothing but blisters. From Westminster we were taken to Baltimore Md. There were many Southern sympathizers in the city, and we saw Confederate flags unfurled from many of the buildings and houses. Many pretty girls waved their handkerchiefs at us that day and blew kisses to us as we marched by, prisoners of war.

From Baltimore we took a boat to Fort Delaware, where I remained a prisoner for 23 months and 17 days. They tried to induce me to take the oath of allegiance, but I told them with spirit that I would stay there 'until my hair was white as cotton before taking their darn oath.' General Schofield, who was in charge of the island, upon hearing me say this, said, 'that's the darndest little rebel I ever saw.' He took an instant liking to me and placed me in charge of one of the wards in the hospital. It sure did me good to be able to 'boss' some Yankees around. I received very good treatment while a prisoner of war at Fort Delaware. In May, 1865, I was paroled and sent home.

Mr. Maggard has been connected with the Houston Transfer and Carriage Company for a number of years. He is at present superintendent of buses for the company, and is also in charge of the Bureau of Information at the Grand Central Station.

MEMORIES OF A PRETTY GIRL

C. L. MARTIN
55ᵀᴴ NORTH CAROLINA INFANTRY
Dallas, Texas
Galveston Daily News
October 7, 1920

A Veteran Participant at Houston is C. L. Martin

Houston, Tex., Oct. 6. – Among the most interesting participants in the Confederate reunion here is Charles L. Martin of Dallas, a member of Dallas News editorial staff. Physically Mr. Martin is not as young as he used to be, but mentally he is youthful and vividly recalls scenes of battles in which he participated years agone.

Manifesting keen eyesight Mr. Martin told of one of the prettiest and most entertaining maids of honor, saying she came from Hickory in Western North Carolina as maid of honor of the North Carolina division of Confederate Veterans – Miss Frank Martin.

Mr. Martin said that Miss Martin was particularly interested when he told her that The Galveston – Dallas News was founded by Colonel A. H. Belo, a North Carolina man, colonel of a regiment of infantry, youngest colonel in the Confederate army at Gettysburg in the memorable charge of Pickett's division up the stormy heights behind which the federals were fighting. Colonel Belo, he said, led his regiment to the summit of Little Round Top, the loftiest point of the ridge, dislodged the federals and held his position until compelled to fall back because of the failure of Pickett's division which had no ammunition for its artillery.

There are some of the immortal Hood's Texas Brigade here, said Mr. Martin. While General Hood, the first colonel of the Fourth Regiment, Infantry, held that regiment in great store, perhaps Company D from Guadalupe County was his favorite company. One of the most popular and humorous members of that company was Lott Calvert of Seguin.

Georgia Monument. Gettysburg NMP.
Tom Miller.

NEVER STOPPED ON THE MARCH

J. M. MATTHEWSON
6ᵀᴴ GEORGIA INFANTRY
Austin, Texas

Was wounded in the left leg at Sharpsburg and in the breast at Gettysburg. Was taken prisoner July 22d, and sent to David's Island where I was kept until we were paroled about two months later, and was treated like a brother. After I joined the Fourth Alabama I never had time to be promoted. We never stopped to eat or sleep and what little we got of either was in the ranks going.[23]

---

23 Frank White Johnson, *A History of Texas and Texans*, (Chicago, IL & New York, NY), 1914, p. 2233.

JOHN BROWN'S HANGING TO GETTYSBURG TO APPOMATTOX

C. H. McARTHUR
7TH VIRGINIA CAVALRY
Houston, Texas
Houston Post, June 25, 1913

One of the veterans who saw service at Gettysburg

C. H. McArthur, aged 79, who resides at 1907 Sabine Street, entered the Civil War at its very beginning. He fought John Brown at Harper's Ferry and witnessed his hanging. Mr. McArthur was a member of Company A, Seventh Virginia Cavalry. He was 25 years of age at the time of enlistment.

A run sure enough, was the Battle of Bull Run, says Mr. McArthur, who, although nearly 80 years old, looks 15 or 20 years younger. "The Yankees we met at Bull Run did not seem to have much fight in them, and it did not take long for us to put them to flight. We, of the cavalry, followed them and struck them on the heads with our sabers."

After Bull Run, I saw service in the Shenandoah Valley. Throughout the war the cavalry was used almost entirely for skirmishing and covering up the retreats. We were under the command of General "Sef" Steward. It was generally our principal duty to guard the ammunition trains, which were constantly under attack by the Northerners.

After the battle of Fredericksburg, we marched on to Gettysburg. During the march we had about 50 skirmishes with the Yankees. They made repeated attempts to capture our ammunition train at the time. Due to this fact, the soldiers were not over-fed while on the march to Gettysburg. Three crackers a day was the ration given us on some days.

The cavalry was not used at Gettysburg, except to guard the flanks. On account of the hilly condition of the country, we were unable to see much of the battle. The noise was terrific. There were over 300 pieces of artillery on both sides and they were kept in use almost incessantly. The ground almost seemed to jar as a result of this great cannonading.

I participated in the greatest cavalry battle, perhaps, in history. It occurred at Brandy Station, Culpepper County, Virginia. There were 18,000 Southern cavalry and 20,000 Northern. We fought all day, and believe me, it was a great battle. Both sides fought gamely throughout. In our previous encounters with the Yankee cavalry we had met mostly the cavalry forces that had been recruited in New York and other New England States. Many of those who constituted the cavalry from New York were not good horsemen, and were tied to their saddles. But in this battle at Brandy Station, we encountered a new element which greatly added in the effectiveness of the Northern cavalry. This new element was comprised of the companies that had just arrived from the West. Many of them contained some of the best natural riders in the country – men who were at home in the saddle.

We had an ideal battlefield. The meadow was level, and there were no fences to retard the charges. The reason for the lack of fences was that the fence rails had been burned by soldiers who had camped there. Although the Yankees fought gamely, we gradually gained the upper hand and drove them across the river by nightfall. They were compelled to leave their artillery and a considerable quantity of ammunition behind. The field was strewn with the bodies of dead horses and soldiers after the battle was over. The fact that the New York cavalrymen were strapped to their saddles because they were unable to ride well, made it possible for us to capture quite a large number of prisoners. As these New York cavalrymen would become wounded, and consequently unable to manage their horses, they would be carried by their mounts into our ranks. A considerable number of dead men were carried into our midst in this manner.

My military career was ended on June 16, 1864, when I was captured and made a prisoner at Upperville, Va. I remained a prisoner of war until Lee surrendered at Appomattox.

Immediately after the war Mr. McArthur came to Texas and has remained in the State ever since. The most of the time he has been a stock raiser and farmer. At present he is living with his son-in-law, R. R. Bradfield of 1907 Sabine Street.

A COMPASSIONATE MINISTER OF THE BLUE

CHARLES C. McCABE
122ND OHIO INFANTRY

El Paso, Texas
El Paso Herald
February 3, 1898

Charles C. McCabe heard the fife and the drum and the bugle which were filling the air with martial music, and he yielded to the tug at his heart, strings which led him to the front where the great Civil War was going on. He was commissioned a chaplain of an Ohio regiment serving in the Shenandoah Valley. In June, 1863, at the opening of the Gettysburg Campaign, this regiment was at Winchester, in the track of the advancing hosts of Lee, then headed for Pennsylvania. The command, to which it belonged, under General Milroy, after a heroic attempt to stem the tide of invasion, was surrounded and in part captured. Chaplain McCabe was busy on the field caring for the wounded and ministering to the dying, and made no attempt to escape, thinking that he and the surgeons, when the facts were known to the Confederate commander, would be released. In this he was mistaken, however, for with the other prisoners he was sent to Richmond, where he and Libby prison were joined in bonds which time will find it difficult to break in pieces. He was a prisoner of war four months, and for a part was at death's door with illness.

A JOYOUS REUNION

JASPER McCULLOUGH
41ST ALABAMA INFANTRY

Abilene, Texas
Abilene Semi Weekly Farm Reporter
June 25, 1909

Jasper McCullough living out on north Mesquite street was made very happy Tuesday morning by the arrival of a brother W. H. McCullough of Walker county, Alabama, who came in to make him an extended visit. The Alabamian is 71 years old and it had been 24 years since they had seen each other. The visitor left home in April, hardly able to travel, going first to Hall county in northwest Texas, and after spending two months there, and after two months there he is feeling young again. He is a Confederate veteran and at the Battle of Gettysburg, was wounded in the side, the ball lodging and it still remains there, and this, he says, gives him considerable pain occasionally.

HARSH LIFE OF A P.O.W.

J. H. McDONALD
2ND MISSISSIPPI INFANTRY

Commerce, Texas

Was taken prisoner the 1st day of July 1863, at Gettysburg and carried to Fort Delaware. I stayed there twenty-three months and eleven days. Twenty-two of my company were carried there and four died. We did not get half rations and only one blanket to the man. I came near freezing but I kept well with the exception of smallpox. There were about a thousand cases of smallpox there at one time.

I was in the battles of Sharpsburg and Gettysburg besides lots of small fights. I was in prison most of the war but I would have preferred to have been with the company, but you see they preferred to have feed us rather than to fight us.[24]

THE DRUMMER'S SECRET

DENTON RECORD CHRONICLE
DECEMBER 11, 1913

Here is an old war story. As a regiment of soldiers was on the march to Gettysburg, some of the soldiers stepped out of line and confiscated a couple of geese, and one of the drummers unbuckled his instrument and put the captured birds in the drum.

Shortly afterward the colonel rode along and, noticing the boy, said sharply:

"Why don't you beat that drum?"

"Colonel," said the drummer mysteriously, "I want to speak with you."

The colonel drew still closer and, bending down his head, said, "Well, what do you have to say?"

The drummer whispered, "Colonel, I've got a couple of geese in here."

The colonel straightened up and gravely said, "Well, if you're sick and can't play, you needn't."

The colonel had roast goose that night.

SERVED IN GENERAL STUART'S HORSE ARTILLERY

W. M. McGREGOR
G. W. BROWN'S COMPANY, VIRGINIA HORSE ARTILLERY
Waco, Texas
Galveston Daily News
July 20, 1903

He of Stuart's Horse Artillery Spent the Day In Waco.
Special To The news,

Waco, Tex., July 19. – General W. M. McGregor, who was orator of the day at the great Bosqueville Confederate reunion yesterday, while in Waco was the honored guest of District Judge and Mrs. Sam Scott. During the war General McGregor commanded on of the batteries of Stuart's Horse Artillery, and was in most of the great battles of Virginia, Maryland and Pennsylvania. He was several times wounded and received promotion for conspicuous gallantry, especially in the Gettysburg campaign, at which time the Stuart Artillery Corps was commanded by Major R. F. Beckham. The battery commanders were Captains W. M. McGregor, James Breathed, R. P. Chew, W. H. Griffin, J. F. Hart and M. N. Moorman. The foregoing batteries checked the pressure of the Federal cavalry on General Lee's rear in the withdrawal from the field of Gettysburg by a plunging fire of canister, which demoralized the troopers in blue and materially reduced their ardor. General McGregor spiked his guns April 9, 1865, to prevent their falling into General Sheridan's hands in fight condition, and finding himself cut off from General Lee retreated through Charlotte and Halifax Counties, crossed the Roanoke River into North Carolina and joined Generals Johnston and Beauregard. On his departure from Waco to-day the General was escorted to the depot by delegations of Pat Cleburne Camp and G. B. Gerald camp, United Confederate Veterans, and Sul Ross Camp, Sons of Confederate Veterans.

---

24   Yeary, *boys in gray*, p. 473.

Valley of Death and the wheat field, Gettysburg, PA. 1903. *Library of Congress.*

A HARSH LOSS

WILLIAM LEWIS MCKEE
18TH MISSISSIPPI INFANTRY
Abbott, Texas

In June 1863, we again crossed the Potomac River and invaded Maryland and Pennsylvania, culminating in the fight at Gettysburg, where Barksdale's Mississippi Brigade went through the noted peach orchard and wheat field, starting in 1500 strong, walking over twenty-five pieces of Yankee field artillery, and on calling the road that night found that we had 750 men left. Here the gallant Barksdale laid down his life on the altar for his country.[25]

A WIDOW'S LAMENT

MRS. C. A. MOORE – WIDOW OF C.M. MOORE
17TH MISSISSIPPI INFANTRY
San Antonio, Texas
San Antonio Sunday Light
November 15, 1884

---

25   Ibid., p. 485.

Lone Star Valor

Written in 1863 by the widow of Captain C. M. Moore, C.S.A. Mrs. Moore is a refined lady of the old school, as will be seen by her composition.

Come All ye good people I pray you draw near,
My sad lamentations I wish you to hear.
I am a lone widow, in sorrow I mourn;
They have slain my dear husband and I'm left all alone.

At the first of the rebellion he offered up all,
And nobly responded to his country's great call,
In the 17th Mississippi, so gallant and brave,
He gladly enlisted his country to save.

Then to old Virginia he quickly did go,
And in many fierce battles he met the great foe;
He soon was commissioned, their captain to be,
In the 17th Mississippi in Company E.
He was in the great battles of Manassas plains,
Where our brave southern troops a great victory gained
In many battles my husband engaged
And he often was where the war tempest raged.

Then to Pennsylvania Genera Lee made a raid,
To conquer the Federals their soil did invade;
And with him did carry the most gallant band
Of brave southern troops we had in our land.

Their amid the great slaughter our dear friends did lie,
And far from their loved ones were doomed there to die,
They left many dear friends who now for them mourn,
In old Pennsylvania they sleep in their tomb.
That time will be long remembered by me,
That battle was fought in the year '63,
In the Gettysburg battle on the 4th of July
My husband was wounded and shortly did die.

Oh! Alas, cruel fate which destined to roam
So far from his loved ones, so far from his home,
Where cannons were dealing their missiles of death,
And bomb shells were bursting in one massive roar.

Will they place a great monument over his tomb,
Inscribing his honor, his glory, his form,
For in old Pennsylvania he sleeps in his tomb,
So far from his loved ones, so far from his home.

Three dear little orphans were left in my care,
No father to protect them their left lonely here;
Our kind heavenly father, I trust them to thee
To guard and protect them wherever they be.

Mrs. Moore was married again to C. A. Dudley, but now at the age of 74 years a widow and in destitute circumstances. Any little contribution by friends or comrades will be received and forwarded to her. Address all communications to the Gospel Crusaders, 308 North Pine street, San Antonio, Texas.

KINSHIP WITH GENERAL GARNETT

MARY LOUISE GARNETT-MCMULLEN
CIVILIAN
Snyder, Texas
Abilene Reporter
March 12, 1939

A birthright tie of kinship with Virginia, the "Old Dominion state" was a highlight of the golden wedding anniversary celebrated last week by Mr. and Mrs. R. L. McMullen, 2311 Avenue N.

Mr. and Mrs. McMullen, who are well known in this territory as pioneer ranchers, were both born in the famous Piedmont Valley of Virginia, and came to West Texas when this sector was still considered the "Texas border."

Mr. McMullen, who came to Colorado City in 1872 as a boy, says his first impression of Colorado "was built around those wooden street cars drawn by horses."

Mr. McMullen studied sheep ranching for several years before going into the sheep business for himself. The McMullen's had one of the most improved ranches in Scurry County in the early years after 1900.

R. L. McMullen was born March 17, 1858 in Green County, Virginia, and his wife near Charlottesville, found a great delight in nearby Monticello, the home of Thomas Jefferson.

Mrs. McMullen's uncle, General Garnett, together with Generals Armistead and Kemper, were three outstanding officers in Pickett's division who fell at the Battle of Gettysburg, July 3, 1863.

Pickett's was one of the outstanding divisions in the momentous Gettysburg battle that marked the "high tide and turning point of the Civil War."

Another one of Mrs. McMullen's kin, General Garland Sims Geirald, who was her mother's father, was an outstanding general in the War of 1812. Mr. McMullen's father and brothers were gallant Civil War officers.

CITY OF MONUMENTS

A. L. METCALF
9TH NEW YORK CAVALRY
Houston, Texas
Houston Post
June 25, 1913
From a Union Veteran

To The Post,

Gettysburg seems to be in the public eye, and the writer has an intense desire to join the grand armies in their pilgrimage to the greatest battlefield ever in history, and more desirous for the fact that he happened to be in that town when visited by the men in gray 50 years ago. Two regiments, the Eighth Illinois and

9th New York Cavalry Monument.
Gettysburg NMP. *Tom Miller.*

Ninth New York of Buford's cavalry, claimed the honor of having brought on the gory battle, whose anniversary we are soon to celebrate. The question was settled, however, by the Battlefield Memorial Association and the following record was made:

"At a meeting held July 3, 1888, a committee of the Ninth New York Cavalry appeared before the board and established to the entire satisfaction of those present that this regiment fired the first shot of July 1, 1863"

The association voted unanimously to allow two tablets in bronze to be placed on our monument vix: "Discovering the Enemy" and 'Picket on Chambersburg Road fired at 5 a. m., July 1."

The bronze alto relievo of a mounted cavalry picket with the legend underneath, "Discovering the Enemy," attracts wide attention. The work is by Casper Bubari of New York, one of the finest artists in the United States. So now I am going for the third time to visit this city of monuments, a place which has so "great a graveyard for so small a town," whose glory rests in the hearts of the living and on the tombs of the dead, the Westminster Abbey of America.

A. L. Metcalf,
Ninth New York Cavalry

A DISTINGUISHED ASSISTANT TO GENERAL LEE

JOEL B. MILLER
AIDE DE CAMP TO GENERAL ROBERT E. LEE
San Antonio, Texas
Daily Express
January 28, 1909

Miller is Well Known

Colonel Miller is one of the most distinguished newspaper men in the South, and likewise one of the best known Confederate Veterans. He was a Colonel and aide de camp to Gen. Robert E. Lee and followed that mighty chieftain throughout his celebrated campaigns through Virginia. Colonel Miller was at the Battle of Gettysburg and was distinguished by the Confederate Government for gallantry during that terrible conflict. He entered the Confederate service as a Lieutenant and left it a Colonel. After the war he founded the *Baltimore Herald* and for years thereafter devoted his service to the profession of journalism. He was for years editor of the *Austin Statesman*. He wields a trenchant and versatile pen, is a college graduate and profound student of science, philosophy and art.

Colonel Miller always declared that he was actuated by patriotic purposes solely in his attack on the text-book adoption. The fact that Confederate veterans throughout the State hearkened to this appeal, and on investigation became as greatly agitated as he, is taken to establish this as a fact, although it has been charged that other motives prompted him. Colonel Miller has a host of friends in Austin and they are not careful to guard their expressions of disapproval. His elimination has revived demonstrations of displeasure which were provoked by the Governor's allusion to the text-book matter in his message.

REUNION WITH MRS. GEORGE E. PICKETT

MICHAEL D. MONSERRATE
3ʳᵈ VIRGINIA INFANTRY
San Antonio, Texas
San Antonio Express
December 20, 1914

An incident of rare and touching interest occurred at the Southern Pacific depot last night during the short time the east-bound train from California was stopped there waiting for the Mexican train coming from Eagle Pass. Among the passengers was Mrs. George E. Pickett, widow of the great Confederate commander whose charge at Gettysburg furnished one of the most memorable pages in the history of the War Between the States. She was accompanied by her son, Major George E. Pickett, paymaster in the United States Army, who is on sick leave. General Chambers McKibbin, commander of the Department of Texas, learning of the presence of Mrs. Pickett on the train, called upon her in company with Mr. Monserrate, vice president and general manager of San Antonio and Aransas Pass Railroad, who was a color-bearer in General Pickett's division and participated in the desperate fighting in the "Bloody Angle." General McKibbin was an officer in the United States Army and was wounded in the Battle of Gettysburg. his brother had been a classmate at West Point with General Pickett, and since the war General McKibbin has met Mrs. Pickett at his old home in Philadelphia, where both have many mutual friends.

View of the hills on the left of our position from the Rebel artillery, last Rebel shot. Alfred R. Waud. *Library of Congress.*

A VIEW OF PICKETT'S CHARGE

R. C. NETTLES
McINTOSH'S LIGHT ARTILLERY BATTERY
Army of Northern Virginia
Marlin, Texas

In August 1861, he enlisted as a soldier in Hayward's regiment, Twelve Months' Volunteers, doing service upon the coast of South Carolina. In March 1862, he went to Virginia and with several of his college companions, joined McIntosh's battery of light artillery, which was afterward attached to General A. P. Hill's division, Jackson's corps. With that famous command, he participated in nearly every engagement fought by Lee's army, from the 'Seven days' battles around Richmond, to the second battle of Cold Harbor in Grant's campaigns against Richmond, fought June 3, 1864. The battery was then transferred to General Hardie's command at Charleston, and served to the end of the war in South and North Carolina. He was color-bearer of his battery and was severely wounded at the battle of Fredericksburg, December 13, 1862. He participated in the three days' battles of Gettysburg. On the third day his battery was in position on the center of the line of battle, held by A. P. Hill's corps, directly opposite Cemetery Hill on the Federal line, and took part in the furious cannonade preceding the memorable charge of Pickett's division. As the division moved forward to the assault the artillery ceased firing and he was afforded a full view of that, the grandest and bloodiest charge of the war.[26]

A SOLDIER IN STONEWALL JACKSON'S FOOT CAVALRY

J. A. NEWTON
44TH NORTH CAROLINA INFANTRY
Troy, Texas
Temple Daily Telegram
August 22, 1913

Biographical Sketch By Andrew McBeath

Mr. Newton was a member of Stonewall Jackson's web-footed cavalry. He was born in Virginia, September 16, 1838, was raised on a farm, attended school of three or four months sessions in log houses, in 1861 he joined the 44th North Carolina regiment, Co. C., Pettigrew's brigade. Stonewall Jackson's corps. First battle was at Seven Pines. He was in the fighting all along the line after that – Drury's Bluff, the Wilderness, was at Fredericksburg where Jackson was killed and where the weather was so wet and cold that the men's clothing would freeze to the ground while they slept and they had to dig the miles' feet out where they would freeze to their tracks. Was in Pickett's charge at Gettysburg and was climbing over that stone fence – famed in history – when he was wounded by a minie ball, stunned by the explosion of a bomb and put out of the fight. In the retreat he forded the Potomac river with the water up to his nose. In this retreat General Pettigrew was killed. He then served at Petersburg and Richmond, where he was captured on the picket line when Richmond fell. He was imprisoned at Fort Delaware until June 24, when he was released and returned to his home. He came to Bell County, Texas in 1890 and lives of the Maedgen Farm four miles east of Troy.

SOLDIER OF THE U.S.C.T.

ISAAC NICHOLS
7TH U. S. COLORED ARTILLERY
San Antonio, Texas
Brownsville Herald
September 23, 1927

Texas Negro, Age 106, Tells of Past

Nichols, Negro, is 106 years old, and that is the main reason his name is in the paper.

He does nothing much except draw a government pension and park his patriarchal bulk of 200 pounds on the front "guttery" of his home and recall the days when mint julip was served like ice tea is now back in Kentucky where he was born.

Isaac has had his days though. He was born in Clark County July 14, 1822; it is shown by papers that came from relatives of his master, Jeff Nichols.

He has seen Robert E. Lee, southern general in the Civil War, and Abraham Lincoln at Paducah,

---

26   *A Memorial and Biographical History of McLennan, Falls, Bell and Coryell Counties,* (book, 1893), p. 682.

Kentucky. Leaving the old plantation in 1863, Isaac joined the Union army at Harrisburg, and was with the Northern heavy artillery at Gettysburg. After the war, Isaac came to Galveston with United States Colored troops, then moved up the Rio Grande by boat to old Brownsville, where his outfit set out inland for the Indian frontier. Isaac came from San Antonio about 13 or 14 years ago.

A HARSH REVIEW OF HOOD'S BRIGADE HISTORIAN

F. P. O'BRIEN
WOOLFORK'S LIGHT ARTILLERY
Army of Northern Virginia
San Antonio, Texas
Daily Express
August 7, 1910

He Calls Attention To Errors
This Correspondent Has Been a Student of the Historical Column.

Editor Express: In the columns of the Historical Reminiscences of May 29, the editor, J. B. Polley, of the department writes that he had a most interesting letter from Leroy Farrington, enclosed was a clipping giving an account of the grand charge of Pickett's division at Gettysburg. He said space would not allow him to publish it in that issue, but he took up half a column to publish to the world in advance one of his, as usual, sarcastic comments to prejudice the mind of those who might read it. Mr. Farrington's letter was not published until July 3, which we and, perhaps, others were anxious to read. Having other matters to attend to and not answering Mr. Polley, for we took a humble part that day and the day previous and carried a souvenir all these years in the shape of a badly crippled arm, received after Pickett's and the other troops making that charge had been repulsed.

We shall tell what we actually saw and know of that battle later; for as Schley said to Sampson, "There was glory enough for all." As to ourself as a soldier (and a very young one) will respectfully refer you to Gen. E. P. Alexander, who is with us yet, thank the Lord, spending the evenings of a useful life on his rice farm, South Island, S. C., his summers at his cottage, "Flat Rock," North Carolina. We served him as an orderly when he was colonel of battalion of six batteries of artillery. The one in which we served was Woolfork's. When General Alexander was promoted to general in chief of the artillery in Longstreet's corps he had us detailed as one of his couriers. They were humble positions, but looked upon as responsible ones. The courier having a wider range for observation than many field officers. We will further state, for the benefit of Mr. Polley, we were a member of the same corps (Longstreet's) that the Texas Brigade was a part of, from its organization after the seven days' battle early in 1862 until the end. Went through the same campaign, took an humble part as a cannoneer, colonel's orderly or a general's courier with the exception of the Battle of Chickamauga, for our battalion of artillery arrived two days late. Had we been there we would not have been in it, as they had a lot of wagon mules to take the places of horses which we left in Virginia at Petersburg, where we took the cars. Our previous experience with mules (we had them to our caissons at Williamsburg and Seven Pines battles) showed that they had no regard for their reputation as well as our own. We took part in two battles that the Texas Brigade was not in – Fredericksburg and Chancellorsville; at the former whole of Hood's Division, with several other divisions, were held in reserve, taking no actual part in the fight, although we have seen in the Historical Reminiscences by Mr. Polley claiming they did. We will also state that our battalion of artillery was always in close touch with Hood's and McLaw's divisions. While there was a full division of Virginians in our corps (Pickett's) we never saw any of their fighting qualities until the third day at Gettysburg. We can honestly say we are proud of them; also of the troops that were on their left, and we hope later to be allowed to tell of that battle as we saw it.

Now, to the point at issue; we quote in part from our "war editor"; in the Express of May 29 he says, "Tackle a Virginian today that has served in Pickett's Division and in telling the story of the third day at Gettysburg he will mention the other commands only incidentally. That these were on the field he cannot and will not deny, but that they took any active part in the charge or displayed any gallantry he will only reluctantly admit." As a Virginian we are not feeling sore, but shocked, and sorry that any man who claimed that he was a member of the Army of Northern Virginia should have published to the world such a statement as above, for he has nothing to back it up, documentary or otherwise; it only emanated from his own sore brain and vitriol pen, as all his past writings will show. Neither he nor any other man/can tarnish the record that Virginia's sons made on every battlefield, from Bull's Run to Appomattox. He took no part in the fight that he so glibly wrote above; he has told us though the Historical Reminiscences that he was in the quartermaster's department and view it from a safe distance-Cemetery Ridge. The printer or his war book must have put him wrong. That was not a safe place; the whole of the Yankee army was there in a bunch, as Pickett's men and the other troops found out. We are inclined to think his safe position was on Seminary Ridge. We would not know where Seminary Ridge was but from the fact General Lee's headquarters was established on it, and it was where our battalion turned off the Chambersburg Pike and traveled over a rough country of hills, dales, and vales, fully three miles from Seminary Ridge, to where or battalion opened a right in Longstreet's from on the second day, and on the same ground where Pickett advanced to the attack on the third. While Mr. Polley had a safe place, even from long-range shots, we deny that he had a fair view to any part of the field that Pickett's men went over, not even when they reached the crest of the ridge., the smoke was too dense.

In a communication we sent Mr. Polley not many moons ago we requested him, if not published in full, to please return it, which he did, stating that it was too personal. We admit it was somewhat that way, but not anymore than what was due to him in the way he answered a former communication of ours. He had a good deal to say about himself in the letter that accompanied it; incidentally he mentions that he is "college bred" that would disqualify him as a mule-driver in the quartermaster's department., and as he was never a commissioned officer it is natural to suppose he was holding down the brave position of quartermaster's clerk. He must have viewed many other battles from a safe distance while holding that position that he writes about with the assistance of his war book. We are inclined to think he held on to it until about June, 64, when General Lee had all able-bodied men holding such positions and similar ones ordered to the front to help fill up his thin lines, that Grant was stretching to almost breaking point with his vast army. As above, he says of Pickett's men, in telling of the third day's fight at Gettysburg, he will mention other troops only incidentally – "consistency thou art a jewel."

Since Mr. Polley has been placed as editor of the Historical Reminiscences he has heroically given the readers of The Express a surfeit of blood, and the Texas Brigade, and we have heard several old veterans remark. "Ain't Polley ever going to let up on Hood and the Texans?" We have heard other veterans remark when discussing the reminiscence columns, "Oh, I never read Polley anymore." We called his attention to this through the Historical Reminiscences columns as to why he did not give credit to the gallant Georgians, Alabamians, Virginians and other troops that fought shoulder to shoulder in the battles he writes of. His curt reply was he "Was writing the history of Texas soldiers for Texas people and for a Texas paper that was not read much outside the state." We beg to differ with him in the last statement as to *The Express* we have found it in several states that we have been in as well as Mexico since our long residence in Texas. We don't think he has done justice even to the memory of General Hood. Reading from him a person would think he never rose any higher than a brigadier general. He commanded the Texans in only one aggressive battle that was June 27, 1862.

Soon after he was promoted to a major generalship, and was such from the second battle of Manassas, '62, up to the battle of Chickamauga, when he lost a leg. Then for a brief time he was commander of the Army of Tennessee. In all his writings we have never seen where he gave any credit, not even mentioning the name of Colonel Wofford (I believe he was a Georgian) who commanded the Texans in the second battle of Manassas and Sharpsburg. Also, good old General Robertson, who commanded them at Gettysburg and Chickamauga, and only once, and that was incidentally, did he mention the name of Gen. John Gregg, whose calm, soldierly bearing was an inspiration (at that critical moment) to all who saw him as he went in with his Texans that memorable morning at the Battle of the Wilderness, who brought them more distinction, commanded them in more battles of almost continued fighting than any man that had ever commanded them and, while gallantly leading his Texans to retake a position that the Yanks had taken from other troops of ours on the Darbytown Road, within sight of Richmond, to the early part of October, '64, that gallant son of Texas, his light went out. General Lee was on the grounds, having come from his extreme right, which was twenty miles or more, where Grant was hammering him pretty much every day. That position he wanted re-taken and came there, as we stated, knowing that his presence would inspire his men to more daring and desperate deeds as it had on other occasions, but the brave Texans, Georgians and Alabamians that made the assault did all that men could do, facing an enemy three times their number, behind breastworks, with magazine guns in their hands. After a great many of their comrades were killed or wounded they were forced to retire, but that gallant son of Texas motto was, as all his battles will show, was "Do or Die." Our beloved chief saw him in his first Battle of the Wilderness as; he was a new man in his army, coming from the Army of the Tennessee with a splendid record. He saw his remains when brought back from his last battle. With hat in hand and bowed head, showing that he felt his death keenly, he remarked: "Texas has lost an honored citizen and statesman and the Confederacy has lost one of her most gallant soldiers." These are facts that Mr. Polley cannot deny. General Lee sent his remains to Richmond, where it was shown as much State honors as Jackson or Stuart, who were both Virginians.

Mr. Polley has told us in the Historical Reminiscences that he received a ball in his foot, put there by a Negro Yank during the above named battle, but he said nothing as to the death of his gallant commander, not even incidentally, although he had acknowledged previously to us in the reminis-cences column that Gregg's name had been left silent and that historians had not done him justice; neither had the men he had commanded. Who today is the historian of the men he had commanded? Is it not Mr. Polley? We beg to add another bit of unwritten history and show the injustice that has been done to the names of other men who commanded the Texans. You will not in our speaking of the brigade we call it "Texas Brigade." That was the name it was known by from its arrival in Vir-ginia until the end, which every comrade today will bear me out. It was never known as Wigfall's, Hood's, Wofford's, Robertson's or Gregg's, only in official reports from the fact that the three Texas regiments, like the Florida Brigade and the Maryland Battalion, were the only organized troops from their respective states in the Army of Northern Virginia, and we have been reliably informed that the name of Hood was prefixed here in Texas after the war, when men claiming to be members of that brigade met at their first reunion. Ninety per cent of the men that were there went with their regiments to Virginia and did some service in the early part of the war; some returned to Texas on account of wounds, sickness, etc., and as Mr. Polley has told us others got transferred or transferred themselves and came back west of the Mississippi. Others joined other commands and done the shouting for the few gallant Texans that were doing hard fighting in Virginia. We attended several of the reunions of the Texas Brigade in the early 70's, and found that bunch of Hood shouters largely in the majority, with very few of the gallant fellows that served under Gregg in Virginia when the tug of war came early in May '64 until the end Very respectfully,

F. P. O'Brien
Lacoste, Tex., Aug. 1, 1910.[27]

---

27   Quartermaster Sergeant J. B. Polley was the historian of Hood's Texas Brigade and wrote two books on the history of the brigade, *Hood's Texas Brigade: Its Marches, Its Battles, Its Achievements, and A Soldier's letters to Charming Nellie*. Sgt. Polley was the contributor of a weekly column titled "Historical Reminiscences," which ran in the San Antonio *Daily Express* for over 10 years.

HISTORIAN OF HOOD'S TEXAS BRIGADE'S REBUTTAL

J. B. Polley, 4th Texas Infantry Regiment.
Texas Heritage Museum-Historical Research Center.

**QUARTERMASTER SERGEANT
J. B. POLLEY
4TH TEXAS INFANTRY**
Floresville, Texas
Daily Express
August 14, 1910

We assume full and exclusive responsibility for all comments and opinions we have made and expressed on and about men, matters and things. For those we are indebted to no person except ourself, no one having been asked or permitted to dictate what we should say, what inferences draw or conclusions arrive at from a given state of facts, what troops and generals praise or condemn, or what conduct hold as praiseworthy or the reverse. For all of our assertions concerning armies and parts of armies and their movements, conduct and achievements we can show the best of written authority; we are not, therefore, afraid that we have led any reader far astray from the truth. We have written "with malice to none," although not, perhaps, with that measure of "charity to all" which would, no doubt, be peculiarly soothing and gratifying to delinquents.

If we have given any "old veteran read of *The Express* "a surfeit of blood," our only sinning was in forgetting that he had not, likely, grown accustomed during the Civil War to either the sight, smell or shedding of it. If we have given him a sur-felt of the Texas Brigade – Hood's Texas Brigade – all that we can do in condonation of our grievous offense is to regret his seeming lack of pride in the achievements of one of the commands hailing from Texas, that helped so valiantly to make history as to win imperishable renown for themselves and their home State. It was of the Texas regiments in that brigade General Lee was writing when, in his letter to Senator Wigfall, dated September 21, 1862 – four days after the battle of Sharpsburg, or Antietam, where the First Texas lost 83 per cent of its men – he said:

"I have not heard from you with regard to the new Texas regiments which you promised to raise for the army, I need them very much. I rely upon those we have in all our tight places, and fear I have to call upon them too often. They have fought grandly and nobly, and we must have more of them. Please make every possible exertion to get them for me. You must help us in this matter. With a few more regiments such as Hood now has, as an example of daring and bravery, I could feel more confident of the campaign."

And it was of Hood's Texas Brigade that General Lee spoke, when on October 7, 1864, being informed by an aide that it was the only command then in line for the assault he had ordered, he said: "The Texas brigade is always ready."

In all our writings of Hood's Texas Brigade we have endeavored to track the lines of strict truth. We feel safe in denying that we never departed from that line, but if we ever did and wandered so far off it as to say that the brigade took part in the battle of Chancellorsville or did any actual fighting at the battle of Fredericksburg, the statements were due to temporary aberration of the mind and not to such ignorance as has led the author of a recent fulmination to assert, in direct contradiction of both Longstreet and Hood, that at Fredericksburg Hood's division was held in reserve. The gentleman who has thus blundered threatens to tell us quite soon the truth about the Battle of Gettysburg. Before he delivers himself of it, it might be well for him to read more history than he appears to have read.

It is alleged that we have not in our reminiscences done justice to commands from other states than Texas, and have been specially and almost criminally delinquent in respect to Pickett's division of Virginians. Like the gentleman who makes that complaint, we can say, quoting substantially his own language, that "while there was a full division of Virginians (Pickett's) in Longstreet's corps we never say any of their fighting qualities until the third day at Gettysburg." In amendment of that statement we take the liberty of adding that we never heard or read of any special gallantry being displayed until about ten days after the battle named. Then the Richmond newspapers reached Lee's army and told us, without mention of other commands that we were engaged, that Pickett's division had on that 3d day of July, 1863, made the most heroic charge ever witnessed by mortal man. Not knowing any better, Southern papers took up the cry and swelled it to such a volume of sound as to drown the protests of the Tennessee, Mississippi, North Carolina and Alabama troops that had joined in the grand onslaught and felt themselves entitled to a share of the credit.

As for Pickett's division it just "lay low an' kep' dark" and swallowed every tidbit of flattery and adulation flung at it by admiring friends, relatives and fellow citizens. It was the first honor accorded it, and why should it not wear it? But there came a time of reckoning when, the war over, the Tennesseans, Mississippians, North Carolinians and Alabamians found time and opportunity to struggle for laurels out of which they had been unjustly cheated. Impartial newspapers and magazines came to their assistance, and a paper war began that continued fierce and acrimonious for a long time and resulted in the complete discomfiture of the Virginians. That their defeat was just, is, we think, very clearly shown in the article published by *The Express* on July 3 last.

The survivors of the paper war sulked in their tents until 1898 – thirty six years after the battle of Gaines' Mill. Then a large detachment of them sallied forth to wrest from Texas an honor awarded it by Generals Lee, Jackson, Hood and S. D. Lee. President Davis and other military and civil officials – their contention being that to Pickett's Virginia brigade instead of to the Fourth Texas Regiment, of Hood's Texas Brigade, was due the credit of being the first Confederate command to penetrate the enemy's lines at the battle of Gaines' Mill and capture fourteen guns of the eighteen that had all day held back the Confederate advance. It was an astounding claim, and the very audacity of it might have won it success had not the Texans been so vigorous in resisting the attack.

Another paper war began and for a while raged furiously. Bare assertion, however, could not win an honor that fighting had failed to gain, and when the leader of the Virginians placed on record the admission that when Pickett's Brigade had approached within fifty yards of the enemy's first line of breastworks, its men threw themselves "involuntarily flat upon the ground" and lay thus flattened out until "the firing of the enemy slackened, and the sun set as it were, in blood, without either side having gained an advantage," the sons of the Old Dominion fled, demoralized from the field of contention; it was useless, they knew, to day that the enemy's lines had been penetrated by the Texans and the guns captured by the same troops, nearly half an hour before sunset.

Still, we admire the Virginia people. While it is true that they act on the theory that "everything is fair in love and war" and nobody can tell what they will claim as rights, perquisites, privileges or prerogatives, they are all other respects honorable and upright, clever and kind, as hospitable as any people the sun ever shone on. During the Civil War their men were brave and patriotic, but while they fought hard and died hard, there are curious figures which seem to indicate that they knew better when to quit than did even General Lee. The class distinctions which prevailed among them, and according to a Virginian of upper class, who has recently published a historical novel, yet exist, made them rather undesirable neighbors in camp to the troops of other States – their aristocrats being unwilling to descend and their pleasantry, as the afore and Virginia home, and hospitality entertained at a Virginia home, and one of the most pleasant memories is of that kindness and hospitality.

We have no reply to make to irrelevant personalities in which, with strange want of taste, some people are fond of indulging. To such persons we offer the sympathy and advice which the old darky bestowed on his master. The master had an oration to deliver, and having committed it to memory, for lack of a more intelligent critic carried the darky, out to a nearby grove to listen to a rehearsal of it. The master had an oration to deliver, and having committed it to memory, for lack of a more intelligent critic carried the darky out to a nearby grove to listen to a rehearsal of it. The master orated, the darky listened, and having concluded with a magniloquent peroration, the master asked: "How do you like it Sam; how do you like it?" "Don't cher feel er heap bettuh, Marse John?" gravely inquired Sam, eyeing his master with affectionate solitude. "Yes, I do feel better, Sam sorter relieved, you know," replied the master. Whereupon with a glad smile on his face, Sam said: "Dish yere nigguh shoah 'spected yer'd feel bettuh, Marse John, w'em yer'd done 'spressed all o' dem wo'ds foin yer buzzum, an' off yer'll go to de house an' tek er dose o' dat ar bile med'cine yer gin ter me do udder day, hil'll hol' off her e'llapse dat yer mout hev."

We have found much enjoyment in the preparation of the articles that have appeared under the general title of Historical Reminiscences and we are glad to have the assurances of many of the readers of *The Express* that they have found them entertaining and instructive. Not even at the beginning, five years ago, did we cherish the faintest hope of pleasing everybody or keeping off anybody's toes. Since all men are equally daring and courageous, strong and enduring, skillful and fortunate there is bound to be a sling to somebody in every true account of an important human event. Truth is a two-edged weapon and if in handling it we have been so awkward as to use the wrong edge and have thus by inadvertence done justice to any man or command we are very sorry; for using the right edge, though, we have no regret.

We wish to acknowledge our great indebtedness to those who have helped us by their contributions. Had they not done so we would many a time have been at our wits end.

In so far as we are or have been on trial for our sins of omission and commission we now submit our case to the jury, asking of it no leniency, but demanding of it the full measure of justice to which we are entitled. Our own conscience approves the course we have pursued, and having the utmost faith in the common sense and fair mindedness of the readers of *The Express* we await the verdict without trepidation.

J. B. Polley.[28]

WOUNDED AT THE STONE FENCE

J. H. PARISH
2ND MISSISSIPPI INFANTRY
Wolfe City, Texas

We did picket duty during the fall and at the expiration of the twelve months, in 1862, we re-enlisted for three years or during the war. We received thirty days furlough and $50.00 bounty and went home, where I remained for fifteen days and then returned to Virginia just in time for the march to Yorktown. We then went to Williamsburg and on to Richmond, and where we fought the battle of Seven Pines.

After this we left on our march across the valley, hungry and barefooted, skirmishing most of the way to Manassas where we fought the battle of Second Manassas. Here I received a wound on the second day in the right arm and was sent to the hospital.

After recovering from my wound I came back across the Potomac and we were engaged in the Battle of Gettysburg where the regiment suffered another heavy loss. At this battle my command opened the engagement. The third day of the fight, Heath's Division was in the rear of a stone fence near where a board fence joined and these men did great work on account of having this fence for protection. I am of the opinion that Heath's men would go as far as any. I have a right to know about this battle, as I was wounded in the foot within six feet of this fence, and was captured here and kept

---

28 The article by J. B. Polley is in response to the scathing article written by F. P. O'Brien, who accused Sergeant Polley of not fighting on the front line at Gettysburg, but having been where the supply wagons were located. Mr. O'Brien also accused Sgt. Polley of only focusing on the Texas Brigade in his weekly article, at the detriment of other regiments that were not in the Texas Brigade.

in the prison hospital for fifteen or twenty days; was there when our men fell back and looked over the field at the dead.

After my capture I was sent to Ft. Delaware, where I remained for twenty-two months. The suffering in this prison was great. Captured July 3, 1863 and was released May 31, 1865.[29]

SENT TO THE DUNGEON

CHESTER PEARCE
18TH GEORGIA INFANTRY
Galveston, Texas
Galveston Daily News
July 1, 1894

Though having been shot 'through and through,' yet Chester Pearce made what the doctors called a 'good recovery,' and, irrepressible, he plunged again into the Confederate army after his exchange. He was in the historic Battle of Gettysburg, rushed on in the murderous charge of Round Top, where he was captured and sent to Fort Delaware. He escaped, was recaptured, placed in a dungeon at Fort Henry among criminals and in time sent to Point Lookout, and was exchanged and was with Lee at the sad surrender at Appomattox.

Marching the prisoners over the mountains to Frederick, MD. Alfred R. Waud.
Library of Congress.

A TREASURED AUTOGRAPH ALBUM OF CONFEDERATE POW'S

A. J. PEELER
5TH FLORIDA INFANTRY
Austin, Texas
Austin American-Statesman
October 17, 1909

Captain A. J. Peeler of Houston, Texas, has presented to the Albert Sidney Johnston chapter, U. D. C., of this city an autograph album of the late Lieutenant A. J. Peeler, formerly of Austin, Texas, containing the officers who were imprisoned at Johnson's island during the year of the war. Lieutenant A. J. Peeler was wounded and captured by the Federal soldiers at the Battle of Gettysburg in command of his company, the Fifth Florida regiment, the captain and aides having been killed, he was the only remaining officer. The colonel of the regiment was killed and Lieutenant Peeler was promoted to colonel of the regiment.

It was gratifying to his numerous friends that he was heard from through a lady of Baltimore to his wife, Mrs. E. J. Peeler (now living in Texas). Though wounded and a prisoner, he was in "good spirits." The following note was kindly permitted to be published:

29   Yeary, *boys in gray*, p. 589.

Baltimore, July 20, 1863.
Mrs. E. F. Peeler, Tallahassee, Fla.

"Dear Madam – I have been attending the wounded soldiers at Gettysburg and among them saw your husband, Lieutenant A. J. Peeler, and am happy to inform you that, although a prisoner of war, he is but slightly wounded, is quite well and is in good spirits. I hope this will reach you and relieve your anxiety. I am, very truly yours, Mrs. Grahan Rigely."

The Houston Post published the following in regard to this war relic, which is especially interesting as the late Colonel A. J. Peeler was a well-known citizen of Austin for many years, a distinguished lawyer and jurist, author of "Peeler's Law and Equity in United States quotes." He died at the age of 48 years in the prime of his life.

"That this album is in existence will be interesting news to many of these who remember the trying ordeals through which the officers in the Confederate army passed in the dungeons of the southern cause. Its leaves are yellow with age and the names are dim in some places, but the book is in a good state of preservation. Among the names in the book are these from Texas: H. Knittle, first lieutenant, Company C, Wauls' Texas Legion, Benton, Texas: former state senator from Washington county. Robert Wright, captain of Company C, Wauls' Texas Legion; R. M. Powell, captain, Fifth Texas, Hood's Brigade, Danville, Montgomery county, Texas. A. J. Peeler, lieutenant in Florida regiment. J. D. Roberdeau, captain, company B, Hood's Brigade. Captain Roberdeau was wounded and captured at Gettysburg and is now living in Austin, Texas. he is the oldest living member of Hood's brigade. Names are found from every state of the Confederacy on the time-mellowed pages of the album. The sentiment was not killed or even suppressed by the rigors of the northern bastille as evidence by the quotations that were inscribed occasionally. Colonel A. m. Lewis of the Seventh Missouri infantry took from the Selly the following appropriate lines and inscribed them to the owner of the book:

"Many meet who never have met,
To part too soon alas; but never to forget."

LEFT BEHIND

JOHN S. PINKSTON
18TH MISSISSIPPI INFANTRY
Waco, Texas

At the Battle of Gettysburg, Pa., I was shot through the thigh and left on the battlefield, when our army had to fall back to Virginia. Was taken prisoner here and sent to Baltimore and then to Chester, Pa., where I was kept till my wound got well, and then was sent to Point Lookout, Md. Was afterwards sick and sent on furlough to our men at Savanah, Ga. I cannot give dates.

Was in the battles of Leesburg, Gettysburg, Fredericksburg, Seven Days Around Richmond, Sharpsburg, Harrisburg, and many others. I was in fourteen heavy battles. I am now suffering from nervous prostration and can hardly write.[30]

WOUND THAT SAVED A SOLDIER'S LIFE

JOHN ORR
6TH LOUISIANA INFANTRY
Austin, Texas

---

30   Ibid., p. 610-611.

San Antonio Express
April 24, 1916

Captain Orr Won Fame For Bravery
Austin Veteran Called By Death – Wound Saved Life In War.

Austin, Tex., April 23. - Captain John Orr, who died in this city yesterday, was one of Austin's most prominent citizens and loyal business men. He was born in Montreal, Canada, February 4, 1841. After an adventurous life in his early days he finally settled in New Orleans, where the was connected with the *New Orleans Picayune* for a number of years. When the Civil War broke out he was elected first lieutenant of a company which he had helped to organize. His company was in Hay's Sixth Louisiana Regiment, and he was soon after appointed adjutant. He followed through some of the bloodiest engagements of the war, being in the Gettysburg campaign and in General Early's division of Jackson's famous corps of the Army of Northern Virginia. At Winchester Lieutenant Orr was severely wounded and was recommended by General Early to be captain of cavalry.

In the official records of the Civil War, Lieutenant Orr is several times referred to for conspicuous gallantry. In reporting the action at Winchester General Hays says: "I desire here to mention that my officers and men won my highest admiration by the cool, steady, unflinching bravery they exhibited in this action, and particularly would I call attention to the conspicuous gallantry of Lieutenant John Orr, adjutant of the Sixth Regiment, who was the first to mount the parapet doing so a severe bayonet wound in the side."

This wound probably saved Captain Orr's life, for his regiment was afterward almost annihilated in the Battle of Gettysburg. In 1863 Lieutenant Orr was captured by the Federal army and was sent along with about 200 other Southern officers to the famous military prison on Johnson's Island in Lake Erie. For eighteen months he remained a prisoner and during this time he was postmaster of his mess of 124 officers. In 1911, forty-seven years after these bitter experiences, Captain Orr wrote an article for the Confederate Veterans and reproduced the entire roll from memory.

VIRGINIAN SHARPSHOOTER AT GETTYSBURG, LATER A TEXAS HOME GUARD

VINCENT F. PACE
4TH VIRGINIA INFANTRY
Dallas, Texas

Born in Pittsylvania county, Virginia on the 24th of March, 1843. In 1861 he enlisted in Company L, Fourth Regiment of Virginia Infantry, this command being attached to Stonewall Jackson's brigade and he himself being assigned to duty as a sharpshooter. In this capacity he participated in nearly all the great battles fought on Virginia soil, and at Gettysburg he was disabled by a severe wound in the arm. Previous to this time he had participated in the Seven Days' fighting around Richmond, and during this period he distinguished himself by his capture of the Union Brigadier General Reynolds. After partially recovering from his Gettysburg wound and was appointed captain of the Home Guards in Montgomery county, and as such cleared his territory of all deserters and other undesirable characters. In 1868 Captain Pace came to Texas and located on a farm near Garland in the northeastern part of Dallas County.[31]

---

31   Philip Lindsley, *A history of greater Dallas and vicinity*, vol. 2, (Chicago, IL, 1909), p. 271.

ASSISTANT SURGEON AT GETTYSBURG

DANIEL PARKER
10ᵀᴴ ALABAMA INFANTRY
Calvert, Texas
San Antonio Express
March 12, 1911

Daniel Parker, the oldest member of the House of Representatives of the Sixty-fifth District, was born in Northfield, Vt., in September 1835, and consequently is 75 years old. He graduated in medicine at the University of Louisiana (now Tulane) in 1860 and practiced his profession from that time until he retired about eight years ago, a period of more than forty years, the last thirty of which were spent in Calvert, Tex., his present home.

He enlisted as a private in April 1861; was appointed assistant surgeon of his regiment in June, 1861, and promoted to be surgeon of the Tenth Alabama Regiment on the day of the battle of the Wilderness. These regiments were part of Wilcox Brigade, Anderson Division, A. P. Hill Corps, and were in the forefront during all the memorable campaigns of the immortal Lee. He was present and participated in the siege of Yorktown, the battle of Williamsburg, Seven Pines, the seven days' fight around Richmond, Second Manassas, Harper's Ferry, Sharpsburg, Fredericksburg, Chancellorsville, including the second Fredericksburg and Salem Church, Gettysburg, the Wilderness, Spotsylvania Courthouse, the siege of Petersburg and was paroled at Appomattox. He had two brothers who lost their lives in that great struggle, one in the Confederate and one in the Federal army.

He volunteered as a detail to remain at Gettysburg after that great battle for the purpose of attending to the wounded who could not be removed and was retained as a prisoner at Fort McHenry for several months.

While he had many interesting experiences he does not claim to have distinguished himself in any way or to have done anything more than to discharge his duty in an inconspicuous manner. He does feel very proud, however, of having been a member of General Lee's army and of having on one occasion taken that great man by the hand. He does not boast of his achievement, but is especially proud of the company he was in.

A GETTYSBURG VETERAN OF MANY WOUNDS

CHARLES PARK
14 VIRGINIA INFANTRY
Dallas Daily Herald
July 4, 1885

Glad He Is Alive

Yesterday was the 22ⁿᵈ anniversary of the Battle of Gettysburg and Mr. Charles Park, who had an arm shot off on that occasion and who received three other wounds, was celebrating his good luck yesterday on being in the flesh.

FIRED FIRST SHOT AT GETTYSBURG

JAMES W. PENDER
STAFF OFFICER, ARMY OF NORTHERN VIRGINIA
El Paso, Texas
San Antonio Express
July 2, 1914

Fired First Gun At Gettysburg
Colonel Pender, Who Lost Millions, Is Dead In El Paso.
Special Telegram to *The Express.*

El Paso, Tex. July 1 – Colonel James W. Pender who fired the first gun at the Battle of Gettysburg, is dead in El Paso. The end came at a local hospital, at the age of 84 years. So far as known he had no living relatives.

When the Civil War began, Pender, an artilleryman, was in the command of General Longstreet. His artillery opened the bloodiest battle of the Civil War, and in this engagement, his cousin, General Pender, was killed.

Colonel Pender came of the American branch of the famous English Pender family. His uncle Lord Pender, laid the Atlantic cable. He married a daughter of Lord Greenville and other members of the family were prominent in English politics. He was born in Virginia in 1831 and was educated at Cornwall Mining School in England.

Among the notable achievements of Colonel Pender was the building of the first railroad across the Andes, connecting Chile and Peru, and the building of the first copper refinery in Japan. He had mined in Ceylon, South Africa, Abyssinia and all of the big camps of North and South America and China.

He made millions of dollars in his successful ventures but he lost it all in other ventures as unsuccessful.

Virginia Monument. Gettysburg NMP. *Patricia Petersen Rich.*

BODIES OF THE DEAD

L. N. PERKINS
50TH VIRGINIA INFANTRY
Plainview, Texas

When we went into Gettysburg the battle had been raging for two days, and we marched over the ground which had been occupied by Gen. Pickett. There were places where one could have walked hundreds of yards on the bodies of the dead – blues and grays together – without ever touching the ground. At one place an old railroad cut was completely blocked with dead bodies.[32]

---

32 Yeary, *boys in gray*, p. 601.

A LEADING FIGURE

HENDERSON W. PERRY
48TH MISSISSIPPI INFANTRY

Lytton Springs, Texas
Austin American
February 11, 1926

Gettysburg Veteran Dies – Henderson Perry Answers Last Call at Lytton Springs.

Henderson Perry of Lytton Springs aged 80 and one of the three surviving members of the George E. Pickett camp of Confederate Veterans who participated in the Battle of Gettysburg, died at his home Saturday after a short illness and was buried Sunday afternoon in the local cemetery at Lytton Springs. A large concourse of friends and relatives attended and the floral offerings were the largest seen there in some time.

Henderson Perry was a leading figure in political circles and was a staunch democrat all of his life and for many years was an active member of the Caldwell County democratic executive committee. He was a native of Mississippi and was in Hood's brigade during the War Between the States and lived in this county for half a century.

GENERAL PICKETT'S RELATIVE

SEVIER PICKETT
SPEIGHT'S BATTALION

Taylor, Texas
Taylor Daily Press
October 5, 1931

"I enlisted when I was 16 and guess I can lick some of those old Yankees yet," said Sevier Pickett, 84, a cousin of the General who led the Confederate charge at Gettysburg.

Pickett is the only survivor of his company, a Speight's battalion unit. He was in North Carolina when the war ended and with five companies walked all of the way to Rusk county, Texas, where his uncle lived.

"We lived on berries and parched corn and my pants were worn off way past the knees," he recalled.

MEMORIES OF GETTYSBURG, FORTY EIGHT YEARS LATER

SAMUEL W. PURVIS
48TH GEORGIA INFANTRY

Sherman, Texas
Sherman Daily Democrat
June 3, 1911

Doesn't seem forty-eight years since Gettysburg. Not many under sixty have an adequate remembrance of it. You're nearly a half century older, comrade. And you, my lady – well, I've seen your daguerreotype taken in the sixties. I don't wonder a certain young officer narrowly escaped court martial for over staying his furlough. And he nearly missed Gettysburg by it, too. To have missed the girl and the battle would have been a calamity. In all the centuries with their innumerable wars there have been few great decisive battles. Creasy names only fifteen between Marathon and Waterloo.

Gettysburg was fought since, but none greater or more decisive before or after. This is hallowed ground. Ever been to Gettysburg? I wish you could before you are a year older. To see its 600 monuments and tablets, visit Cemetery hill, Round Top, Little Round Top, Culp's Hill, cross that mile wide plain over which from Seminary Ridge thundered Pickett's awful charge. Walk through the Devil's den, the Peach Orchard and the Wheatfield. If your heart doesn't swell almost to bursting, if your nerves do not thrill almost to exaltation, if you do not say to your guide, "I must walk or suffocate," then I do not know the youth of our generation.

I have recently been over the ground "just once more." It is changed where shot and shell crashed through forest then – the birds are now building their nests. The drumbeat is hushed, the bugle peal has died away, the soldiers that endured hunger, thirst, weary marches, charged up mountain side, faced death in camp and field and filled the world with their glory are passing away, the blue and the gray be together in death. The green corn of spring is now breaking through their commingled dust. The dew from on falls upon their union in the grave. From the battlements of peace in the clearer light of the spirit world they surely say, "It is well." So shall we.

Louisiana Monument Gettysburg NMP. *Ray Fincham.*

BAYONETED IN THE BREAST

N. J. RAWLINGS
14ᵗʰ LOUISIANA INFANTRY
McCauley, Texas

I got back to my command just in time for Gettysburg. That was the hottest fight for the time I was ever in. We charged the breastworks three times, and the fourth time we were successful. I was shot in the left leg and bayoneted in the breast. I don't know how I got out of the breastworks, but the next morning I was in the woods with a number of others, and Dr. Campbell dressed our wounds. Owing to my wounds I got a fest of four months and would have been glad to have gone to mothers' just then, but could not.[33]

---

33   Ibid., 632-633.

THE BRAVE 26ᵀᴴ NORTH CAROLINA INFANTRY

S. N. RICHARDSON
18ᵀᴴ NORTH CAROLINA INFANTRY
Galveston Daily News
June 15, 1895

North Carolina Confederates

Alvin, Tex., June 11. – To The News: Some days since the writer noticed a communication to The News relative to what troops suffered the heaviest percent of loss at any one battle of the war. The flowing is an extract from a speech of Hon. Alfred M. Waddell of North Carolina, delivered in Raleigh on the occasion of the unveiling of the monument erected by the women of that state in commemoration of the confederate dead on May 22 last, as published in the North Carolinian. It gives a bit of history that swells the heart of every Tar Heel as memory carries him back to the dark and bloody days of the war. We are proud of this record and while many of us are loyal to other states where circumstances have placed us, we love to know that the Old North State stands without a peer, when mentioned by patriotism and sacrifice. Hear Mr. Waddell:

"I tender her poll lists of voters of 1861, 113,000, and the total of her confederate rank and file, 125,000. I point to the fact that she contributed nearly one-fifth of the soldiers of the confederate army; that she lost one-fourth of those killed in battle and more than one-fourth of those who died of wounds, and one-third of those who died of disease. I cite the appalling and unprecedented fact that at Gettysburg her ever memorable, Twenty-sixth regiment lost 90 per cent of men carried into action. I put in evidence the fact that on several battlefields of Virginia she left more dead and wounded than all the other southern states combined. I proudly show that her Thirty-second regiment floated the standard of the Confederate States at a point farthest north it ever reached. I proudly show that one of her sons, commanding a confederate ship, was the only ship to carry the confederate flag around the world. And finally I show that when the end came and her banners were furled both at Appomattox and at Greensboro, she stacked twice as many rifles as any other state in the confederacy. This is the answer, the glorious answer, which North Carolina makes to those who ask where she was and what she did during the War Between the States.

This record of 90 per cent lost in one engagement by the Twenty-sixth North Carolina stands without an equal.
S. N. Richardson
Eighteenth N. C. Regiment.

ONLY THIRTEEN KILLED AT GETTYSBURG

THOMAS E. RIDDLE
12ᵀᴴ TENNESSEE INFANTRY
Austin, Texas
Austin Sunday American-Statesman
May 27, 1951

Thomas Evans Riddle, 105, Texas Confederate Home for Men, Austin, spends time playing dominoes with attendants, listening to news on the radio or taking a slow walk around the yard using a cane.

A private in the 12ᵗʰ Tennessee Infantry, Riddle fought under lee at Gettysburg. Made an honorary Texas colonel 69 years later, along with the state's other receiving Confederate veterans. "People still argue about Gettysburg," Riddle says. "Some say as many as 2,000

Thomas E. Riddle.
12th Tennessee Infantry Regiment.
Austin History Center.

were either killed. But I know how many were killed. Thirteen, that's all. I was there and we buried every one of them right there on the field.

PICKETT'S CHARGE REPORT

GALVESTON DAILY NEWS
MAY 19, 1894

Gettysburg Field
The Lines That Mark the Different Positions of the Contending Troops. Awaiting The Assault. The Column of Attack – Characteristics of the Charge – The Terrible Loss of Life – Gallantry of the Troops.

A representative of The News recently visited the battlefield of Gettysburg by invitation of Major W. M. Robbins, who has been appointed Confederate member of the Gettysburg battle field commission in place of Gen. Forney, deceased. An appropriation of $60,000 has been recommended by the congressional committee, and will probably pass. The purpose is to establish the lines of battle and mark the different positions of the troops at different times of the engagement, lasting through the three days. Col. John H. Bachelder, a graduate of West Point, went to Gettysburg immediately after the battle and spent eighty-five days, conversing with all there who had participated in the engagement, and made very full extracts of these conversations with the wounded from both sides. He has devoted the greater part of his time since then in making maps and collecting information about this battle field, and is one of the commission at the present time. With Col. Bachelder and Major Robbins, The News representative went to the point where the first guns were fired when the battle was opened. The whole day was spent following the different maneuvers until they finally reached the culminating point. Col. Bachelder stated that he had written an account of the charge on the third day, calling it Longstreet's charge, which is here reproduced. This charge has generally been called Pickett's charge, but Col. Bachelder calls it Longstreet's charge, because it consisted of his command, comprising sixteen North Carolina regiments, eighteen Virginia regiments, and one battalion, three Tennessee regiments, two Alabama regiments and three Mississippi regiments.

The statement is a result of careful investigation from every source attainable, including the wounded found at Gettysburg immediately after the battle-prominent among whom may be mentioned Lieut. Col. Martin of the fifty-third Virginia, Major Cradup of the forty-seventh North Carolina and Col. Frye, commanding Archer's brigade, and many others. The gentlemen named occupied different positions in the columns were wounded in the assault, and I attach great credit to their statements: and last, though not least, the location of the dead as I found them on the field. As the column of attack was composed of troops from five different states and of three divisions brought upon the field under different circumstances, moving from different directions, over different surfaces to one common center, it is important to a clear understanding of the whole that the circumstances connected with the movements of each be carefully considered.

Meade Awaiting The Assault.

It will be understood that this charge followed immediately the great cannonade of the third day, a cannonade in which at least 250 pieces of artillery were engaged, by which it was hoped, at the time believed by the Confederate commanders, that the guns of the northern army would be silenced and its infantry demoralized. And it was under the decisive impression that this result had been accomplished that Gen. Alexander, to whom Lieut. Gen. Longstreet had assigned the responsible duty of determined the desired moment for the assault, notified Gen. Pickett that the time had arrived, which was silently acquiesced in by Gen. Longstreet. The fire of Gen. Meade's guns had slackened all along the line, but from a cause not understood by the confederate commanders then, or generally known by the public now. During this cannonade Gen. Warren chief engineer of the army of the Potomac, remained upon Little Round Top, from whom commanding summit an unobstructed view of the whole field was had. Toward the close of the cannonade, after studying its results carefully, he signaled to Gen. Meade that "we were doing the enemy very little harm, nor was he injuring us," and in his opinion "he was only filling the valley with smoke, under its cover," and advised "that the firing cease." (I give the telegram from memory, not having my notes at hand.) The order was immediately issued to "cease firing.' In the meantime, Gen. Hunt, chief of artillery of the army of the Potomac, had ridden during the cannonade along the entire line, cautioning his battery commanders to husband their ammunition, and also to prepare for the infantry charge which would undoubtedly be made. Fresh batteries were brought to replace those disabled and others were supplied with short range ammunition. The infantry crouched behind such slight cover as it could find, and the destruction of life was far less than might naturally have been expected from such a fearful bombardment. Later, Gen. Warren telegraphed Gen. Meade that the commencement of the charge would be announced by the opening fire of Hazlett's battery of rifled guns from the position he occupied at Little Round Top. And thus forewarned, Gen. Meade awaited the grand assault.

The Column Of Attack.

In the meantime Lieut. Gen. Longstreet had been assigned the duty of forming the column of attack, for which the only fresh troops available was Pickett's division, which had come upon the field that morning. Heth's division which was also selected opened the battle on the first day. Gen. Heth had been wounded, Gen. Archer captured and the division was generally badly "cut up." Pender's division had also participated in the same engagement, in which Scales' brigade lost every regimental officer save one in killed or wounded, including its commander. This division was also without the magnetic presence of its gallant young commander, Gen. Pender, who was wounded unto death on the second day. Two brigades of Pender's division were in the assaulting column. Scales' and Lane's, under the command of Gen. Trimble; the other two, Thomas and McGowan's from an advanced position covered its left flank; while Wilcox's and Perry's brigades of Anderson's division were ordered to cover the right, and Wright's brigade was held in a convenient position to act as reserve. But these three brigades had made a most gallant attack on the day before, nearly severing the line of Gen. Meade's army, during which all lost heavily. Hence it was upon Pickett's division fresh in the field and "anxious for the fray," that Gen. Lee depended to make the directing movement in the assault, and to it was given the advance position. The main line of battle of the two armies occupied respectively Cemetery and Seminary ridges, distant from each other 1560 yards, more or less as the ridges diverged from parallel lines. Between these two ridges is an intermediate ridge, which, commencing near Cemetery hill, runs south-westerly, intersecting Seminary ridge at a distance of two and one-half miles; along the crest of this ridge runs the Emmettsburg road, which was enclosed with stout post-and-rail fences, and on its crowning summit was the famous peach orchard the salient of Gen. Sickles' line on the 2d and after from which his troops were driven after a desperate engagement. This commanding position was seized by Gen. Alexander the same night and occupied by his artillery on the 3d, while Pickett's division, supported by Wilcox's and Perry's brigades, was brought up under its cover to within 900 yards of the point to be assailed, where it lay during the cannonade. This ridge falls off as it runs toward the north, until, failing to give shelter to the troops, Armistead's brigade was placed in the second line. In the charge which followed the right of Pickett's division, after passing through the artillery, almost immediately changed direction to its left and crossed the Emmettsburg road, the fences of which, however, had been generally prostrated at this point during the previous day's engagement.

An Embarrassing Circumstance.

Several houses, barns and other outbuildings lay in its line of march, while nearer the point of attack a number of small rocky knolls covered with scrub-oak bushes were eagerly sought as cover by the men. The left of the division moved to the north of the buildings. At this time the most embarrassing circumstances occurred. The order had been given the column to "dress on the center," but, either the terrific fire of canister and musketry so thinned the ranks that, or from some other cause, to order to "close to the left," a large portion of the right of this command was compelled to move by the left flank; and this, too, within the easy musketry range of the enemy's lines. Had the direct march continued to the right of the column would have struck Stannard's brigade of Vermont troops – but when Pickett's line closed to its left two of Stannard's regiments also moved by the flank, and when Pickett resumed the direct assault, by direction of Gen. Stannard and Gen. Hancock, who were in the thickest of the fight, these regiments "changed front forward on first battalion," had opened fire on Pickett's flank, while Gibbons' division still kept up the fire from the front. Turning to the movements of the left wing of the column – in the formation of troops it was found that the same topographical features which caused Armistead's brigade to be placed in the second line made it necessary to post Heth's division, Gen. Pettigrew commanding, on the posterior slope of Seminary ridge, in rear of the general line of artillery, while Scales' and Lane's brigades, Gen. Trimble commanding, lay in Pettigrew's rear. In the charge which followed these troops, after passing the artillery and the fringe of timber on Seminary ridge, advanced over 1300 yards without obstruction or over save a short distance through the valley, joined further on by Pickett's line as they moved, and together crossed the Emmitsburg road, within an average of 500 feet of the enemy's line. Here the fences proved a serious obstruction. They broke up the alignment, which, under the heavy fire, it was difficult to correct.

Characteristics Of This Charge.

The advance of the column was not characterized by that dash and enthusiasm which usually attends an infantry charge of shorter duration. All seemed impressed with the importance of saving their strength for the final struggle. Slowly but determinedly they moved forward notwithstanding each man knew that every step brought him nearer "the jaws of death." It was not until half across the plain that the column encountered a serious artillery fire, but against which, as a man presses against a blinding storm, they moved steadily on, as if impelled by a will greater than their own – some might unseen power which they could not resist. Solid shot plowed through their ranks, spherical case rattled in their midst, and canister swept them by hundreds from the field. Yet on they pressed unflinchingly. As they rose the acclivity and crossed the road they met a withering fire of musketry – a perfect shower of lead. They staggered, halted and returned the fire, and with a wild "yell" dashed on to their dreadful doom, the left of Pickett's and the right of Pettigrew's divisions charging right up to the stone wall in their front. This stone wall was not of the same height, nor was it continuous in a direct line, but formed an angle. That portion which was assaulted by the right of the column was lower and advanced about 100 feet, which gave an echelon formation to the defense. And Pickett's division and the right of Pettigrew's and Trimble's commands struck this advanced position just that much sooner than the troops to their left; but the left of the column continued to move on toward the second wall, threatening the right and rear of Gibbon's division, which held the advanced line; Gen. Webb, whose brigade was on the right, had hurried back to bring up his single reserve regiment from the second line. But before this could be accomplished the first line broke under tremendous pressure, which threatened its front and flank and fell back upon the reserve.

The Terrible Loss Of Life.

Hay's division, at the retired portion of the wall, which was much stronger, remained unbroken through whose well-directed and terrible fire no foe could pass. Several regiments where thrown forward from the right of Hays' division, which, with a number of batteries had continued to enfilade the left of the column – already weakened and commencing to break. The destruction of life was fearful, and in the hopelessness of despair hundreds broke for the rear or threw themselves to the ground for protection; others pressed to their right and continued the contest at the angle of the stone wall. Of this portion of the engagement Col. Shepard, in his report of Archer's brigade (which had the right of Pettigrew's division), says: "The line both to the right and left, as far as I could observe, seemed to melt away, until there was but little of it left. Every flag in the brigade except one was captured at or within the works of the enemy. The first Tennessee had three color bearers shot down, the last of whom was at the works, and the flag captured. The thirteenth Alabama had three in the same way, the last of whom was shot down at the works. The fourteenth Tennessee had four shot down, the last of whom was at the enemy's works, and the flag was only saved by Capt. Morris tearing it from the staff and bringing it out beneath his coat. The fifth Alabama also lost their flag at the enemy's works. There were seven field officers who went into the charge, only two of whom came out." Garnett had fallen dead just after reaching the road, Kemper was desperately wounded, Pettigrew and Trimble had also been place horse de combat. Hancock lay bleeding upon the ground, Gibbon was being taken wounded from the field; Webb, too, was hit, Sherrill and Smyth both disabled, the former mortally; Stannard had received a painful wound, but his troops continued to pour volley after volley into Pickett's flank. Frye, Marshall and Lawrence, Pettigrew's and Trimble's brigade commanders, and thousands of others lay bleeding on the field.

A Great Act Of Battle.

At this moment (for it was all the work of only a few minutes and almost simultaneous occurrence) Armistead's brigade, which had followed closely, dashed up to the wall already abandoned by Webb's right. That, seeing that his men were inclined to use it as a defense, as the front line was doing, Gen. Armistead for the first time drew his sword, placed his hat on its point, raised it high in the air, and springing over the wall cried: "Boys, we must use the cold steel; who will follow me?" Lieut. Col. Martin with less than 100 men responded to the call, only four of whom with their officers to the crest, passing as they advanced Gen. Webb, who was returning to his front line. At this moment Hall's and Harrow's brigades, the fighting having ceased on their front, rushed to their right and struck Armistead in flank. Webb's second line advanced at the same moment. Both Armistead and Martin were instantly shot down, forty-two of the men who crossed the wall lay dead, and few if any returned unhurt to tell the tale. Thus ended this great act of the battle – one of the most gallant charges recorded in history. Gen. Alexander ordered up Wright's brigade to attack as a relief to Pickett, but Gen. Longstreet directed him to stop the movement, remarking that "it was useless and would involve an unnecessary loss, the assault having failed." Gen. Longstreet then ordered Gen. Wright, with all his officers and a portion of his own staff, to rally and collect the scattered troops, behind Anderson's division. The supplementary movement of Gen. Wilcox's command, his own and Perry's brigades, occurred about twenty minutes later. Gen. Wilcox, who had been directed to cover the right of the attacking column, now received orders to advance, which he did; but on reaching the crest of the intermediate ridge, and seeing nothing of Pickett's splendid column that had so recently passed him, he considered it had carried the line the position and passed over Cemetery ridge, where he commenced to follow. But he soon met a most fearful fire of canister from McGlivery's brigade of artillery and several detached batteries, and a flank fire of musketry from Stannard's brigade, by which his line was broken up and large numbers were lost in killed, wounded and missing. In this brief description of an important movement, I have left unsaid much that ought to be written, untold many movements of individual commands that should not be lost to history, and frequently for want of space, I have been unable to make as full descriptive connection between events as I should have been glad to do so. Events of nearly simultaneous occurrence are necessarily separated in the description.

The Gallantry Of The Troops.

It is sometimes asked, "Which troops conducted themselves most gallantly in this grand assault?" But this is a question very difficult to answer. To do so one must take fully into consideration the condition of each command when the charge commenced, the distance which each had to move, the character of the obstructions which each had to overcome, the cover by which each was protected, the relative strength of the defense assailed, and the character of the troops which each met. These and many other points of minor importance must be fully considered before one attempts to pass in judgment upon this question. Indeed, it is my opinion that whoever visits Gettysburg will no longer wonder why the position was not carried, but will rather exclaim with surprise that any troops could have reached the point they did and live.

PRIVATE TO MAJOR

JOHN ROCH
22ND MASSACHUSETTS INFANTRY
Proctor, Texas
Dublin Progress
November 7, 1902

In his youth he was apprenticed to a machinist but all thought of this was put aside in 1861, when in response to President Lincoln's call for volunteers he enlisted for three months service he was mustered into service in the Taunton Light Guards. At the expiration of this service he was mustered in the Twenty-Second Massachusetts Infantry, with which he would be connected for the period of three years, serving in the Army of the Potomac. His duties were often arduous and he was wounded five times in battles, at Gaines' Mill he was shot through the neck at the charge of Fredericksburg he was shot through the left leg and at the memorable Battle of Gettysburg was shot through both thighs and the left breast. He entered service as a private but later breveted a major for bravery.

General George A. Custer. *Library of Congress.*

General Thomas Rosser. *Library of Congress.*

LASTING FRIENDSHIP WITH GENERAL CUSTER

THOMAS L. ROSSER
5TH VIRGINIA CAVALRY
Charlottesville, Virginia
Weimar Mercury
July 16, 1908

General Thomas L. Rosser of Charlottesville, Va., who was yesterday nominated to be a brigadier general of volunteers, has an unusually diversified history. He was nominated to West Point from Texas in 1857, and would have graduated with the class commissioned June 24, 1861, but when

Texas left the union, Rosser resigned from the academy and started for Richmond. Rosser's father was a Virginian and a kinsman of Governor Henry A. Wise, and so when Wise was made brigadier general he took young Rosser on his staff as ordinance officer.

When the cavalry of General Lee's army was reorganized in June, 1862, Rosser was made colonel of the Fifth Virginia cavalry. While a cadet Rosser, who was the best horseman in his class, was detailed as assistant to the cavalry instructor. One of those who profited by Rosser's teaching was General George A. Custer, and the two then formed a friendship that lasted until Custer's tragic death. When Rosser left the military academy he said this to Custer:

"George, this will be a great war. Let us promise each other that our old friendship shall not be interrupted by anything, and if we meet on the field it will be as friends."

On June 9, 1863, the only really great cavalry fight of the war occurred at Brandy Station in Virginia, or Fleetwood, as the Confederates called it. Custer was then captain and aide de camp on the staff of General Pleasanton, who was then commanding the cavalry corps of the army of the Potomac.

General Stuart was covering General Lee's movement into Maryland, the beginning of the Gettysburg campaign. There was about 12,000 horsemen on each side at Brandy Station. It was the first time the cavalry of the two armies had ever met unsupported by infantry. The fight lasted all day. In the thickest of it, as he always was, Custer was almost surrounded by the Fifth Virginia. At first he had not observed who was leading it, but in a moment he saw his old room-mate and friend, Rosser. The two recognized each other about the same time. "Hello, George," said the tall young colonel of Virginia's crack regiment, as he dropped his saber's point in salute.

"How are you, Rosser," replied the other.

"Let that officer go," called Rosser to the men who were pressing Custer about to cut him down. They obeyed wonderingly.

"You did very right," said General Stuart when Rosser told him the story after the fight. "These things soften the barbarities of war."

After the surrender Rosser had nothing to do in Virginia. He did not care to go back to Texas, so he struck out for the northwest and for a year or two disappeared. The Northern Pacific railroad was being built at this time. General Custer, then lieutenant colonel of the Seventh cavalry, with eight full troops of his regiment, was guarding the working parties against the Sioux, who were away out near what is now Fort Buford.

One day as Custer was riding idly along the line of excavation he was struck by the physical shape of a section boss, a tall, picturesque young fellow, whose heavy beard and bread-brimmed hat rendered further recognition difficult. The man was driving his force of 250 Irishman with tremendous energy.

"That fellow's been a soldier somewhere," said Custer to his brother Tom, "I can see it in every move he makes. I'll find out."

"Hello, my man," called Custer to the brawny Irish boss of a gang, "who is that with the red shirt and broad rim hat who is bossing this section?"

"Sure, general," responded the other, "an' I dunno sir, but he do be a terrible cusser."

At this moment the subject of the conversation drew nearer. "By jove, I've known that fellow somewhere," said the young lieutenant colonel.

"I say," he began, addressing the stalwart boss, "where have I known you?"

The other never looked up, but kept on with his work. In a moment he replied, "Why, confound you; I taught you to ride at West Point."

In a second Custer was out of his saddle and had his arms around the big man's neck.

"Haven't you something better than bossing a section for a West Point man to do?" said General Custer to William Milner Roberts, chief engineer of the road, that evening.

"Why, yes, of course I have; but what do you mean?"

Custer then told him how Rosser, having nothing better to do had taken pick and shovel in his hands and gone to work on the Northern Pacific as a railway laborer.

Rosser was made assistant to the chief engineer of the line and pushed his working parties through the Uncapapa and Sans Arc, all on the warpath, and Bois Brnic Sioux country, having many a sharp fight with the northern tribes before he could in security run his lines. Finally General Rosser became chief engineer of the entire line. Knowing just where the road would run, he invested his wages so prudently that in a few years he had $50,000. He invested it carefully, and now lives near Charlottesville on the finest estate of the whole country side. Why he quit all of this and his charming wife, to put on the blue no one but himself can say. General Fitzhugh Lee, one of those brigades and afterward a division Rosser commanded, asked for his appointment and got it. Rosser will go to Lee's corps, the Seventh.

LOST BOTH LEGS AT GETTYSBURG

A. D. SADLER
61ST VIRGINIA INFANTRY
Galveston, Texas
Brenham Weekly Banner
April 10, 1890

Texas farmer gets off a pun by remarking that the difference between Capt. Sadler and Mr. Wortham as candidates for state treasurer seems to be that one wants a legacy and the other hast no legatee. Mr. Wortham claims the office as a legacy from Uncle Frank Lubbock by virtue of having served for a number of years as his clerk. Capt. Sadler is a gentleman who visited Brenham recently and whose presence here and whose candidacy were noted in the local columns of this paper. It will be remembered he had both legs shot off at the Battle of Gettysburg.

BOUNDARIES FOR THE BATTLEFIELD

Galveston Daily News
June 6, 1890

The Confederate Lines
Marks And Boundaries Proposed A Gettysburg. A Bill Before Congress Appropriating $300,000 for the Purpose – that a Simple Tablet Marks the Desperate Valor of the Confederate Soldier.

Washington. June 5. – [Special] – There is a bill before congress appropriating about $300,000 for the establishment of the works and boundaries of the Confederate lines at the battlefield of Gettysburg and for the purchase of such grounds may be necessary to place it in the hands of the government.

A story told by Robert Cowart of Dallas on Judge Aldridge of the same place is applicable here and conveys the point intended for by the friends of the measure. Judge Aldridge, while in Chicago, went to the cyclorama off the Battle of Gettysburg. It was just after the first cyclorama had been unfolded to the gaze of the American people, and they naturally attracted great attention. On this occasion there where hundreds of northern visitors present, and the man whose duty it was to explain the points of the picture waxed eloquent over the acts of heroism of the Union troops. "There," said he as he pointed to a spot on the canvas, "was where they came within a pistol shot of our brave boys, who poured into them such a deadly volley that they recalled. "There," pointing to another spot, "they came up and almost grasped the guns of our heroes. Their Struggle For Supremacy was in vain, as their saviors of the Union grasped them in their embrace and crushed the life out of them. He went on, in this style for half an hour, at the end of which time he wiped his brow and asked if anybody would like to ask any questions about any matter they did not understand. Aldrich, from whose face no man has ever yet been to interpret the working of his mind, in a timid way intimated that he was befogged and would like to ask one question. As he was the only person who had responded to the request for interrogatories, very naturally all attention was fixed on him. The talker of the show told him not to be backward, but go ahead. The question was "Why were they fighting?" The showman turned red and bean to expectorate in a dry sort of way. His confusion was not aided by the slight titter, which grew into a roar of laughter as the crowd saw the point.

"Who Were they Fighting."

This is not right. The war is a thing of the past. On this field of Gettysburg we had an illustration of American valor and partiality – should not exist. No Southern man will deny the courage of the Union soldier on this occasion. The politician of the North is losing his influence in the matter of the war and the Northern people are free to admit the courage of the Confederates. The stately monuments to Northern heroism are loosely without the humble stones – to these on the other side, telling who was fighting and how they fought. These humble stones, marking positions, may too, after times be shadowed by monuments which will grow from the generosity and pride of the Southern people, who know so well how nobly their people fought.

The best of strife has almost abated. It will have been gone forever in ten years. With it will have gone a great interest in it. The Northern people understand this, and hence have perpetuated this love for their soldiers in enduring brass and marble, that future generations may know what heroes preceded them. What are the Southern people doing? Broken in purse and in spirit, they have not had the means to do that which their hearts would have had them do, and they have moaned over their dead, as needing no further monument than that of the great love and pride for them which is forever in their souls. There are dozens of men who will vote

Against The Measure

because it is a good policy to impress voters with the idea that their representatives are economical and averse to spending public money. The majority of them are from the South, but I hope that on this occasion they will agree that this is not an extravagance but a justice to their people, and that they belonged and of which they each and every one expresses himself as being so proud. The field of Gettysburg has always been an interesting one to me though I had never seen it till a few days ago when a delegation from Washington went to it in what was meant by the bill herein before alluded to. Among my friends in Texas, I count many men who were in the terrible fight, and who time and again explained it to me, but not till I stepped foot on this ground and saw it all could I comprehend anything of the horror that must have hung over this spot which, no nestling in the bosom of the Alleghenies, in the abiding place of plenty and peace. Colonel Batchelder, who has made a study of the battle from the day it was fought to the present time, pointed out every point in the field on which we tarried for four or five hours. His addresses at such point, in explanation, was eminently fair and at no time were marked by such eloquence as draw from Judge Aldridge the inquiry as to who were the men who were fighting against the Federal army. I am no soldier – I have neither experience nor theories, but after

Looking At Every Point

and hearing the details of the battle, I am impressed with the following idea. The Confederates started up the Shenandoah valley into the Cumberland valley, which is but a continuation of the former, in order to capture Harrisburg. The Federals ascertaining that the Confederates had left Virginia pursued them at once. So they nearly marched side by side till they were near Gettysburg. Here there is a small ridge in the valley which divided and concealed each from the other's view. The valley becoming more narrow it was impossible for the two lines to prevent a clash. And here is where they clashed. I stood on the very spot on one side of the town where the first gun was fired which commenced that general engagement was at hand. General Reynolds of the Federal army was killed in a little grove of timber about a hundred yards away, and scarcely two hundred yards from that point in the fatal ditch as which so many Mississippians met defeat and so many North Carolinians met death. A country road rose at right angles with this ditch, which is a railroad but about ten feet in depth and about two hundred yards in length. Along this road now are monument after monument telling of the regiments of Federal soldiers which stood there during

The First Day's Fight
A Mississippi regiment attempted to get through the railroad cut. They came into it and were caught like rats. Two Federal regiments poured volley after volley and contended a surrender. This bloody work being done, the federals ensconced themselves is the sore spot. A North Carolina regiment came on the scene just after this catastrophe to their comrades; come over a small rise a quarter a mile away; came marching in line as if on dress parade; came within forty steps of this chasm when a Wisconsin regiment poured into them such a leaden death that the line fell as it stood, the men almost shoulder to shoulder. I went to where they fell, I looked for the railroad cut. The human eye could not have detected its presence had not the signs of telegraph poles been there. Twenty-three years afterward a great crowd of northern people stood upon the brinks of this bloody chasm, looked down into it, went away and viewed the spots where so many of the confederates breathed their last, and I heard but one remark, and that was: "How dreadful; how dreadful." In the edge of town is a seminary On its top is a kind of bell-shaped tower. In this General Lee stood, so the guides say, and reviewed that battle which meant so much to him and his people. Further on is famous Seminary ridge, across which Longstreet hurled 18,000 men. The guides say that Lee was nearly out of ammunition. Historians do not dispute this. Longstreet believed

The Charge Was Ill Advised
But ammunition running scarce there was nothing to be done but this. It was bayonet now. Along the top of this hill there were three lines of federals, one just behind the other, while in front of them for a mile and a half were the batteries of the federal army shotted to the muscle for the charge which they knew must come. And still in advance of the batteries was a stone fence, behind which was another line was another line of federals. The fence is there, its stones are gray and mossy, but it stands as it stood that day, a veritable breast plate for the heart of the union. The line back behind the batteries are clearly defined by monuments, which tell simply the name of the command, regiment, or company and the horrors of the fight by the number of men who met their death upon the spot.

A little grove of trees, some of which are no larger than a strong man's thigh, is between the monuments and the fence. It is surrounded by an iron fence and is not more than thirty yards in diameter. It must have been a cluster of bushes. I asked why it was railed in. The reply was that it was the point which each confederate soldier was commanded to reach. It was the common point for the charge. The stone wall is just on the edge of the valley or meadow, and this grove of trees about fifty feet back. The valley or meadow that lies spread out under this elevation is about seven-eighths of a mile in width. From

The Crest Of The Hill
or Cemetery ridge it appears to be perfectly flat, but an inspection will show that from the trees on the other side is an ascension – not heavy, but just enough to tire a man to walk it. In those trees on the opposite side were the confederates. Back of them a short distance was their artillery. The guides say this roared on the federal troops on Cemetery hill for an hour and a half, when from out on the green foliage a third line, as if of gray smoke, came swiftly on. There were no drums beating. There were no bands. There was no hurrahs. Silently and swiftly, as if the teeth were on the lips, and every muscled strained as if this was to be the last of mortal work, it glided across the green award, while from the eminence above a very hell of shrieking shells and hissing balls were poured into it. Round shot was used. Men fell, but men closed up. Shrapnel was poured in. Men fell, but man closed up. Grape shot tore down company after company, but never was there a lag, never a falter. Only a hun-

dred yards from the wall! Behind it men knelt down and said nothing. They knew what the line of gray meant. They know that now.

The Life Of The Union

was with them. A failure meant its death. If over that wall they came the blood of the years before had been spilled in vain. Only seventy yards away, and if hell had vomited its worst it could not have been more frightful. Volley after volley was poured on the host, which still came on, though death had ridden through them so often that there was but a fringe of that great line which marched from the fresh woods beyond. The wall was nearly reached. The wall was reached, but there were not more than a handful of that 18,000 who had made that fearful charge to mount it. But they mounted it. What could they? Behind them were their comrades stricken in death. Why should they fear death now that death had played with them for that fearful distance they had passed? They mounted the wall; they passed it; they struggled on, fighting seeing their numbers; gathered around and sent them to the dust. Five men went further than the rest. They succeeded in getting over the wall and seventy yards into the federal lines. Among was General Armistead of Virginia. He died, and a simple tablet marks the spot, and marking it marks the high water mark of the confederacy. On it when I saw it was a little read rose. It was a simple but

A Grand Tribute

to a soldier who, conscientiously doing his duty, had done it for his life's worth. Down in that meadow peace is typified. The cow bells' sweet music is heard on every side. The birds sing from every bush, and some of them nest in the bushes growing over that dreadful wall. The houses in the distance are as white as snow, and the great red barns look fat with their contents. Like a gray veil in the distance is the Cumberland range of mountains. It was nearly nightfall when we left. The cows were coming home, making the air resonant with the music of their bells, the whippoorwill had begun to call to his mate from Big Round Top and Little Round Top, where death once held such high carnival, and over the entire valley, from mountainside to mountainside there came a feeling of blessed and sweetest peace.

MONUMENTS ON HALLOWED GROUND

J. Z. H. SCOTT
10TH VIRGINIA CAVALRY

Galveston, Texas
Galveston Daily News
March 3, 1902

Old Field Of Battle – Judge Scott Tells Camp Magruder How It Looks There To-day.

It is my purpose this evening to confine myself as far as I can to an account of one particular expedition, which I took in company with one of Lee's paladins to examine the battlefield of Gettysburg. neither of us had been there since July 4, 1863. On that occasion we were buried with many cares and duties and had neither the leisure nor composure needed for a careful comprehensive study of the situation. It had not then been mapped and measured to within the fraction of an inch, nor marked to show each position and by what occupied. If all this information had been available to General Lee in those days you and I might still be living, as we lived then, under Confederate colors of blessed memory.

"But to my tale. My companion and I started from Harrisburg in the historic Valley of Virginia, all of which was debatable land in those times, for it was occupied alternately by our armies and those of the enemy, once, twice, even four times in a single year. The old valley turnpike along which, to and fro, hurried Jackson's sinewy men to strike in turn Milroy, Banks, Fremont and Shields all within the space of 30 days, is now paralleled by railroads from Waynesboro and Staunton to the Potomac and as we speeded by we looked out for the cars on the scenes of strife at New Market, where the V. M. I., Cadets, boys from 11 to 18 years of age, charged and captured artillery served by veterans; at Mount Jackson, at Kernstown, historic witness of pitched battles to Harper's Ferry, first made famous by the infamous John Brown, his capture there by Generals Lee and Stewart under orders from the Federal government and his righteous execution by the Virginia authorities.

"In those days even such wild abolitionists as Garret Smith and William Lloyd Garrison strained their charity to pity the misguided zeal of this team whose fanaticism turned to insurrections, secularism and murder. But latterly a President of the United States in journeying through the land has gone far out of his way to stand uncovered at John Brown's grave to do worship to his memory. Can we wonder that six months ago he himself should parish at the hands of a murderer of the same type as the man whose crime he thus honored? Civilization rejoices that John Brown and Czolgosz have paid the supreme penalty for their equal crimes against organized society.

"The site of the Fire Engine House at Harper's Ferry, long known as John Brown's Fort, is marked by a monument erected by his sympathizers and laudatory of the man and his crimes. The building itself was taken to a Northern city many years ago to serve as an object of religious veneration to the haters of the South, in that region. In the Museum of Art in New York, I saw prominent among the paintings one of John Brown going to his execution, and showing also a grateful negro woman holding her child forth for a sanctified kiss from the aged martyr. We of the South are asked and expected to forgive and forget the injuries received at the hands of the people of the North, while they, good souls, perpetuate in every way the memory of those crimes which drove the South to desperation.

"Harper's Ferry is famous also as the scene of the capture by Stonewall Jackson of some 11,000 Yankee troops in 1862. When Lee moved to Frederick City the evacuation of Harper's Ferry by the Federal troops there became a military necessity. In his great surprise they remained, as it afterwards appeared, by the direction of Halleck, and it became necessary for Lee to rid his flank and rear of menace from that direction. Jackson was detached to hem the garrison on the south and west, while McLaws took position on the Maryland Heights and Walker occupied Loudon Heights on the Virginia side. The capture was assured as soon as Jackson crossed the Potomac and marched through Martinsburg to the rear of Harper's Ferry; the rest of the work was a mere matter of detail. From Harper's Ferry my companion and I travelled by rail, through Pleasant Valley to Hagerstown, and thence, after some vexatious delays and missing connections, over and through the mountains by Fairland to Gettysburg, reaching our destination in the late evening. Our progress, conformed, of course, to railway schedules, and herein differed from our approach toward the same spot 37 years before. General Lee made our schedules at that time, and we had less troubles and anxiety about them. In the morning we engaged, transportation of our host, who was also a competent guide, and arranged to make the tour of the field in company with a gentleman and two ladies of our one way of thinking and two ladies of the Northern persuasion.

"We first went out on the Cashtown road, along which Heath moved on the village on July 1, and bearing to his north and east covered the ground over which Early and Roads, marching to the sound of Heath's battle, assaulted the Federal right and after desperate fighting drove them back on their center and through the town to Cemetery Hill in its rear. Turning back toward the Seminary we followed the ridge of that name, which was occupied by Hill and Longstreet during the second and third days of battle and from which our assault were made. We followed the Confederate line, some two miles, I suppose, to Round Top, the extreme Confederate right, and in its vicinity examined the Federal stronghold on Little Round Top and the Devil's Den in front of it, occupied during the battle by Southern sharpshooters. Returning toward the town, we passed along the Federal position on Cemetery Ridge from Little Round Top to Cemetery Hill and saw the field for the first time from the enemy's standpoint. In the evening we drove eastward to the scene of the cavalry engagement on the 3d of July between Stewart and Gregg and thence returning and followed the Federal line from their extreme apex on Cemetery Hill. Our right for the most part was along roads constructed by the Government in pursuance of a design begun early and in continuous execution to make the entire battlefield a National Park, and locations of troops, batteries, headquarters, etc., are clearly marked in the greatest detail so far as the Federal position is concerned. Pieces of field artillery cohabitates the identical guns used in the battle are on the ground and pointed in the direction of their fire during the battle. In great part, but not so completely, the Confederate position is similarly marked and illustrated.

"The most prominent and conspicuous feature of the field is the line of monuments that crowns Cemetery Ridge, almost continuously from one end of it to the other. Each division, each brigade, each company, and in some cases the individual has erected some shaft, tablet or figure to tell the place where they crouched to the earth during the two days' battle, while Confederate lines of battle marched erect a mile or more across the open plain, torn from start to finish by the concentrated fire of 200 cannon to meet and pierce the infantry lines on those heights. Ninety-eight thousand "present and equipped for duty," according to Meade's official report, with 360 cannon, so bravely held those heights against the attack of 62,000 Confederates, according to the estimate of Colonel Walter Taylor, Adjutant General of Lee's army, that supreme honor was held to be due to each here who thus witnessed the shock of almost two Confederates to every three in the Federal army, That is the meaning of the monuments I have mentioned. Among them I recall two that attest most happily, however unintentionally, the transcendent glory of Confederate arms on that field. One is the statue of a Yankee Captain by the name of Brown, as I remember: It is of heroic size, seemingly gilded, and shines afar from a pedestal of some height. At his feet is seen a hatchet, never falling sign and emblem of a "tough story." In his hand he holds a sword and the tradition is that having left his manly zeal for the welfare of his command on the march, outrun his respect for some well-meant orders of his superiors, he was put under arrest and so remained during part, if not the whole of the battle. He would not be restrained, however, and into the struggle went with his men, carrying a hatchet in lieu of the sword of which he was deprived when he was arrested. He dealt with the enemy so valorously that in place of (or in addition to) the hatchet he exanimated at the end of the battle, a Confederate officer's sword. Hence the statue (bronze or gilt) to commemorate the heroic courage, required to wait stationary on Cemetery Ridge in comparative security, while that Confederate officer led his men over an open plain, swept the 300 cannon, to give Captain Brown a chance to get the sword, most probably from the Confederate's dead body. Whose is this glory told by this monument?

"Another statue, gilt or bronze it matters not, is of a Federal infantryman in the act of striking something in front of him with his clubbed rifle. In pretended simplicity and ignorance, I asked our guide what that meant "There," he replied, "is where they came to blows with their muskets." "Ah!" I mused, "Someone must have been pretty close to them at that time." Whose, I ask you now, was the credit, the glory of that strife, the men who, three to two, waited the assault, or the depleted lines that had reeled and staggered through a hell of wounds and death and destruction to reach superior numbers and undaunted meet them hand to hand?

"There is one monument, yes, two, not exactly one, but a little inside of the Federal lines, to which the attention of the casual visitor is not called. The furthest inside is called 'high-water mark' and indicates the extreme reach of Confederate troops. The other is near at hand and bears the name of Lewis Armstead. Here he fell, than whom no worthier, truer or braver Southerner fell that day. (Remember always that they had marched a mile through the artillery fire I have mentioned), and placing his hat upon his drawn sword and waving it high in air as a rallying and guiding signal, he urged his men forward to complete the success he so desperately earned. He fell, as I have stated, and his men, no longer held by his magnificent daring. After advancing a little farther, gave way and the day was lost. I do not mean to say that it would have been otherwise had he lived, for the supports intended to follow failed to cooperate with him and without them he could not have held the place which he won. Around these two monuments clusters more of glory than around all the others combined. I felt that I trod on holy ground consecrated by such patriotism and lofty courage, reckless of consequences when Gray led the way.

"Official returns show that in the Battle of Gettysburg out of 28,000 effectives Meade lost 23,019 leaving 75,000 still available after the engagement. Out of 62,000 General Lee lost 25,451 leaving in round numbers 41,500 in the close of the fight. Meade prudently remained on Cemetery Ridge nor is it recorded that even Captain Brown violated general orders not to go down to the plain where lee waited for them all day on July 4, and whence Ewell only marched late on the 5th, two days after the battle. Seventy-five thousand Federals to 42,000 Confederates on equal ground was considered a game too hazardous for Meade to play, and turning slowly to the southward, he marched back east of the South Mountains, while Lee, uninterrupted, retired by a parallel route on the west.

"I cannot conclude the imperfect remarks about the battle and battlefield of Gettysburg without mention of Major Robbins, one of the Commissioners in charge under the United States Government of the park and its furniture. He sought us out, accompanied us over a great part of the field and gave us much valuable and interesting information, was an officer in Law's Brigade that occupied the Confederate one in front of Little Round Top, for many years was a member of Congress and is now an exotic denizen of a Pennsylvania village.

Riding Around the Federal Lines

J. Z. H. Scott
10th Virginia Cavalry
Dallas, Texas,
Galveston Daily News
January 19, 1904

He was sent through Thoroughfare Gap to see if the enemy were all gone; returning found that Stuart had started on his raid around Hooker's forces via Rockport, Md., Hanover and York, Pa, and was already far in the enemy's lines. Scott's party retraced their steps, followed the infantry across the Potomac at Williamsport and to Chambersburg, thence to Gettysburg with Longstreet's division; arriving there on the morning of the second day. Reporting to Gen. Robert E. Lee in person, and stating the cause of the absence from the command, he directed Scott's party to keep a lookout on the right wing of the army, where he expected a cavalry demonstration on his trains. The second day of the battle was spent in executing these orders. The next day, Stuart having joining the left wing of the army. Scott's party rode around the rear of the Confederate army and resumed duty with the regular command.

During the evening of this, the last day of the fighting at Gettysburg, the cavalry was heavily engaged on the left. Next morning the withdrawal began towards the Potomac. In some way, (not now recalled), Scott became separated from his command, going to the West of the Cumberland Mountains, or hills, to Williamsport. On the day following his arrival there, Kilpatrick undertook to capture the place, where at the time all of Lee's supply trains were concentrated. Gen. Imboden mustered all of the stragglers and offered such resistance detained Kilpatrick until Stuart attacked him from the direction of Hagerstown, and drove him eastward toward Booneville. Scott rejoined his command and with it was engaged in reconnaissance, scouting and picket service around Hagerstown until the 12th of July, when the command was driven to the southwest, while Scott was out in front, and on his return to the place where he had left his command, it was occupied by the Federals. Thinking that the Confederates had retired the way where they had come, he rode through the Federal lines towards Hagerstown and got deeper and deeper into their midst without knowing it until it was too late. He was captured after about half an hour's hard riding around the lines, looking for an outlet, and spent some six weeks in the Baltimore city jail, and thereafter, until Dec 22 or 23, at Pt. Lookout, Md.

BULLET RIDDLED UNIFORM COAT

W. N. SCRUGGS
6TH ALABAMA INFANTRY
Bastrop, Texas
Bastrop Advertiser
October 15, 1898

Mr. Scruggs was in Alabama when the great Civil War broke in upon the quiet of our peaceful nation.

Lending then a willing ear to the call of his state, he volunteered on the first call for troops, and next to the name of the noted Gen. John B. Gordon was written with the name William N. Scruggs, a volunteer in the 6th Alabama Regiment.

At Gettysburg Mr. Scruggs regiment occupied the center and he led his men to those heroic charges from which so few of them returned, and he himself with the skirts of his coat bullet-riddled and cut into strings and shreds.

A BAREFOOTED REBEL

ROBERT S. SHEPARD
4TH GEORGIA INFANTRY
Quinlan, Texas

Was slightly wounded in the Battle of Gettysburg behind the ear. My command fought in a wheat-field, just ready for the binder, where we did good work. We killed and captured all in our front, then double-quicked for half a mile to cut off all others coming from town. I came out of Pennsylvania barefooted, but I enjoyed that fight after the scare left me.[34]

TAKEN PRISONER AFTER THE BATTLE

Battle of Gettysburg Prisoners belonging to General Longstreet's Corps captured by Union troops marching to the rear under guard, July 3, 1863. Alfred R. Waud. *Library of Congress.*

JACOB M. SHUFFORD
23RD NORTH CAROLINA INFANTRY
Colorado, Texas

Enlisted in the Confederate Army March 15, 1862, in Lincolnton in Company B, Twenty-Third North Carolina Infantry, Early's Brigade, D. H. Hill's Division, Jackson's Corps, Army of Northern Virginia, George Seegle, first Captain and John Hoke, first Colonel.

Served in the same army until captured. Suffered in prison from cold and hunger, being thinly clad and always hungry. Was in prison for nineteen months – one month at Washington, twelve months at Point Lookout, Md., and six months at New York.

I was taken prisoner on the retreat from Gettysburg in August, not far from Blue Ridge Moun-

---

34   Ibid., p. 682.

tains; was cut off from the command by being on the skirmish line. Was in the battles of Williamsburg, Seven Pines, Seven Days' Fight in front of Richmond, Chancellorsville and Gettysburg, and in many skirmishes.[33]

CAPTURED AT THE PEACH ORCHARD

H. H. SIMMONS
21ST MISSISSIPPI INFANTRY
Coleman, Texas
Democrat-Voice
March 2, 1923

H. H. Simmons

Captain Henry Harper Simmons of Coleman, departed this life February 26, 1923, in the 85th year of his life. He was born at Preston, Mississippi, January 22, 1837, was the son of Colonel Stern Simmons and Elizabeth Harper Murray Simmons; he was one of the youngest of a family of sixteen children, of which one remains living, Dr. James L. Simmons of Clarksdale, Miss.

Capt. Simmons was one of the first to respond to the call of the South, going out with Barksdale's Brigade, twenty-first Mississippi Infantry, Company F, Tallahatchie Rifles. He served with Lee and Longstreet in Virginia and Maryland and was in all the battles this glorious brigade participated in from Virginia to Gettysburg. At Gettysburg in the second day's charge on Peach Orchard Hill, leading his men as captain of Company F under Colonel Humphries, he fell, as it was thought mortally wounded. He was captured by the Federal troops, was imprisoned at Ft. McHenry and Point Lookout, where he remained prisoner for eight months, and being a cripple for life, having lost his left leg in battle.

In exchange of prisoners, Captain Simmons was discharged and made his way back to Augusta, Georgia in eighteen sixty-four. He was married the following September. To Miss Maria Juliette Boiselair. After marriage he returned to his home in Mississippi; came to Texas in 1884 and has spent the last fifteen years in Coleman.

MEMORIES OF FALLEN COMRADES

J. A. SLATER
6TH U. S. REGULARS
Galveston Daily News
October 15, 1894
Tales From The Fort

A Batch of Stories Told on the Corner and in the Hotel Lobby Sad War Reminiscence

Fort Worth, Texas., Oct. 12 – A few evenings since, while at the Arlington Inn, The *News* reporter found party of veterans of the late war conversing. Among the number was Capt. J. A. Slater, of Burlington,

The battlefield of Gettysburg. The Valley of the shadow of Death. Between Big Round Top and Little Round Top. Timothy O'Sullivan. *Library of Congress.*

Vermont, who was enroute north from the City of Mexico, and had stopped over a day with some friends. Said he: "There are incidents that occur in the lives of all men that live forever in memory and grow brighter with the flight of years. July 2, 1863, just before the fighting began in earnest, on that day at Gettysburg. I was with Brig. Gen. Stephen H. Weed, who was temporarily commanding Gen. G. K. Warren's brigade; Col. Patrick H. O' Rorke of the 140th New York volunteers and First Lieut. Charles F. Hazlett, commanding a battery of rifled cannon in the regular artillery. About us on all sides were evidences of the impending storm. We had all been friends and had shared hardships and privations of war together, and as a lasting bond of friendship had sprung between us. My companions were all West Pointers. Weed had graduated in 1854, and was but 20 years of age; Hazlett in 1851, and was but 25; O' Rorke at the same time, and all the head of his class, was but 27. All were in their prime, splendid specimens of younger manhood, and apparently on the threshold of a useful and brilliant career. A little later Gen. Warren rode up and ordered Pat O' Rorke's regiment to occupy a position near Little Round Top. Hazlett's battery of rifled cannon was planted squarely upon it. The firing began, and soon it seemed to me as if the air was choked with the leaden hail. O' Rorke fell mortally wounded while charging at the head of his regiment. A moment late Steve Weed was in the death agony at the summit of Little Round Top. I saw him fall, and as he did so he beckoned faintly to Lt. Hazlett, who was doing deadly work with the guns. The latter ordered his men to continue firing and then bent over Gen. Weed to receive his last command. The whole sad scene is vividly depicted before me now – O Rorke a short distance to the left of that fatal spot, dead, Weed just to his right dying, with Hazlett bending over him to catch his last words. At this juncture it seems that all the demons in hell had broken loose and both the blue and gray were doing terrible execution. I saw Gen. Haslett as he knelt over the body of Gen. Weed, I saw him tenderly clasp the hand of his dying general and bend low to catch his last earthly message, destined, however, never to be known, for at that very moment the brave Hazlett fell a corpse upon the breast of his friend and associate. A confederate bullet had pierced him squarely in the forehead. During the last remainder of the fight, I think I must have lost my senses, for I have never been able to recall a single additional event of that terrible battle, but all previous to this is clear in my mind. The fact that only a moment before I had been gaily chatting with my friends, all of whom were cold in death in close proximity to me, seemed to have completely overwhelmed me. I was, prior to that time, a light hearted, happy man, but since I have been saddened and there has seemed to me to be a crushing load upon my breast. I loved the brave trio as only soldiers who have faced death together can love, and I often wonder how it was that my poor soul was then spared and the earthly career of three such useful soldiers terminated.

Capt. Slater's reference to death of Gen. Weed recalls to mind the fact that his diploma, handed him on graduation from West Point forty years ago, was found recently in a barrel of waste in New York City. How it got there or where it has rested all these years is a matter of mystery. Suffice it to say, that it is now in the hands of his descendants, who greatly prize and treasure it.

A WELL-TRAVELED PRISONER

B. T. Smith, 12th Alabama Infantry Regiment. *Harry Hogue.*

B. T. SMITH
12TH ALABAMA INFANTRY
Athens, Texas

Born March 9, 1838, near Marianna, Fla. Enlisted in the Confederate Army at Manassas Junction on the 28th of Aug., 1861, as private in Company K, in the Twelfth Alabama Infantry, R. T. Rodes' Brigade, D. H. Hill's Division, Early's Corps, Army of Northern Virginia. My first Captain was Will C. Price, and first Colonel, R. T. Jones. Was wounded at Gettysburg on the 1st day of July 1863, through the left side. Was also wounded at Strausburg through the left thigh. Was taken prisoner at Gettysburg and was taken to Baltimore and then to City Point, Va. Was also taken prisoner when wounded and carried to Point Lookout, Md. Was in the battles of Seven Pines, Seven Days Around Richmond, South Mountain, Sharpsburg, Fredericksburg, Chancellorsville, Spotsylvania, Culpepper Court House and many others of less importance.[35]

SOUVENIRS OF THE BATTLE

D. P. SMITH
16TH NORTH CAROLINA
INFANTRY
Pittsburg, Texas
Austin Weekly Statesman
July 21, 1881

Major D. P. Smith, of Pittsburg, was wounded in the shoulder at the Battle of Gettysburg, and ever since has suffered with the wound at times, by small pieces of bone working out. A few mornings ago he felt a pain in the shoulder like a pin sticking him and on examination felt something out of the skin. Calling on his wife she got hold of it and pulled out a needle. He cannot account for its being there, unless some of the bandages were fastened with it when he was first wounded.

North Carolinia Monument. Gettysburg NMP. *Tom Miller.*

A TREASURED HORN

H. H. SMITH
11TH MISSISSIPPI INFANTRY
Beaver Station, Texas
Evening Messenger
October 19, 1900

History of a Horn.

Mr. H. H. Smith, a native of Carroll county, Mississippi, who lives near beaver Station, in Wichita county, Texas, was a son of Capt. H. H. Smith. Between this last named and James Cobb, Jr., the father of Mr. W. E. Webb of Wichita Falls there were strong ties of friendship. In the early spring of 1861 James Cobb, Jr., volunteered in Company K, eleventh Mississippi infantry of the Confederate States and marched away with his command to defend his native southland against invasion by the United States army. After long service and active participation in many battles on the fields of Virginia under the immortal Lee, he gave up his life in the celebrated charge of Pickett's division against the stronghold of Cemetery Ridge at Gettysburg.

Before leaving him in Mississippi he gave to Capt. H. H. Smith, father of Mr. H. H. Smith, as a token of remembrance a hunter's horn, which he himself had, with his own hands, dressed and adorned, and which the two friends had used in many a fox and deer chase. Capt. Smith died some

---

35   Ibid., p. 686.

years since in Texas. Upon his deathbed he gave the horn to his son, H. H. Smith, with the paternal injunction that he should sacredly keep it and faithfully deliver it to the sons of the friend of his young manhood. Through all these years the horn has been carefully preserved and Mr. Smith, having met, one day last week, Mr. W. E. Cobb of Wichita Falls, it was safely delivered into his hands with the injunction of his father that it should be faithfully kept by him and his brothers as a token of the love and esteem which he bore for their father.

YULETIDE GREETINGS

MICHAEL SPENCER
PARKER'S COMPANY, VIRGINIA LIGHT ARTILLERY

San Antonio, Texas
San Antonio Express
December 24, 1911

Remembers One-Time Foe
G. A. R. Veteran Sends Christmas Cheer to Confederate.

Former Common Pleas Judge David F. Pugh, of Columbus, Ohio, who served with a West Virginia regiment on the Union side, yesterday sent a basket filled with dressed chickens, fruits and delicacies to Michael Spencer of this city, who served in the Confederate army and who was commended for gallantry in the charge of General Pickett's men at Gettysburg. Pinned to the basket was a card on which a short Christmas greeting. The note concluded:

"This will help pay back some of the chickens we took down south."

Judge Pugh has long been prominent in the local movement in caring for the graves of the Confederate dead in Camp Chase Cemetery, on the outskirts of Columbus, and in other efforts to wipe out all animosities resulting from the war of the '60s.

A LADIES MAN

C. A. Sterne, General and Staff Officers,
Non-Regimental Enlisted Men C.S.A.
Stuart Whitaker.

C. A. STERNE
GENERAL AND STAFF OFFICERS, NON-REGIMENTAL ENLISTED MEN, C. S. A.

Palestine, Texas
Temple Daily Telegram
July 4, 1921

None of Palestine Veterans Seem to Be Out of Running
Another Confederate Who Will Visit Temple In September Heard From.

In echo of the recent assertion of Adjutant C. A. Sterne of Palestine, 90 year old Confederate veteran, that time has passed him up and youth, and youth and vigor are still his, word has been received that his company commander, Capt. T. C. Spencer of Palestine, has grown jealous of his compatriot's reputation for liveliness and doesn't care to be "left in the shade" when he arrives in Temple for the Confederate reunion in September.

Following is a letter from Comrade Sterne by Adjutant Patterson of Temple:

"I was agreeably surprised to find my late letter to you published in the Temple Daily Telegram, and the complimentary notice by its editor. I am not seeking notoriety, have no complaint, and no harm has been done, but our dignified commander, Captain Spencer, is manifesting a spirit of jealousy since reading the article, and he charges that his adjutant and the Hon. Adjutant at Temple are combining to leave him in the shade's seclusion on our visit to your city.

"Our commander is a courtly old Virginia gentleman of the "first families." He made his last double quick march in the field of Gettysburg, Pa., in the wake of General Lee's army. He learns that ladies' man, especially popular with old ladies, and requests that you are select not the youngest, but the widow of an old veteran, with snow white hair and bright sparkling eyes for his partner during the reunion.

"He explains that as an elder in the Presbyterian Church he is disqualified from engaging in an old fashioned Virginia reel, but will manifest his devotion to his partner, by a bouquet of roses and a promenade to the nearest ice cream parlor."

Adjutant Patterson is doing his best to fill all the wants and wishes of Temple's honored visitors.

CHILDHOOD MEMORIES OF THE BATTLE

SAMUEL BOYD STEWART
CIVILIAN
Armstrong County, Texas

Samuel Boyd Stewart was born February 7, 1857 at Gettysburg, Pennsylvania. He was the second child to Charles William and Mary Ann Burrell Stewart. A brother, Ambrose, was older and a sister, Katharine, and a brother, Charles, were younger. Their home was located at the foot of the Alleghany range. The most outstanding incident in Sam Stewart's childhood was the Battle of Gettysburg which he witnessed. He never forgotten how the houses shook with the tumult of cannon, some four hundred of which thundered for two days; he also remembered the fright and anxiety of the people and the gruesome destruction.

Sam Stewart learned the lumbering business under his father's guidance. When he was fourteen years old, he began hauling limestone to the kilns at the coal mines. When he was sixteen, he drove a six-horse team over the South mountain and hauled charcoal to an iron foundry which was located between the North and South Mountains.

In 1882, Sam and his brother Charles rode the train to Albuquerque, New Mexico. They were met by their father and brother who had made the same journey a year earlier. The next several years they were employed in driving sheep across New Mexico and Texas. In 1890 the sheep were sold and the Stewarts turned to cattle. During the four following years Sam Stewart became well acquainted with the trail to North Dakota.

In 1897 Sam Stewart was married to Miss Nancy Joanne Stribling of Throckmorton, Texas. The couple came to Armstrong County to make their home and lived there until death except for short moves to college towns to give the advantages of college education to their children.[36]

---

36   Armstrong County Historical Society: *A Collection of Memories, A History of Armstrong County, 1876-1965*, (book, 1965), p.258.

CUT OFF FROM HIS COMMAND

T. H. STEWART
3RD GEORGIA INFANTRY
McGregor, Texas

During the second day's battle at Gettysburg five of us got cut off from our command. The others got back, but I was reported missing, killed or captured. I was fortunate enough to have a well-filled haversack, and when that was exhausted I went to the house of a good woman who gave me all that I could eat and refilled my haversack.[37]

The Angle – Longstreet at Gettysburg. *Mark Maritato.*

ARTILLERY SUPPORT FOR PICKETT'S CHARGE

J. B. STINSON
23RD ALABAMA BATTALION SHARPSHOOTERS
W. M. OWEN
MCINTOSH BATTALION, CONFEDERATE ARTILLERY
SHERMAN, TEXAS
Sherman Daily Democrat
August 12, 1912

Confederate Veterans Hold Their Regular Session.
Dr. J. B. Stinson read to the camp the following recollection of the third day at Gettysburg, written by Col. W. M. Owen.

Longstreet had fought up to the Emmitsburg turnpike, and the fields were strewn with the dead of both armies. Pickett's division had just arrived from Chambersburg, where it had been left to destroy

---
37   Yeary, *boys in gray*, p. 720.

a railroad and was now in line. A strange silence prevailed in both armies. The federals occupied the crest of Cemetery Hill and Little Round Top, and the officers upon each line of battle looked at each other across the intervening space through their field glasses. We were with the artillery officers, sitting upon our horses, in a little oak grove near the peach orchard, awaiting the opening of the fray, when a courier rode up and handed Col. Walton a dispatch. It was from Gen. Longstreet, requesting Col. Walton to come to him where he had established headquarters on the field. We put our horses to a gallop and when we reached the spot indicated met there several division commanders and Gen. R. E. Lee.

A plan of attack was being discussed, which was finally concluded as follows: At a given signal – which was to be the firing of two guns by the Washington artillery at the peach orchard – all of the Confederate guns in position were to open upon the enemy's position, to prepare the way by battering them for our infantry to advance to the attack. The assaulting division was to consist of Pickett's division, supported on its left by Heath's division of A. P. Hill's corps and upon its right by Wilcox's division.

Opening the Ball.

Returning to the position of the Washington artillery, we quietly awaited the order to open the ball. At 1:30 p. m. a courier dashed up in great haste, holding in his hand a little slip of paper, torn evidently from a memorandum book on which, written in pencil and addressed to Col. Walton was the following:

Headquarters: July 3, 1863 – Colonel; Let the batteries open. Order great care and precision in firing. If the batteries at the peach orchard cannot be used against the point we intend attacking, let them open upon the enemy on the rocky hill. Most respectfully,

J. Longstreet
Lieutenant General Commanding.

The order to fire the signal guns was immediately communicated to Maj. Fableman, commanding the Washington artillery and the report of the first gun rang out upon the still summer air. There was a moment's delay with the second gun, a friction primer having failed to explode. It was but a little space of time but 100,000 men were listening. Finally a puff of smoke was seen at the peach orchard, then came a roar and a flash and 128 pieces of Confederate artillery opened upon the enemy's position and the deadly work began with the noise of heaviest thunder, echoing and re-echoing among the hills and valleys of Pennsylvania.

The federal artillery, numbering almost as many guns as the Confederate, replied immediately, and the battle of the 3rd of July had opened. Shot and shell tore through the air and plowed great furrows in the fields and crashed through batteries, tearing to pieces men and horses. Lee, with the flower of the southern army flushed with the late victories at Fredericksburg and Chancellorsville, looked on and calmly awaited the dreadful shock.

Pickett's Virginians.

For forty minutes the dreadful din continued, until the cannonneers, exhausted with their work, and almost fainting from the heat of that July day, being ordered to cease firing, slackened the fire, and finally hardly a gun was heard from either combatants. Then Pickett's brave Virginians – heroes of many battles – stood up and formed for the assault, their gallant commander riding up and down their lines, talking calmly to his officers and men. But Longstreet could not bear to give the order to throw these men across the plain and against the breastworks of the enemy and when at last Pickett said: "Shall I go forward sir?" Longstreet turned away his head. Then Pickett, proudly and impetuously said, with the air of an old crusader, "Sir, I shall lead my division forward."

The loud orders from the officers now rang out. "Attention! attention!" and the brave fellows, realizing the hot work before them, could be heard calling out to friends and comrades a few files from them, "Goodbye boys! goodbye!" Suddenly the final order came from Pickett himself, who, superbly mounted, and his long hair waving under his kepi, seemed the very incarnation of war, "Column forward! guide center!" and the brigades of Kemper, Armstead and Garnett moved forward in common time, their gay battle flags fluttering over their heads as they passed over the green award. It was nearly a mile they had to charge and the enemy's artillery, again opening, made great gaps in the ranks, which were closed up as fast as made.

Heth's division, under Gen. Pettigrew, now emerged from the timber and followed Pickett on his left flank and in echelon, Wilcox moved out upon his right. Pickett's lines were seen to halt and under a tremendous fire he changed his direction by an oblique movement, beautifully, coolly and deliberately made. They then advanced again, and the Confederate artillery reopened upon the enemy, firing over the heads of the advancing lines.

Federals on the flank.

Forward the brave Virginians went until at last they were within the range of the federal infantry behind the stone walls on Cemetery Ridge. Then the blue line arose and with loud cheers poured a deadly fire into the Confederate ranks. The Confederates responded with a wild yell and pushed on unfalteringly. Now a body of federals were seen emerging from a clump of trees on the left of Pettigrew's North Carolinians. Taken by surprise, they faltered, staggered and fell back, as the best troops will do when realizing they are taken at a disadvantage.

Pickett's men had crossed the federal liens and had laid their hands upon eleven of the enemy's cannon and were in the full flush of victory when news came to Pickett from Longstreet, conveyed by Col. Latrobe, of his staff, whose horse was shot under him as he crossed the field, of the disaster that had befallen his supports. He galloped back to try and rally the fugitives, but all in vain – they could not form under that storm of shot, shell and bullets. Then, finding himself unsupported, each of his flanks assaulted, his generals Kemper, Armstead and Garnett and all of his field officers killed or wounded, his men falling by scores around him, he threw away his empty pistol and with his great soldier heart almost breaking, he gave his order for his remaining braves to fall back.

WOUNDED AT SEMINARY RIDGE

A. J. TABOR
14ᵀᴴ GEORGIA INFANTRY
Bryan, Texas
Bryan Weekly Eagle
February 22, 1923

Served in Confederate Army.

Deceased was born in Mitchell county, Georgia, August 13, 1842. When the call "to arms" sounded in the War Between the States, although only nineteen years old, he responded, and served valiantly in the Confederate army during the four long years of that bloody struggle. He was a member of the 14ᵗʰ regiment, with Dr. T. C. Munger as captain in A. P. Hill's division. He took part in the Battle of Gettysburg, when Seminary Ridge was captured; he was wounded in this battle. After recovering from his wounds and again joining his company, Private Tabor was captured, between Fredericksburg and Orange Court House, in the Wilderness. As a prisoner he was carried to Point Lookout and was held there for two months, later being transferred to prison in Elmira, New York. While in the New York prison, he, with many other soldiers incarcerated there, had that dread disease, smallpox.

THE CANNONS ROARED AND MUSKETS RATTLED

D. P. TAYLOR
17ᵀᴴ GEORGIA INFANTRY
Dowden, Texas
Polk County Enterprise
March 17, 1910

From An Old Confederate Veteran 75 Years Old.

I depend upon my memory for these few things I am going to tell you as they were impressed and kept in my mind. I'm almost sure they are nearly correct.

My father James Taylor was born and raised in Virginia. He moved from that State to Charleston, South Carolina where he married my mother Miss Sallie Richardson. I was born June 10th, 1834. In the year 1837 my father moved to Baker county, Georgia. In February 1839 he died.

December 20th, 1857 I married Miss Martha Deason. In 1860 I joined the Missionary Baptist church, and was baptized by Rev. Bartley Sims, which faith I hold to, up to the present time.

High Tide at Gettysburg. Charles Stanley Reinhart.
Library of Congress.

I enlisted in the Seventeenth Georgia Regiment, Company G., in Milford, Baker County, Ga, 21 of March 1862. My Captains were composed of the following: first, A. C. Jones; second, A. B. Nichols; third, J. Darley.

My first Brigadier General was Bob Toombs of Georgia; second Benning, of Georgia; Hood's Division, Longstreet's Corps and Lee's Army of Northern Virginia. I will here try to mention a few battles that my brigade was more or less engaged in: Battle of Seven Pines, Va., from 31 of May to June 1, 1862; Seven day's battle before Richmond, 26 of June, to July 1st, 1862. Second Manassas, August 28 to 30, 1862; Antietam, Sept. 17, 1862; Chancellorsville, May 1 to 3, 1863; Knoxville, Tenn., Nov 18, 1863; Battle of Cold Harbor., June 3, 1864; Atlanta, Ga., July 20, 22, and 28, 1864; Explosion at Petersburg, Va., July 29, 1864. We then took up the line of march for Gettysburg June 18, 1863 is a day the writer will never forget, it being the day in which Hood's division of Northern Virginia broke up camp at Culpepper Courthouse Va., and resumed their march northward on the Gettysburg Campaign. Benning's Brigade was composed of the following regiments. The second, fifteenth, seventeenth and twentieth Georgia. Hood's division was composed of the following Brigades: Hood's (Texas), Benning's (Georgia), Anderson (Georgia) and Law's (Alabama). On or march to Gettysburg the heat was so intense that men were overcome and fell along the roadside with sunstroke, almost as thick as falling in battle. However, we continued our march across the mountain At Ashley's Gap and came to the Shenandoah River which we waded and turned eastward to Martinsburg and on to the Potomac River which we waded. Went to Hagerstown, then to Glencastle, Pa., and from there to Chambersburg where we remained until the first of July when we received orders to go to Gettysburg which we reached on the 2nd of July. In this battle I received a wound in the corner of my left eye that destroyed the sight and also a wound in the arm at the same battle. Gentleman I am here to tell you that the cannon roared and the muskets rattled and it was a hot time at old Gettysburg, Pa., on the 2nd and 3rd of July 1863.

When General Lee retreated from Gettysburg on the morning of the 4th all the artillery on both sides was engaged: It was reported that there were 300 pieces, and from the report I think there was, or probably more. I was one of the boys' who went with Lee in every invasion he made on the enemy's country except when Early invaded Pennsylvania, July 5, 1864. On those long marches I have gone lots of days without food, barefooted and without much clothing but we had to go all the same.

There were other battles pitched and skirmish fighting that I have not mentioned. If there are any of my command that sees this I would like for them to write to me. I came to Texas in 1872 and have lived in Polk county every day since.

D. P. Taylor
Dowden, Texas.

DESTROYED EYESIGHT

D. P. TAYLOR
17TH GEORGIA INFANTRY
Dowden, Texas

I was wounded on the 3rd day of July, 1863, in the corner of the left eye, which destroyed its sight, and also in the left arm at the same battle.[38]

LEFT ON THE BATTLEFIELD FOR TWO DAYS

J. W. THOMPSON
4TH ALABAMA INFANTRY
Groesbeck, Texas
Houston Post
November 12, 1909

Thompson – Groesbeck, Texas, November 9. J. W. Thompson Sr., long a resident of this county and one of the most prominent citizens, died this morning at 1:20 o'clock after an illness of about three months. The cause of his death was a general breakdown and bladder trouble. He was 65 years of age. James Wilson Thompson was born April 7, 1846, at Harpersville, Shelby county, Ala. This was his home until the war between the States, when he enlisted in company C, Fourth Alabama regiment, before he was 18 years of age. He served through the war, and was under Lee, Jackson and Longstreet at different times; was wounded at the battle of the Wilderness, and lay on the battlefield of Gettysburg for two days with a wound in the head. After the Battle of Gettysburg he returned south with General Lee's army and surrendered at Appomattox. After the surrender he returned to his Alabama home and on December 31, 1867, was married to Miss Susie Nelson, who survives him; three children were born to this union ten children – five boys and five girls.

---

38   Ibid., p. 740.

HORRORS OF THE BATTLE

J. W. TINKLER
5ᵀᴴ TEXAS CAVALRY

Houston, Texas
Houston Post
December 22, 1913

Dick Dowling Camp Met.

Prompted to decry the efforts of those who were urging war with Mexico, J. W. Tinkler, historian of Dick Dowling Camp, who was the principal speaker at the meeting of that organization in the City Hall Sunday, gave a graphic description of the horrors attending the Battle of Gettysburg, in which he participated. He detailed the story of the conflict and told about the fighting which occurred around Round Top between the Confederates and Federals. The meeting was presided over by R. D. Chapman in the absence of Commander J. J. Hall. George A. McCurdy acted as adjutant.[39]

J. W. Tinkler. 5th Texas Cavalry.
Houston Post.

SUMMARY OF SERVICE

ALF H. H. TOLAR
18ᵀᴴ NORTH CAROLINA INFANTRY

Houston, Texas
Houston Post
May 28, 1911

Alf H. H. Tolar was born in Cumberland County, North Carolina, April 26, 1843: was the seventh son of Robert Tolar and Francis Autry Tolar. He had three younger brothers and one sister. Nine of the boys entered the Confederate service at the beginning. Alf H. H. Tolar enlisted at Elizabethtown, Blanden county, April 23, 1861, in the first company organized in that county. He entered until the reorganization in 1862, when he was elected second lieutenant of his company, which was known as the Bladen Guards, until the organization of the Eighteenth North Carolina regiment, when the guards took the number of H. in the regiment. Soon after the reorganization the Eighteenth regiment was one of the five regiments compiling the Second North Carolina brigade. General L. O. B. Branch was the first brigade commander. The brigade was ordered to Virginia and was included in the organization of General A. P. Hill's Light division. Through the campaigns that followed, Hill's division and Branch's brigade participated in every battle and acquitted themselves as true North Carolinians in every engagement. Lieutenant Tolar commanded sharpshooters during the memorable campaign from Richmond to Gettysburg, and in that battle was so severely wounded that he was relieved from field service and assigned to the enrolling service. After the Battle of Gettysburg, Lieutenant Tolar was promoted to the captaincy of his company as a reward of merit, the general knowing he would not be able for field service again, but his appointment being over the first lieutenant and ranking officer, Lieutenant Tolar requested that the company vote on who should have the command as captain, the first lieutenant or himself, and the colonel ordered the election, and the result was Lieutenant Tolar received sixty-one votes and his opponent three. He then went before the medical board and was relieved and at his re-

---

39   According to the Civil War service records, J. W. Tinkler was a soldier in the 5ᵗʰ Texas Cavalry. The 5ᵗʰ Texas Cavalry did not fight at Gettysburg, or east of the Mississippi at any time during the Civil War.

quest assigned to the enrolling duty in North Carolina, where he served as such until the close. Captain Tolar was wounded four times during the war and was in about twenty-five pitched battles besides the many battles with sharpshooter in front of his command on the advance from Richmond to Gettysburg. To describe all three battles and skirmishes would require more space than could be told in this sketch. Captain Tolar discharged his duty in every station as a soldier and in his more mature years is proud to number himself among the soldiers of a cause that was lost, but which was just.

Wounded in Three Battles

Alf H. H. Tolar
18th North Carolina Infantry
Houston, Texas
Houston Post
June 22, 1913

To The Post:

Your issue of this morning states, "*The Post* would be pleased to have the name and photo for publication of any veteran living in Houston who saw service at Gettysburg." I take pleasure in furnishing you the name of Alf H. H. Tolar, captain of Company K, Eighteenth Regiment, North Carolina troops, who is an old resident veteran who served with great credit all through the war: was wounded in three different battles, Cedar Run, Frasier's farm, and seriously wounded at Gettysburg in the last charge on the left of pickets line, under General Hill. He is the last of nine brothers who fought for the Confederacy, and to whom a monument of mercy and honor has been erected in North Carolina.
Philp E. Peers.

The battle of Gettysburg. Currier and Ives. *Library of Congress.*

Lone Star Valor

Anxious for the Fight

Alf H. H. Tolar
18ᵗʰ North Carolina Infantry

Houston, Texas
Houston Post
June 25, 1913

Alf H. H. Tolar of 2604 Pease Avenue is another Houstonian who participated in the Battle of Gettysburg. He enlisted in the Confederate Army in Blanden County, North Carolina, April 26, 1861, when 17 years of age. He was a member of Branch's Brigade of the Army of Northern Virginia.

My first experiences in a real battle was at Hanover's Courthouse, Virginia, where our force of 3000 fought against 20,000 Federals. We fought desperately from 2 o'clock in the afternoon until after sundown, after which we retreated under darkness to Asheville, the birthplace of Henry Clay.

At Asheville we joined Major General A. P. Hill's division, Lieutenant General Stonewall Jackson's corps of the Army of Northern Virginia. At our next battle, that of Fair Oaks, General Robert E. Lee was placed in command of our forces.

I was engaged in the seven days' fighting around Richmond, Va., every day. We finally got the best of the Yankees, who embarked on their boats and left Richmond in our possession. At Richmond we spent some time in resting up after our strenuous week of fight the 'Yanks,' but it was not long before we were preparing and organizing for the campaign up the river.

At the battle of the Wilderness we had a hard fight with that brave Yankee leader, General 'Joe' Hooker, who was in command of the Northern Army of the Potomac at that time. We had as hard a battle as that at Gettysburg, but we finally succeeded in surrounding the Federals and making them retreat in confusion. We were considerably aided in this battle by the dense canebrakes which enabled us to surround the Yankees to a great extent. It was from these dense canebrakes that the name "The Wilderness" originated.

I was in command of the sharpshooters off our brigade during the skirmish that took place between the advance guard of the Confederate army during the march on Gettysburg and during the desultory firing that took place before the regular battle begun .This work was somewhat relieving for us, as the worst part of the war is inactivity and waiting before a battle begins. Soldiers are always anxious for the fighting to commence in earnest because in the excitement of battle fear and worry is unknown, while the nervous strain that soldiers are under while resting on their arms before the battle is very great. Once the firing begins and the order of 'forward march' is made, an irresistible and indescribable something takes possession of soldiers that makes them anxious to get into the fight no matter how small the chances of them escaping alive.

I was in Pickett's famous charge. I remember a humorous situation that has not recurred to me for many years. When we had gone a considerable distance down the hill where we formed in line of battle we came across a man and his wife who very excitably dragging a trunk out of their red brick house. As we passed them the air was full of bursting shells and cannon balls were beginning to shatter their house. The old man was greatly mortified that his house happened to be situated in the line of fire, and as I passed him I heard him say, 'My God, is this what you call war?'

The principal cause of the defeat of the Southern army at the Battle of Gettysburg was the fact that a gap of quarter of a mile wide was left open in our left wing. General Ward's Federal brigade took possession of the gap and turned our flank. We were being fired upon from three different directions and the consequent charge was something terrible. I kept fighting gamely, although I saw my comrades being cut down like wheat before a scythe. I was finally wounded in the groin from a shell which exploded a few feet in front of me. I was carried off the field by an Irishman in my company by the name of Mike McConish. I was taken to the field hospital, but my wound was not dressed until the morning following the battle.

When Mr. Tolar became able to get around on crutches he was assigned to the enrollment department in the North Carolina district. He served in the capacity of recruiting officer until after the war. Mr. Tolar was the founder of the Colorado Clipper of the Colorado Clipper of Colorado, Mitchell County Texas. During the last 10 years he has been in the real estate business in Houston.

SWEARING AT THE ENEMY

Grapevine Sun
December 20, 1913

Pious Advice

A veteran told a story recently about a very pious chaplain. The chaplain was as brave as he was pious, and was distributing cartridges on the firing line at Gettysburg when he overheard a veteran swearing blasphemously at the enemy. "Blank them to Blank!" He murmured: "the Blankety blank Blankety Blanks"

"Brother, brother," admonished the chaplain dealing out cartridges, "don't cuss the poor fellows – kill 'em."

CITATION FOR BRAVERY

ALF H. H. TOLAR
18TH NORTH CAROLINA INFANTRY
Houston, Texas
Houston Post
July 2, 1927

At Gettysburg he won a citation for bravery on the field of battle - the highest honor that could come to a soldier under Lee and Jackson. And he was seriously wounded. The losses at Gettysburg had been terrific. On the last of those three days of fighting two Confederate officers were left to carry forward the last charge - Captain Tolar and one other. Captain Tolar got within 20 feet of the Federal works and was shot down. Carried to the back of the lines by one of his men, he was deposited on a litter and forgotten. Later on, the wagon train, which held his litter, was captured by the Federals and he escaped by crawling out of the wagon and over a stone fence into a wheat field. After hours of hiding, he was found by two of his soldiers. Fitzhugh Lee came up about that time and recaptured most of the wagon train and Captain Tolar was conveyed to the nearest hospital. But after three months spent in and around hospitals he was retired from active service and assigned to the enrolling service in North Carolina, where he remained until the close of the war.

NEVER TAKEN PRISONER

H. M. L. TORBETT
2ND GEORGIA INFANTRY
Devine, Texas

Was wounded by grape shot in the shoulder below Petersburg, Va., in the forehead at Petersburg, Va., and in the back when the army was on the move to Gettysburg. I determined never to be taken prisoner and never was. Was made first Sergeant after the Battle of Gettysburg. Was in the hospital on account of deafness for two weeks which was the only time I was away from my company during the war. Was in the Seven Days' fight around Richmond, at Gaines' Mill, Chancellorsville,

Gettysburg, Petersburg, Drewry's Bluff, and numerous others. Our first fight was at Sewell Point, Va. Saw the engagements between the Merrimac and the Monitor. Saw the Merrimac sink and fire the Cumberland, and Congress, in the mouth of James River [40]

NEVER TRAVELS NORTH

S. L. TOWNSEND
WAUL'S TEXAS CAVALRY
Houston, Texas
The Eagle
June 25, 1931

For the first time S. L. Townsend of Houston is visiting Bryan and the Texas Hood's and Green's Brigades. Captain Townsend is a member of Dick Dowling Camp and has attended every meeting of the United Confederate Veterans except two, the reunion held at Washington and Gettysburg. "The Yanks are too much for me. I don't want to go when the reunion is held in their cities," said Townsend.

STIRRING MEMORIES OF LONG AGO

W. W. UPSHAW
9TH LOUISIANA INFANTRY
BELTON, TEXAS
Temple Daily Telegram
July 2, 1911

Sword carrying cavalryman confronting infantryman.
Battle of Gettysburg. Alfred R. Waud. *Library of Congress.*

Veterans Indulge In Reminiscences
Former Confederate Soldiers Talk of
Stirring Times of Forty-Eight Years Ago.
Special to *The Telegram*

Belton, July 1 – An interesting reminiscence was opened this morning when a group composed of Captains Jas. Boyd and T. W. Traylor and County Treasurer W. W. Upshaw the latter asked the question,

"What does today remind you of?" Then it was that the other two remembered that forty-eight years ago today they were in pursuit of the Army of the North in its famous retreat into Pennsylvania. The night before the United States army had rushed their horses and cattle across a bridge over the Susquehanna river near a little village named Yolston and had set fire to the bridge. The north flank of the army which was composed of the Army of Northern Virginia, in which were fighting the three friends of this morning's reminiscence, were detailed if possible to save the bridge and make it passable in order that the southern army might advance and the cattle and more particularly, the horses might be recaptured and driven back to the south side of the river. The bridge was too much burned to be safe for crossing and the army was soon ordered to advance to Gettysburg where the next day the memorable battle was fought.

Peter Hammersmith and H. H. Little of that city and N. E. Edmonds of Route 3 were members of the Army of Northern Virginia and were also participants in the pursuit of the federal army and later in the Battle of Gettysburg.

---

40   Yeary, *boys in gray*, p. 753.

SIXTY FIRST ANNIVERSARY OF THE BATTLE

W. W. UPSHAW
9ᵀᴴ LOUISIANA INFANTRY
Belton, Texas
Belton Journal
July 1, 1924

Today Is The Anniversary of Gettysburg

Commander W. W. Upshaw has called attention to the fact that today is the sixty-first anniversary of the Battle of Gettysburg.

He states that on the day of the battle, he marched 25 miles and fired his gun until his shoulder was sore.

Mr. Upshaw expresses the deepest thankfulness that he has been spared for sixty-one years and is strong and well enough to be busy and enjoy life and the companionship of his friends.

V. B. VINSON
WASHINGTON ARTILLERY OF NEW ORLEANS
R. A. BRIGHT
STAFF OFFICER OF GENERAL GEORGE E. PICKETT
Houston, Texas
Houston Post
March 6, 1904

General Pickett's Charge.
Full Story of it as Told by a member of His Staff – Statement as to Where the General Was Located During the Charge

The subjoined story from the pen of Mr. R. A. Bright recently published in the Richmond (Va.) Times-Dispatch, deals with many interesting and disputed subjects. The article was written by a member of the staff of Major General Pickett and was furnished The Post, by Captain V. B. Vinson of this city.

Editor of the Times-Dispatch.

Sir: The following statement of what I saw and heard on the third day at Gettysburg was in the main written about thirty years ago, and was rewritten for publication in 1903, but the issue of it was prevented until now by an attack of gout by which I suffered. I earnestly wish that it had come out before the death of my corps commander, the brave General Longstreet.

Early in the morning of Pickett's Virginians, 4700 muskets, with officers added, 1,000 strong, moved from the camping ground of the second day, two miles in rear, to the battlefield, and took position behind the hill from which we charged later in the day. Then came the order from head-quarters: "Colonel E. P. Alexander will command the entire artillery in action today, and Brigadier General Pendleton will have charge of the reserve artillery ammunition of the army." Later, General Pickett was informed from General Longstreet's headquarters that Colonel Alexander would give the order when the charge would begin. Several hours later the batteries on both sides opened. Had this occurred at night, it would have delighted the eye more than any fireworks ever seen.

English Gordon.

Shortly before the artillery duel commenced, I returned from looking over the ground in front, and found General Pickett talking to a strange officer, to whom he introduced me saying, "This is Colonel Gordon, once opposed to me in the San Juan affair, but now on our side."

In explanation of this I will state here that the San Juan affair occurred on the Pacific coast when

General Pickett was captain in the United States army, and when he held the island against three English ships of war and 100 English regulars, he having one company of United States infantry and part of another company. General Winfield Scott was sent out by this government to settle the trouble.

After the introduction, Colonel Gordon, who was an Englishman, continued speaking to General Pickett and said:

"Pickett, my men are not going up today."

The general said, "But, Gordon, they must go up; and you must make them go up."

Colonel Gordon answered. "You know, Pickett, I will go as far with you as any other man, if only for old acquaintance sake, but my men have until lately been down at the seashore, only under the fire of heavy guns from ships, but for the last day or two they have lost heavily under infantry fire and are very sure, and they will not go up today."

This officer was on foot, there was no horse in sight, and he must have come from Pettigrew's brigade on our left, only some 200 yards distant.

I have written and asked about the command to which this officer belonged, but have met with no success.

Three times General Pickett sent to Colonel Alexander saying, "Is it time to charge?" The last messenger brought back this answer: "Tell General Pickett I think we have silenced eight of the enemy's guns and now is the time to charge." (Some Federal officers after the war informed me that they had only run these guns back to cool.)

Brigadier General George E. Pickett.
Library of Congress.

Mounted Officers.

General Pickett ordered his staff officers, four in number (Major Charles Pickett, Captain Baird, Captain Bymington and myself), to Generals Armistead, Garnett and Kemper and to Dearing's artillery battalion, which earlier in the day had been ordered to follow up the charge and keep its caissons full. Orders to the other staff officers I did not hear. But I was sent to General Kemper with this order:

"You and your staff and field officer to go in dismounted: dress on Garnett and take the red barn for your objective point."

During the charge I found Kemper and Garnett, apparently, drifting too much to the left, and I believe it was because the red barn was too much to Kemper's left. General Pickett would have altered the direction, but our left being exposed by the retreat of Pettigrew's command, our men and 10,000 more were needed to the left.

When I reached General Kemper, he stood up, removing a handkerchief from under his hat, with which he had covered his face to keep the gravel knocked up by the fierce artillery fire from his eyes. As I gave the order, Robert McCandish Jones, a friend and schoolmate of mine, called out, "Bob, turn us loose and we will take them." Then Colonel Lewis Williams, of the First Virginia regiment, came to me and said, "Captain Bright, I wish to ride my mare up," and I answered, "Colonel Williams, you can not do it, have you not just heard me give the order to your general to go up on foot?" and he said, "But you will let me ride; I am sick today, and besides that remember Williamsburg." Now Williamsburg was my home and I remembered that Colonel Williams had been shot through the shoulder in that battle and left at Mrs. Judge Tucker's house on the courthouse green. This I had heard, for I missed that fight, so I answered, "Mount your mare and I will make an excuse for you." General Garnett had been injured by a kick while passing through the wagon train at night had been allowed to ride.

Colonel Hunton of the same brigade also rode, being unable to walk. He fell on one side of the red barn and General Kemper on the other side. So there were eight mounted officers, counting General Pickett and staff, mounted in the charge.

Colonel Williams fell earlier in the fight. His mare went up rider-less almost to the stone wall and was caught when walking back by Captain William C. Marshall of Dearing's battalion. His own horse, Lee, having been killed, he rode Colonel William's mare away after the fight. When I returned to General Pickett from giving the order to General Kemper, Symington, Baird and Charles Pickett were with the General, they having less distance to carry their orders than I, as Kemper was on our right, and Armistead not in first line, but in echelon.

Where Pickett Was.

The command had moved about fifty yards in the charge. General Pickett and staff were about twenty yards in the rear of the column.

When we had gone about 400 yards, the general said to me: "Captain, you have lost your spurs today, instead of gaining them." Riding on his right side, I looked at once at my left boot, and saw that the shank of my spur had been mashed around and the rowel was looking toward the front, the work of a piece of shell, I suppose, but that was the first, I know of it. Then I remembered the Irishman's remark, that one spur was enough, because one side of your horse went, the other would be sure to go.

When we had charged about 750 yards, having about 500 hundred more to get over before reaching the stone wall, Pettigrew's brigade broke all to pieces and left the field in great disorder. At this time we were mostly under a fierce artillery fire; the heavy musketry fire came farther on.

General Pettigrew was in command that day of a division, and his brigade was led by Colonel Marshall, who was knocked off his horse by a piece of shell as his men broke, but he had himself lifted on his horse and when his men refused to follow him up, he asked that his horse be turned to the front. Then he rode up until he was killed. If all the men on Pickett's left had gone on like Marshall, history would have been written another way. General Pickett sent Captain Symington and Captain Baird to rally these men.

They did all that brave officers could do, but could not stop the stampede.

Longstreet's and Freemantle.

General Pickett directed me to ride to General Longstreet and say that the position against which he had been sent would be taken, but he could not hold it unless reinforcements were sent to him. As I rode back to General Longstreet I passed small parties of Pettigrew's command going to the rear; presently I came to quite a large squad, are, very foolishly, for I was burning precious time, I halted them, and asked if they would not go up and help those gallant men now charging behind us. Then I added, "What are your running for?" and one of them, looking up at me with much surprise depicted on his face, said, "Why, good gracious, Captain, ain't you running yourself?" Up to the present time I have not answered that question, but will now say appearances were against me.

I found General Longstreet sitting on a fence alone; the fence ran in the direction we were charging. Pickett's column had passed over the hill on our side of the Emmettsburg road, and cold not then be seen. I delivered the message as sent to General Pickett. General Longstreet said, "Where are the troops that were placed on your flank?" and I answered, "Look over your shoulder and you will see them." He looked over and saw the broken fragments. Just then an officer rode at half speed, drawing up his horse in front of the general, and saying, "General Longstreet, General Lee sent me here and said you would place me in a position to see this magnificent charge. I would not have missed it for the world. General Longstreet answered, "I would." Colonel Freemantle; the charge to order. Captain Bright, ride to General Pickett and tell him what you have heard me say to Colonel Freemantle." At this moment our men were near to but had not crossed the Emmettsburg road. I started and when my horse had made two leaps General Longstreet called, "Captain Bright." I checked my horse and turned half around in my saddle to hear, and this is what he said: "Tell General Pickett that Wilcox's brigade is in that peach orchard (pointing) and he can order him to his assistance."

Wilcox and Pickett.

Some have claimed that Wilcox was put in charge at its commencement – General Gordon says this; but this is a mistake. When I reached General Pickett he was at least 100 yards behind the division, having been detained in a position from which he could watch and care for his left flank. He at once sent Captain Baird to General Wilcox with the order for him to come in; then he sent Captain Symington with the same order, in a very moments, and last he said: "Captain Bright, you go," and I was about the same distance behind Symington that he was behind Baird. The fire was so dreadful at this time that I believe that General Pickett thought not more than one out of three sent wound reach General Wilcox.

When I rode up to Wilcox he was standing with both hands raised waving and saying to me, "I know, I know." I said, "But general, I must deliver my message." After doing this I rode out of the peach orchard, going forward where General Pickett was watching his left. Looking that

General James Longstreet.
Library of Congress.

way myself, I saw moving out of the enemy's line of battle, in head of column, a large force; having nothing in their front, they came around our flank as described above. Had our left not deserted us these men would have hesitated to move in head of column, confronted by a line of battle. When I reached General Pickett I found him too far down towards the Emmettsburg road to see the flanking troops, and he asked me the number. I remember answering 7,000, but this proved an over estimate. Some of our men had been faced to meet this new danger, and in so doing somewhat broke the force of our charge on the left. Probably men of the First Virginia will remember this.

At this moment our left (Pickett's division) began to crumble and soon all that was left came slowly back, 5000 in the morning, 1800 were put in camp that night, 3,500 killed, wounded and missing.

We moved back, and when General Pickett and I were about 800 yards from the position from which the charge had started. General Robert E. Lee, the peerless, alone on Traveler, rode up and said: "General Pickett, place your division in rear of this hill and be ready to repel the advance of the enemy should they follow up their advance." I never heard General Lee call them the enemy before; it was always those or these people. General Pickett, with his head on his breast said: "General Lee, I have no division now, Armistead is down, Garnett is down and Kemper is mortally wounded.

Then General Lee said: "Come, General Pickett, this has been my fight and upon my shoulders rests the blame. The men and officers of your command have written the name of Virginia as high today as it has never been written before." (Now talk about "glory enough for one day!' why this was glory enough for one hundred years.)

Lee and Kemper.

Then turning to me, General Lee said: "Captain what officer is that they are bearing off?" I answered, General Kemper, and General Lee said: "I must speak to him," and moved Traveler towards the litter. I moved my horse along with his, but General Pickett did not go with us. The four bearers seeing it was General Lee, halted, and General Kemper feeling the halt, opened his eyes. General Lee said: "General Kemper, I hope you are not very seriously wounded."

General Kemper answered: "I am struck in the groin, and the ball has ranged upwards: they tell me it is mortal," and General Lee said: "I hope it will not prove so bad as that, is there anything I can do for you, General Kemper?" The answer came, after General Kemper had seemingly, with much pain, raised himself on one elbow.

"Yes, General Lee, do full justice to this division for its work today."

General Lee bowed his head, and said: "I will."

I wish to mention here that Captain William I. Clopton, now judge of Manchester, told me after the war that while General Pickett was trying to guard his left, he saw twenty-seven flags, each with the usual compliment of men, move out on our right flank, but we did not see this, as all our thoughts were fixed on our left flank.

Captain Symington and Captain Baird could each give many interesting incidents if they could be induced to write for publication. My article of the 26th of December, 1903, in the Times-Dispatch should be read before this account to show how and when General Pickett's command reached Gettysburg.

Personal.

Should I write again, it will be about 4000 prisoners we guarded back to Virginia. Kemper's supposed death bed, and General Lee's not to General Pickett, a few days after Gettysburg. To those seeking the truth about this great battle, I will say, the very great losses in either commands occurred on the first and second days. The third day, at this exhibition, was most decidedly Virginia day, and a future Virginia governor, Kemper by name, was present. I wish here to state that some of my men of Garnett's brigade told me they saw up at the stone wall, mostly the latter, of two other states, and in answer to my questions as to numbers and organization, answered, numbering in all, less than sixty and without formation of any military kind, Alabamians and North Carolinians.

Now as to the position of Armistead's brigade in the charge. He was ordered to go in on the left of Garnett, but Captain Winfree, a most gallant officer of the Fourteenth Virginia, now living in this city, agrees' with my memory, that Armistead's brigade went in between Garnet and Kemper. I also wish to give such information as I can to Senator Daniel, who asked for it in the Confederate column of the Sunday's Times-Dispatch, 24th of January, about the losses of Pickett's three brigades on the third day. No official returns came to us until long after the battle, because no one was left to make report, and hardly say one was left to receive such report. General Pickett's staff officers who encamped the command on the night of the third day counted 1800. I find Senator Daniel since the war always turning from Washington to Virginia, like the needle to the pole, but strange to say, during the war I found his always turning from Virginia to Washington as though he wanted that city. Very respectfully,

Ro. A. Bright,
Formerly on the Staff of Major General George E. Pickett

Howell S. Wallace. 9th Georgia Infantry Regiment. *John Clay Elisor.*

HAIL OF DEATH

HOWELL S. WALLACE
9TH GEORGIA INFANTRY
Coleman, Texas

When I got my command the army was on the move to cross the Potomac River at Williamsport, Md., and we went across the corner of the State of Maryland into Pennsylvania and camped at Chambersburg, and the next day was the memorable Battle of Gettysburg. Our command did not get there in time for the first day's battle, but were on hand the second, and Anderson's Brigade, Hood's Division, Longstreet's Corps, was right in the center. It is hard to realize that men could live through such a hail of death, but some did. I was wounded in the calf of the leg, and as Gen. Anderson passed along I told him I was wounded, and he told me to do the best I could for myself. I started to the rear, dragging one foot. I had to go across a wheat field, and very slow at that. Part of the way was in the range of bullets, and I could hear them and see the wheat falling all around me. With much difficulty I got to Hood's Division Hospital. The doctors had taken charge of a large barn and converted it to a hospital. Late in the evening I went up to the hospital to see if I could find any of my comrades. The sight I saw was too horrible to relate, if I could. At the back door I saw what seemed to me to be a wagon load of arms, legs and hands. I turned and walked back, and never went there anymore. The next day Gen. Picket's Corps engaged the enemy, and the carnage was terrible. James Robinson, who was wounded in the foot, was with me a little way from the house under an apple tree, and he made use of a remark that I have never forgotten. He said: "Do you hear that noise?" I told him that I did. He said: "That is the wisdom of wise men." This was the third day. On the next day things were in a general stir, and I saw something was going on, but did not know what it was. Gen. Anderson was wounded in the thigh and was brought out there for treatment, and I asked about the movements of the army, but he would not tell me. I did not want to fall into the hands of the enemy, so he told me to leave when the wagon train left. That was enough for me, and I finally worked my way back to Richmond and reported to the doctor in charge of the hospital at Camp Winder, and he gave me a furlough and I went home and at the end of thirty days went back to my command.[41]

Informing a Father of His Wounded Son

Nicholas Weeks
3rd Alabama Infantry
July 8, 1863

Dear Sir,

Your Son, Sgt. Nicholas Weeks of our Company was wounded in the Battle of Gettysburg, Pa., on the 1st July. He was wounded in the left leg & is a very painful one, though not dangerous. He was left at Gettysburg under the charge of a good Surgeon; Lieut. Ledyard of our company is with him. Should I hear anything from him will advise you of the fact.
Respectfully
Jno. H. Hunsethal
1st Segt. Comd'g Co. A
3rd Ala Regt [42]

A Good Samaritan

Nicholas Weeks
3rd Alabama Infantry

Mr. N. Weeks Sr.
Mobile, Ala

Your kind favor of the 11th inst. came safe and containing $16/100 which you desired me to hand to Mr. Robert A. Matthews. I called at the 3rd Ala. Hospital this morning & Mrs. Judge Hopkins informed that Mr. Mathews had gone home to Mobile and advised me to pay the money over to a gentleman by the name of "Neville" a wounded soldier of the 3rd Alabama. Reg't, who was going home to Mobile in a few days who would hand the money over to you or pay it to Mr. Mathews as you might think best. I also learned from Mr. Neville that I am very sorry to write you & that

---

41 Ibid., p. 773-774.
42 Letter, Jno. H. Hunsethal to Nicholas Weeks Sr., July 8, 1863, Nicholas Weeks, Jr., Papers, 1861-1865, 1901-1903, Dolph Briscoe Center for American History, The University of Texas at Austin.

Nicholas was wounded in the left leg below the knee cap but Mr. Neville did not know whether he was brought away from the Battlefield by your men or left at Gettysburg & fell into the hands of the enemy. He has not been brought here, so far as I can learn, but if he should be brought here or you can learn his whereabouts & I can do something to alleviate his suffering believe me my dear Sir, I will take great pleasure in doing so.

My family lives about 50 miles from here on the James River although I am still attending (?) in the city. When they hear of Nicholas being wounded they will grieve over it as if he is sent to this city & I can have him transferred to private quarters I will try & persuade him to go up to my farm to private quarters for it is a good healthy country & can have good medical treatment there, with my kindest regards to yourself & family, I remain you most humble servant.

E. Boyle [43]

DELICACIES AFTER THE BATTLE

NICHOLAS WEEKS
3RD ALABAMA INFANTRY
July 23? 1863

Dear Father,

I wrote to you on the 4th when our army evacuated this place & also requested Major Sands to write to you. My wounds is by no means dangerous, & is doing very well. – Our having to remain up here, has without a doubt been the greatest advantage is very cool, - and we have been supplied with every delicacy - & with under clothes by association called the Sanitary Commission, principally from Baltimore. Wines, Legumes, Lemons, Jelly's, Butter Crackers, concentrated Beef, which makes splendid soups. - & all such things in abundance. – We are in a barn near the battlefield. I was wounded on the first days fight July 1st. – I was walking at the time I was wounded, the ball striking some distance below the knee, on the side coming out at the calf.

We have had a very pleasant time considering. There are six of us (of our regiment) here together in a room. All very clever fellows – Men detailed from the regiment to wait on us. - & Surgeons from the Brigade were left to attend us.

Give my love to all,

Yours affectionately,

Nicholas

Lt. Ledyard is here & has lost his leg below the knee, - but is nearly well already. – Poor McKerrel is dead.[44]

GETTING ON REMARKABLY WELL

NICHOLAS WEEKS
3RD ALABAMA INFANTRY
Hospital Near Gettysburg
August 11, 1863

Mr. N. Weeks
Mobile, Ala.

---

43   Letter E. Boyle to Nicholas Weeks Sr., July 18, 1863, Nicholas Weeks, Jr., papers, 1861-1865, 1901-1903, Dolph Briscoe Center for American History, The University of Texas at Austin.

44   Letter, Nicholas Weeks Jr. to Nicholas Weeks Sr., July 23?, 1863, Nicholas Weeks, Jr., papers, 1861-1865, 1901-1903, Dolph Briscoe Center for American History, The University of Texas at Austin.

Dear Father,

I am still near Gettysburg, and getting on remarkably well. My wound is doing very well and I will be able to travel home in the course of a few days. – My health is very good. I never enjoyed better.

I wish you would see Mr. A. E. Ledyard & let him know that his son William is recovering very fast, from his wound. –

Do not be uneasy about me, there is not the least danger of my wound. - & we received every foreseeable care & attention.[45]

HEALING FROM WOUND VERY NICELY

NICHOLAS WEEKS
3RD ALABAMA INFANTRY
Hospital near Gettysburg
Sept 1, 1863

Dear Father,

I am still in hospital near Gettysburg, expecting to be sent off daily for exchange or parole, as my wound is almost entirely well. – I suffer no pain from it whatsoever, but my knee is quite stiff yet. I am able to go all about with the assistance of my crutches. My health was never better than now & I am strong & stout as I ever was. We fare very well. Our food is very good. We are in tents, but have good bedsteads, everything kept very cleanly. We get a clean change of clothes & sheets every week. Tell Ma not to be uneasy about me, we are well treated, and it is probably but for our wounds that we were left here, for the weather has been very cool around here and that is very favorable for the wounded. I have never had the least inflammation about my wound.

Give my love to all, kiss them all for me. I hope it will not be many days ere I will be with you. Yours Affectionately,

N. Weeks Jr.

Lt. Ledyard is doing well, - let his father know – N.[46]

TELEGRAPH NOTICE

NICHOLAS WEEKS
3RD ALABAMA INFANTRY
The Southern Telegraph Company
Received at Mobile, Sept 29, 1863

Telegraph from Richmond, 29, To. N. Weeks, City Treasurer

Arrived here yesterday from Baltimore. I am well. – Nicholas Weeks. 9/220.[47]

---

45   Letter, Nicholas Weeks Jr.to Nicholas Weeks Sr., August 11, 1863, Nicholas Weeks Jr., papers, 1861-1865, 1901-1903, Dolph Briscoe Museum for American History, The University of Texas at Austin.

46   Letter Nicholas Weeks Jr. to Nicholas Weeks Sr., September 1, 1863, Nicholas Weeks Jr., papers, 1861-1865; 1901-1903, Dolph Briscoe Museum for American history, The University of Texas at Austin.

47   Telegraph, Nicholas Weeks Jr. papers, 1861-1865, 1901-1903, Dolph Briscoe Museum for American History, The University of Texas at Austin.

DETAILED MEMORIES OF THE BATTLE

NICHOLAS WEEKS
3RD ALABAMA INFANTRY
Galveston, Texas
Galveston Daily News
April 4, 1904

Nicholas Weeks, 3rd Alabama Infantry Regiment.
Alabama Department of Archives and History.

Members of the camp were prepared to listen to the address of Capt. C. N. Weeks. Captain Weeks' was a soldier in the Battle of Gettysburg and was wounded at that place, and his address consisted of an interesting account of the invasion of Pennsylvania. During his talk he read several interesting letters written by himself to the folks at home regarding their marches and closed with a eulogy on the united country as it now stands. The address was listened to with rapt attention, and at its conclusion the camp gave him a vote of thanks. Following is the address in full:

Capt. Weeks Address.

Comrades – Our venerable and most worthy adjutant notified me a fortnight ago that I would be expected to make you a little talk at this meeting, and not to disappoint him, I will try. I had prepared nothing until last night, and but for some letters written by me to my folks at home while on the march to Gettysburg I would not have the temerity in this skeptical age to say that "we were even there." I noticed a letter from a comrade published a short time ago that strongly appealed to me. It appears that he had previously made a statement of facts about his experience in some battle, and immediately other fellows came back at him in contradiction, and to use his own forcible language they made him out "all sorts of a liar." In as many different places. Time narrows the vision of the mind, while age illuminates the imagination and we old veterans grow skeptical. We are prone to see too little other than our own shadows in the late evening of life when looking back to those stirring times.

"Our brigade" did all the fighting, it would appear whether in the Army of Virginia, Tennessee or Texas, from what particular State it matters not that "our brigade" came. Esprit de corps is praiseworthy, but is it not a sad commentary on the intelligence of our comrades that they should have to be marshaled great hosts to do battle when "our brigade" did it by its lone self? Why the Government should have fed, clothed and sometimes paid the entire fighting force of the country talking in "everything from the cradle to the grave" for the four long years when "our brigade" would have sullied is past finding out. If we are to judge events in the past by the lights of today – that is by what we read. Armed with these quaint little documents I will venture in a homely way to tell of our trip to Gettysburg without attempting a description of the battle. I have them here as a proof of what I say – proof enough even for Col. Stafford –and they are as true now as they were then. Only a few words in pencil on bits of rough paper, sent back to loving ones at home to relieve anxious hearts, oftentimes written by the light of the camp fire when the day's march was done, with an inverted skillet or the stock of a musket for an improvised desk.

It appears that we started on this journey June 4, as the following will show:

"Bivouac, Spotsylvania Courthouse. June 4, 1863. – We are twenty miles from our old camp, having marched it since this morn at 8 o'clock. We were on picket when we received marching orders. There is no telling where we are going. Some say we are bound for Pennsylvania, others say for the valley. Gen Lee only knows. Don't be uneasy if you do not hear from me often, as my chances for writing are but slim now. We take up our march tomorrow morning early."

The next is from:

Bivouac Near Culpepper Courthouse, Va., June 8, 1863. – We are now under command of Lieut. Gen. Ewell. He has a part of Gen. Jackson's old corps – three divisions. He is a very superior officer and the troops have the greatest confidence in him. We arrived here yesterday and from all appearances will be on the move tomorrow again. Hooker is reported to have fallen back to Centerville beyond Manassas. The men are all in good health and fine spirits. My health is very good, but I don't relish these long marches. Twenty miles a day is considered an ordinary day's marching, but is pretty "heavy" when you have a musket, forty rounds of cartridges, blanket and three days rations to pack."

We had been lying in camp since the latter part of December, after the Fredericksburg fight. Except the week we had taken off in early May to chase Hooker out of the Wilderness, and evidently grown fat and lazy on a pound of flour and a quarter of a pound of bacon a day. Hence I found twenty miles a day "heavy" marching, but it was not long before we had trained down to our marching and fighting weight and could do thirty miles a day without punishment.

As I remember, Ewell went down the valley with two divisions to assail Milroy in front at Winchester, while our division pushed rapidly along the eastern slope of the Blue Ridge Mountains to get behind and cut off the retreat to Harper's Ferry. Nothing of moment occurred until we crossed over the mountains and surprised a brigade of cavalry at Berryville. We must have moved with celerity, for they were not expecting us. We dropped in just at their dinner hour, and my! what a feast awaited us – well worth a week's march and a fight. The pork and beans were done to a turn, and was the first square meal we had since the feast at Chancellorsville out of the Eleventh Corps haversacks. They evidently left in haste, and in Indian style, judging from the saddles' bridles, jackets and blankets left behind. They had no more use for the common things of life than a bridegroom. We tarried long enough to put the pork and beans where they were needed, and swap blankets; the old for the new. That morning two old farmers joined us. They were bitter in their denunciation of Gen. Milroy, who they said compelled them to take the oath of allegiance before they were permitted to sow a grain of wheat. We promised them that when we captured the gentleman they could have him. We pushed on, with no hope of overtaking this cavalry on flying horses, but to get well between Winchester and Harper's Ferry. We next came upon our friends again at Martinsburg, where we captured some 2,000 infantry and the finest battery of light artillery I had most ever seen a Michigan battery, every horse a deep bay, fat and sleek, and bearing the brand 1 M. B. on the shoulder. Before making the attack Gen. Rones had a regiment or two of infantry mounted behind Jenkins' cavalry, each cavalryman had an infantryman on his horse, and away they went posthaste to the rear of the town. The battery had opened a brisk fire on us as we advanced, but as we neared their position the firing ceased, the battery disappeared and great volumes of smoke arose. The enemy had set fire to their stores concentrated there as they retreated, and it was said that 12,000 bales of hay were ablaze. We passed through to the outskirts and halted. In a little while the entire garrison quietly came back and surrendered. Not a man or horse was hurt. Their avenue of escape had been blocked.

I had rather an unpleasant experience before the general assault was made. Our brigade was ordered forward to us to support a rifled piece that had been placed in on an exposed position. We climbed up the hill in front obliquely, and when I was about twenty feet from the top the welcomed command was given to halt. I was in big luck for once in my life, but "it was ever thus from childhood's hour," for then followed the order to "close up to the right," and close up we did until I was on the very apex of the hill. The command to "lie down" came but for one time I didn't obey with my usual alacrity. I tried in vain to keep up the movement – "close up to the right," give way to the left, but it was no go. To aggravate the situation, I was next to the color bearer, as fearless a fellow as ever breathed, who had refused a commission because he would have to give up the colors, and he kept on waving the flag to attract the fire of the battery. It was fun for him, but I felt like the frogs when the boys were chunking. He succeeded in drawing the fire all right Every shell that came either barely cleared the hill or struck a few feet below, exploding and throwing dirt all over us. Finally one struck not more than a couple of feet under me. As it penetrated the earth, I could feel the ground sink and my heart, too, with a sort of a gone about the stomach that was disgustingly sickening. No explosion followed this time, and I felt better. The suspense was but seconds, but it seemed ages. I was consoled with the knowledge that two shells had been seldom known to strike the same place, and we correspondingly happy. We had Milroy's retreat safely cut off, when the news came that Winchester was surrendered, and as we moved away to the Potomac River. We learned afterward that he and his staff passed down the road within an hour after we had left. The garrison at Winchester surrendered, but not so the General. He must have been afraid of the farmers, and the farmers went back home in disgust.

Another reads:

"On the banks of the Potomac River, June 16, 1863. – We will cross into Maryland today, A part of our division is already across. We have run the Yankees out of several towns already. No damage done to us as yet. We are now opposite to Williamsport, Md.

"Bivouac near Greencastle, Pennsylvania. U. S., June 22, 1863. – You will see by the heading of this letter that we are in the Union at last, but reckon 'Old Abe' would feel much easier if we would secede again. We have met with but little opposition so far, but anticipate some work in a few days. We marched through several towns to the tune of 'Bonnie Blue Flag." The boys are in excellent health and spirits. "It will be impossible for me to write often, as the mails are very irregular,"etc.

Our regiment was on provost duty in Chambersburg a few days after this, as will be seen by the following letter, written from,

"Carlisle, Pennsylvania. June 18, 1863. – We arrived here last evening, after a march of twenty-six miles in about thirteen hours. The Yanks have offered little or no resistance as yet. You may hear some stirring news from here shortly as it is impossible a brush. The army is faring splendidly up here. Everything is in abundance. All private property is respected. We are the advance division. Our regiment was on provost duty in Chambersburg, a couple of days ago and our money was taken by the citizens in payment for goods almost at the same rate as Yankee greenbacks. Coffee at 40 cents, sugar 15 cents, calico for ladies dresses at 40 to 50 cents per yard, etc. I find the people an ignorant and deluded race in regard to the war and slavery. They are blind to all of Lincoln's faults. They speak like little children, if you tell them that they brought on the war they will deny it, and reply that we fired on For Sumpter, and all such answers. Then, again, there are some Copperheads. They hate the Abolitionists as bad as they do Rebels, but want peace on any terms. The wheat crop is very fine, cattle and horses in abundance, which are taken for the army," etc.

As you will observe, there were "Copperheads" then as now, "against the Government." We had lots of fun guying them. They would come into our camp, sneaking around, and as if we belonged to the "Golden Circle," and tell us that they were Copperheads and opposed to the war. But they received poor comfort from us. The boys would invite them to take a musket and join us. On their refusal to do so they would get roundly cursed as a lot of traitors that ought to be shot, and sometimes get a kick for their reward, with the admonition that we had a lot of their cowardly breed down our way who called themselves, "Union men," with no other principle than the fear of getting their worthless carcasses punctured. The people of Chambersburg could well afford to sell to us for Confederate money on a basis of "greenbacks, "as there was precious little of it along, for we had not been paid for a long time and what little we did get had long since passed into the hands of the sutler for coffee at about $10 a pound and wages at $11 a month, our pay didn't go very far.

We were now within seventeen miles of Harrisburg, and expected to occupy the capital of Pennsylvania the next day. But for reasons unknown in us we were sent down the Baltimore pike in a southeasterly direction, crossed the mountains at a place called Mount Holly or Poker town and camped that night at Heldlensburg. There rumors were rife of words of Yankees, bonafide "blue bellies" – no militia- and parks of artillery just beyond. We marched back in a southerly direction on that morning. July 1 we were at a route step when in the distance, to the south and west of us, we heard the booming of cannon. The command of "close up, double quick," was given, and away we went to join in the fray, and we got into it, and it was Gettysburg. Three day afterwards I wrote the following home: "Hospital Near Gettysburg, July 4, 1863. – I received a slight wound in the leg on Wednesday, July 1. It may be possible that I will be left here in case the army moves. As the ambulances were used entirely for the officers, I nor the physicians thought it prudent for me to walk about much at present. Don't be uneasy; I have plenty of good company along. My wound is slight and I am in the best of health," etc.

This was given to a comrade that passed by to bid me "good bye old fellow." The army was falling back. I had the bone of one leg shattered and a flesh wound in the other. How it happened and what happened afterward I will tell some other time if your patience is not exhausted.

To the noble women on both sides is due the credit of the heroic deeds performed in that heroic period of our history. It was only after we crossed the line into Pennsylvania that we began to appreciate the reason why the Yankee with his proverbial good sense and lack of sentiment, as we then thought, would rather be dead in Virginia than alive at home, and why he bartered thrift and comfort for death. We had congratulated ourselves in the belief that the St. Lawrence and not the Potomac River was the ultimate destination of McDowell's troops at Bull Run from the pace they set on their return in 1861.

When the Federal fleet came to the rescue of McClellan's army, and it took water at Harrison's Landing in 1862, we were sure that they were convinced of the folly of attempting the subjugation of the South. Again at Fredericksburg, when Burnside's madness hurled them into the vortex where death held such wild carnival that Lee exclaimed: "Blood enough had been shed for one day," and lastly, Hooker's folly with his 100,000 soldiers in the Wilderness, would have given them such a longing for home that even bounties would lose their charm. That was the way we viewed the situation then. But "a change came o'er the spirit of our dream," when we invaded the land of "brotherly love." The men were civil enough, but patriotic defiance was everywhere in evidence in the flashing eyes of the women, especially the young ones. If there were any Quakers there they were not in petticoats. I can assure you. The girls were full of fight and hate, without fear or love in their hearts for their enemies. They had no "these" and "thous" for us, but "you horrid, ragged rebels" was hurled at us on every side, much to our admiration and it amused us to hear them say "I declare they look just like our own men," as if they expected us to have horns and devil's tails. We soon found out that they, like our own glorious women, had bolded the front doors and barred the back gates against skulkers. The stay-at-homes were objects of loathing and contempt when their country called for men. This solved the mystery why the Yankee preferred to meet death in Virginia, and we forgave him. A soldier's dream of reward is the welcome smile of his sweetheart, and the seers of battle are as jewels in her sight. Man would not fight if it were not for lovely woman, nor would the love of country exist without her. So all credit to her for the deeds of valor and patriotism.

How our world has changed we were making history then. Unwittingly cementing a great nation that we thought to dismember. How mysteriously the invisible hand of destiny works out its ends. The country had passed the scope of the politician with his compromises. The soldier was called in with the sword and the opiates of the quack had given way to the surgeon's knife. The disorders were removed at the priceless cost of patriots' blood, but the body was healed and has grown strong under the ken of the wisest, we built better than we knew. Our country today occupies the proudest place in the front rank of the great nations of earth.

"LITTLE PIECES" OF THE BATTLE

NICHOLAS WEEKS
3RD ALABAMA INFANTRY
Galveston, Texas
Galveston Daily News
June 6, 1904

The Scenes At Gettysburg
Captain Weekes Tells What He Saw at That Memorable Battle – No One Division Did It All.
Capt. Weeks Address.

Comrades – You were promised a feast for today, and I am sorry to report that Col. Mott's absence from the city prevents him from addressing you. Accepting the adage that "half a loaf is better than no bread," I will act in is plead, but you all know that little was expected from a substitute in war times, and you will accordingly please be kind enough to expect even less than that little from me," in this weak, piping time of peace.

At the last meeting I gave you an account of our trip to Gettysburg, and promised at some other time to tell you what happened there. Some of you were generous enough to say that what I told interested you. It was a crude, unvarnished statement of facts, fortified by letters written from points along the march, with no attempt to draw upon the imagination – just simple, stupid truths. Proceeding along this same line, I will read you some extracts written to Gen Battie a year ago about Gettysburg. We were both there, he at the head of a regiment and I, at the tail end of a company. We didn't see very much of the battle, only little pieces of it directly in front of us. The line of battle extended miles, and we were only in one place at a time; had plenty to do all the time and had no time to take note of what our neighbors were not doing. Besides, it was a little smoky thereabouts, which interrupted with a view of the landscape, even if we hadn't been kept busy dodging shells and trying to say our prayers at the same time. We did help to bore a hole through the enemy's line of battle on the first day, which they resented with some violence. Others did the same and met with a little discourtesy.

From the letters I referred to I will quote in part as follows:

My dear General – It didn't used to be a sin to fight on Sunday, and cant much harm now for two old 'vets' to have a little war talk on the good day. What you say about the regiment at Gettysburg is exactly what I recollect, up to the time I was knocked off my place. As a proof that my memory is pretty good. I will briefly relate some minor incidents, only by way of collaboration, without attempting any dissertation of the battle. A part of A. P. Hill's corps, which evidently had come up by the Cashtown road, had opened the ball.

We were halted in a clump of woods. Gen. Rhodes soon after hurried up with a battery of Carter's artillery, which took its position with us and opened up, and so did the enemy, who used shrapnel on us almost exclusively. Our regiment was moved off at a right oblique across an open field, and was between Daniels and Iverson's men when it had reached its destination. We were under the impression that our regiment was detached to join with Daniel's brigade, which was a new one in our division and we thought in its first baptism of fire. We did not know then or suspect even that a mistake was being made.

The enemy's infantry was concealed in the woods in our front, but their artillery was in evidence everywhere. Our first attempt to carry the enemy's position was unsuccessful. Then a second assault was made, with no satisfactory result. We were subjected to an aggravating fire of musketry in front and artillery enfilading both flanks. We seemed to be in a pocket, and were impatient to get to work again as a relief from the strain. Col. Forsyth expressed the opinion that our sharpshooters were in front engaging the enemy in the woods. This, the peerless George Ellison volunteered to find out. He advanced to within a short distance of the woods, and standing on a little mound deliberately fired and loaded his gun three times in the midst of bursting shells, for it seemed as if every shot was directed at him, and returning reported,

'Nothing in front but Yankees.

In our exposed position it was evident that we were in danger of being captured, and you decided to rejoin our own brigade. We were moving by the left flank under a galling fire when Gen. Ramsener rode up and asked you, 'What troops are these?' On being told, he said he had sent two of his regiments to O'Neal's support and asked, 'Will Alabamians fight alongside of North Carolinians?'

With a yell we took position on the right of his remaining regiments. He rode out to the front a little distance, turned around, ordered officers to the front of their commands and said, 'Men, we can take that stone fence, and by the gods we can hold it too!' Lifting his hat above his head as he wheeled his horse about, and giving the command, 'Come on!' he dashed forward. He was mounted on a small-sized white horse. We did not fire a shot on the charge, so fast was our pace, and our officer being in front, nor did he once glance back to see if we were following. I saw when a shot struck Lieut. Ledyard, who was leading our company, breaking his leg, yet he bounded on with his leg dangling until he fell. A sergeant only, but next in command, I had to take his place. I thought the Yanks would never leave that wall. How I longed to see just one go. We were nearly up to them, when to my great relief they started: in the next instant we were jumping over the fence. The gallant Ramsener was the first, clearing the wall on horseback. He immediately called for two men from each company. I detailed Bob Hearn and John Stephens of the cadets. With this squad he disappeared around behind the woods we had just previously attempted to take. We were now in the breach, shooting both ways. Gen. Ramsener came back afoot, and hearing someone say that we were firing on our friends, said, "There are no friends there: they killed my horse, Give them __l! He ordered his aid or orderly, a bare-headed lad of apparently 15 years to 'Go tell Iverson to press them in front, that I am in their rear. Which Iverson's brigade evidently did, for prisoners soon came pouring in a stream by us like water through a Mississippi crevasse. Here we rejoined our own brigade, and were soon on the way to Gettysburg. We went through the town, going south under a hot fire from house tops, windows, and cellars as well as from retreating soldiers in front. There were none of our people between us and the enemy, not on that street, at least. Whether 'we were first to enter Gettysburg' or not, I wouldn't positively assert, but we neither met or passed any Confederates on the way through. We reached the southern outskirts of town and were halted at the foot of the hill. Why we were not permitted to follow up the victory and finish the job that evening we could not understand. Next came the fatal order to fall back to the railroad. Some said Gen. Ewell was tired and thought we were. The mutterings of disapproval by the men at this order, at first sullen, 'Oh, that Stonewall Jackson were only here!' could be heard on every hand, and was echoed in every heart. You were brought back to the field hospital on Schneider's farm wounded in the thigh, and Maj. Sands below the knee; Col. Lightfoot of the Sixth Alabama, with arm shattered; Lieut. Ledyard, leg off; Shanghai Donaldson, shot in neck, shoulder and hip; poor young McKerrell through the stomach, and some 300 or more dead, dying and mutilated lying around. These are some of the things seen and heard by a man in the ranks. My memory is not infallible, besides in me subordinate capacity the opportunities for knowing we were very limited, hence I am wide open for correction. When the last taps will have been sounded, I hope at the great reveille there will be none absent, not even your humble sergeant.'

The Army of Northern Virginia at the time was composed of nine divisions of infantry, with an average of about 6,000 effective men to a division. The casualties were, in round numbers, 23,000, officially reported, to which, if added to the slightly wounded, that were not allowed to be counted, would easily swell that figure to 25,000, or say nearly 50 per cent of the whole number actually engaged. So you can see that it was impossibility for any one or two or even four divisions to have done all the fighting and suffered all the losses without going to extinction, and this applies as well to the troops from any one State.

The Yankees played no favorites in the game. It mattered not whence we came, whether from Maryland or Texas, Arkansas or Florida, all were alike to them, 'terrible rebels.' The losses were as nearly equally divided between the several commands as the chances of battle permitted. Some necessarily lost more than others, but all losses-a-plenty.

The questions are often asked, "Why Gen. Lee selected such a place for the battle?" and "Why he did not press the advantage gained on the first day and occupy the heights?" It was because Gen. Lee did not arrive on the scene until the first day's fight was done; otherwise the result would have been different, perhaps. Through a drawn battle, it was in effect the most potent factor in the annals of our country's history it was there the tide of Confederate hoped touched high water mark, and ebbed where the two great hosts of contending America death struggle for the survivor of principles dearer than life. Three days the frightful carnage raged, and they drew apart in breathe and rest. No fear and no boasting, but gore and glory enough for both. Fifty thousand dead and wounded was the measure of their desperate courage. The Federal heroically stood his ground, the Confederate reluctantly failed in his purpose. Each satisfied to have won the respect of the other; to have done more was impossible.

Comrades, if at some future time you find yourselves suffering from an exuberance of patience, and you find relief in no other quarter, I will reluctantly come to your assistance with a tale of prison hospital life, or something else that I know for a fact, if you prefer; but I do not expect to be called upon very soon again after this dose. I thank you for your flattering indulgence. God bless you.

ANGELS OF MERCY

NICHOLAS WEEKS
3RD ALABAMA INFANTRY
Galveston, Texas
Galveston Daily News
June 7, 1909

Comrade Nicholas Weeks' War Experience. Kindly Act of Express Agent.
Comrade Nick Weeks' Address.

Comrades: At the meeting before the last I gave some personal experiences as a wounded prisoner at Gettysburg which were not exaggerated, but pretty rough, and will now present a less somber view of the picture, all from memory. I was not the most unfortunate there, but on the contrary, was peculiarly favored throughout, not only that I was one of the few who came through with both life and limbs, but in very many ways, which I will endeavor to show, but cannot explain. The first wound I got that day was a shot in the center of my left knee, and using my gun as a crutch had gone but a couple of steps when another shot struck my right leg. I sat down then to contemplate the fatality of bragging. It may be thought superstitious, but I have never bragged on man or beast, nor even on fishing, but what I was doomed to disappointment. On our triumphant (?) march through Pennsylvania to the tune of "The Bonnie Blue Flag" the boys would ask, "How will you feel if the Yankees catch you up here?" My invariable reply was that they will have to get me in both legs before any catching would be done; that there was not a sharpshooter in all the Federal army who could draw a bead fine enough to find my legs – so very slim was I then. But they did that very thing and made me sorry that I had bragged.

Two comrades, Jim Harrison of the cadets and Tom Macon of the Gulf City Guards, dragged me back behind the line of battle, and for this I was doubly fortunate, for I fell into the hands of a brave, noble woman, who, melting with compassion at the sight, bathed my wounds and bound them up with her apron torn into bandages. Not content with having done this much for me, she washed the grime and powder smoke from my face. When I attempted to thank her for the kindness done an enemy in her own hand, "Hush, she said, "I know neither friend or foe: all is suffering humanity for me." Then bursting into tears, with face adverted, she pointed to some Union colors lying in the street, she cried out in heartbroken sobs: "All but that! My God! I cannot stand the sight of my country's flag trailing in the dust!" (Of this I think that I have spoken before.) Twice in the early '70s I went back to Gettysburg in search of this grand heroine, but could never find a trace of her. If I had the means a spotless marble shaft towner above all around would be erected there to "the American woman."

A few days after our army had marched away and the usual torrential rains after battles had set in, three horsemen appeared. The oldest one of them was touched to the heart at our deplorable condition. He explained that they were searching for the federal wounded, to rescue them from the rising water in low places. He was reluctant to leave us to our fate, but duty to his own called him away. He asked if we knew anyone North who might help us. The answers were in the negative. He went on to say that there were many southern sympathizers in Baltimore who would kindly contribute to our relief, if they knew of our condition. But none of us had acquaintances there. At last he asked where we were from, addressing William Ledyard and me. When told, he said there was quite a rich man in Baltimore formerly from our town, a Mr. John W. Wicks, in the sugar trade. We both had heard of such a person having once lived in Mobile, but it was before our time. The gentleman who was speaking to us gave his name as G. H. Hunt, interested in iron works in or near Baltimore, saying that a letter mailed to him from any person care of the Christian Commission would reach him. I think that was the address he gave us.

The first Sunday after this visit, a Mr. Kingdon, an Episcopal minister, hunted us up and did much for our relief. He came at the instance of Mr. Wicks. As I remember, he was an English subject from Jamaica, and procured a pass through the lines to preach in a little church somewhere. Mr. Wicks soon after came himself and gave us most generous aid, but the authorities got after him, we were told and he left us almost immediately. A Mrs. DeForest came to us, who put up a tent on the grounds. She was known as the "White Angel," as she always dressed in immaculate white linen. She was an angel to us. At all hours of the day and night she could be seen moving among the trees caring for the sick and dying scattered about in the woods. To our great sorrow, she too had to go. There was a Mr. Johnson connected at one time with the Panama Railroad. I, and his nephew, Patrick Henry Smith, who were untiring in their efforts to help us. But like the others, they, too, after a few days, fell under the ban of suspicion, as did generous, whole-souled Mrs. Cate, the wife of a Baltimore lumber dealer, and we missed them sadly. The Baltimore people who came to us were supposed to be from Philadelphia, Harrisburg and other loyal places. I recall the names of Mr. and Mrs. Poinsal and their splendid niece, Miss. Laura Mantel of Montier, Mrs. Wilcox of 77 Lombard street, Baltimore, who gave me this address in case I made my escape from prison. Thee was Mrs. Sawyer and also Mrs. Banks, the beautiful wife of Baltimore's mayor, and the lovely Virginia girl, Miss. Ella Strath of Charlestown, sister of the surgeon of the Stonewall Brigade. She comforted the poor dying boys with assurance that all Confederate soldiers were bound to go to heaven, and she believed it. There were some others, whose names I do not recall at the moment. I had no means of keeping a record, and if I had I would not have written down names for fear of getting people in trouble with the federal authorities. We were without a chaplain, and the soldiers that died were deprived of the consolation so dear to the Christian heart, except the few whom the good ladies attended in their last moments during the short times they were permitted in the grounds.

I recall a scene that was not an exceptional occurrence. A poor fellow was dying of pyemia. Kneeling over him with ear close to his lips to catch the last words to his mother was a young woman, who reported them to another girl, sitting on the ground with pencil and paper in hand, taking down the message. When he ceased to speak they realized the end was near and rising on their knees, their voices tremulous with emotion, sand through their tears, "Nearer, My God, to Thee," and when his spirit had taken its flight they threw their arms about each other and sobbed aloud.

The South had no large cities from whose slums to draw, and most of the young men in the ranks were well raised, of good morale and generally devout, and to a large extent farmer boys. It did seem hard that they had to be denied the comfort of religion at such a time as this. I referred to my previous talk to a lady who had "snatched me back to life." Like many others I was attacked with pyemia, chill followed chill, suppuration had ceased and I knew death was close at hand, and turning to my comrade, said that I would soon be gone, for him to tell my father how I fell, that I had never complained nor asked the enemy for even a drink of water. At this juncture Mrs. Sawyer (?) approached us and offered me tobacco, pieces of castile soap, a sponge, and bandage, all of which I gratefully declined, explaining that I would not be here but a little while longer and for her to save them for others who needed and could use them. She was much distressed at this and said she had a bottle of brandy that might do me some good. I knew stimulants of that character were used in cases of snake poisoning and my affliction was similar in effects. She moved up close to me and dropped the bottle on the ground near my hand and slipped it under my head (she, like the other ladies, carried these articles in a false pocket or bag under their skirts). When she had gone and no sentinel was in sight, I knocked the neck of the bottle off with my knife. Being too weak to sit up, much of the spirits was spilled in my efforts to drink from the broken bottle while lying down. But I got enough to serve the purpose. This was in the evening early and I did not wake up until the next day about noon. Ledyard told me the burial squad had come for me twice already that day. But my good fortune was still with me; the crisis was past, and though feeble, hope and life then slowly began to rise.

By way of credential I submit here with two letters, one from me written at Gettysburg, and the other from John Hurxthal from Hagerstown, Md. Sergeant Hurxthal came over to the field hospital on the eve of the army's leaving to see and say good-by to the wounded. He held his gun stock so that I could write a few lines home, which he would mail for me. He read it and promised to confirm it in every particular. This was done to save anxiety to my dear mother, whose heart would break soon enough when the truth would come. We understood each other, and when good-by was said, it was forever, as we believed. I carelessly wrote of a slight wound and that I would be well in a few days and paroled, etc. God forgave the lie, for, like Uncle Toby's oath, "the accusing spirit which flew up to heaven's chancery with the 'lie' blushed as he gave it in, and the recording angel as he wrote it dropped a tear upon the word and blotted it out forever."

PLACED IN THE SAME HOSPITAL TENT

NICHOLAS WEEKS
3RD ALABAMA INFANTRY
DAN S. HOOKER
32ND NORTH CAROLINA INFANTRY
Galveston, Texas
Galveston Daily News
July 1, 1913

They Were At Gettysburg – Two Galvestonians Received Wounds Fifty Years Ago Today.

Fifty years ago today two Galvestonians, wearing uniforms of the gray, struggled in that fight mass of humanity at Gettysburg, and before the sun had set in a smoke-obscured sky were lying in the same hospital tents with severe wounds. They were Dan S. Hooker, master of the schooner *Daisy,* and Nicholas Weeks, city auditor. Another Galvestonian participating in the battle was William Schadt engaged in the manufacturing business. Mr. Schadt was in Hood's Brigade. Messrs. Hooker and Weeks were in Road's division, a part of Jackson's old corps.

"Weeks and I were wounded at the first battle," said Captain Hooker on Monday, "and lay in the same hospital tent. By a strange coincidence we were on the same steamer, the *City of New York*, as prisoners of war, and came to Galveston in the same year – 1872. In spirit we will be on the old battlefield Tuesday."

FORMER FOES BECOME FIDDLER FRIENDS

"COL." PATTEE
24TH MICHIGAN INFANTRY
J. C. WILES
47TH GEORGIA INFANTRY
San Antonio, Texas
San Antonio Express
November 20, 1919

At the Majestic

They say politics makes strange bedfellows but the political game has a close second in modern vaudeville. An apt illustration of this is that of Col. Pattee and Maj. J. C. Wiles, members of the "old Soldier Fiddlers" appearing at the Majestic this week.

Fifty-six years ago both these men participated in the great Battle of Gettysburg. Their own regiments were opposed to each other in many a fierce charge in that great fight, and there is no doubt that Col. Pattee and Maj. Wiles were often in close proximity. It would have been sure death to have even intimated to either of them at that time that there was a possibility of their appearing together on a public stage and clasping hands in friendship. But today the two warriors are bosom friends, and with two other veterans of the great civil strife, are showing vaudeville audiences a real novelty in the musical line.

The four cronies are just "fiddler'." They scorn the term "violinists." Such a thing as a musical education is unknown to them.

LEFT FOR DEAD ON JULY 3RD

D. H. WILLIAMS
13TH MISSISSIPPI INFANTRY
Corsicana, Texas
Corsicana Sun
May 3, 1916

Left For Dead
D. H. Williams, Ninety-One Years Old, Wounded At Gettysburg.

Mr. D. H. Williams of Barry was in town today. He is ninety-one years old, but doesn't look it by quarter of a century. He is active in body and his mind is perfectly clear. Mr. Williams is a Confederate veteran and saw much service in the war. He was wounded three times but only one of these wounds, he says, was serious. He was in twenty-feet of the man who shot him down at Gettysburg. This occurred about noon on July 3rd, 1863. About the same hour that night he regained consciousness and left the battlefield. The other wounded had been carried away, he being left for dead. Mr. Williams said that his brother was told by a comrade who was standing by him when he received the wound, that he "never saw a man killed deader," meaning that to the comrade death seemed to have come the instant the bullet struck him. Mr. Williams' brother spent the night looking for him and just at daylight ran face to face with a squad of Federal soldiers. He fled and although not less than forty shots were fired at him he escaped injury.

RECEIVED THIRTEEN WOUNDS DURING THE BATTLE

ED C. WILSON
3RD LOUISIANA INFANTRY
Electra, Texas
Courier-Gazette
July 27, 1921

Received 13 Wounds At Gettysburg
Judge Ed C. Wilson of Electra Here for Ex-Confederate Reunion.

Justice of the Peace Ed C. Wilson of Electra, Texas, arrived in McKinney this morning to attend the Ex-Confederate and Old Settlers picnic and reunion. Mr. Wilson is 78 years old and served through the four years struggle in the war between the states. He is a native of Louisiana and enlisted in the Confederacy in that state at the outbreak of the Civil War. He enlisted in the 3rd Louisiana Infantry under General P. G. T. Beauregard. However, after reaching Virginia he was made a scout and spy under General Lee. At the Battle of Gettysburg Mr. Wilson received thirteen wounds. During the entire war he sustained thirty-two wounds. The worst was when he had his thumb shot off and received two other saber wounds in the back of the head.

At the Battle of Gettysburg Mr. Wilson said his father and four brothers were killed in the battle. His father was 67 years old when he was killed.

Mr. Wilson visited McKinney about twenty years ago. This is his first visit here since then. He was loud in his praise for McKinney.

Mr. Wilson is aide-de-camp on staff of Commander-in-chief U. C. V.

SENTENCED TO BE SHOT

ED C. WILSON
3RD LOUISIANA INFANTRY
Electra, Texas
Pampa Daily News
July 17, 1933

Civil War Vet Of Electra Was Once Sentenced To Be Shot By Union Army, But Dug Way Out

Electra. July 17. – Head erect, shoulders which scarcely betray their weight of years and with a swift, firm step that still shows something of the military training that began in April, 1862, when he enlisted in the Third Louisiana Infantry at New Orleans. Col E. C. Wilson, who celebrated his 91st birthday on Monday, July 10, at his home here is probably the busiest and most active survivor of the Civil war.

Col. Wilson, the only survivor of his regiment so far as has learned and the last of his family.

He participates in every patriotic parade, ceremonial or service in Electra He serves as registrar of vital statistics for his town and precinct in Wichita county and uses a typewriter efficiently in making out his reports.

When Col. Wilson came to Electra in 1911 a score or more Confederate veterans were living in this vicinity. They dwindled to 11 in 1926 and in 1933 only two remain. Joe McCracken and Col. Wilson. The two carried out the U. C. V. ritualistic ceremony over a majority of their deceased comrades, Col. Wilson serving as chaplain.

Col. Wilson was born in New Orleans. His mother's maiden name was Sabatier and she was a native of France. His father was part French. He was attending school when the call to arms in behalf of the Confederacy was sounded. He and several of his schoolmates enlisted at the same time and were rushed immediately to the eastern coast in time to participate in the battle before Fort Sumter. He was given the rank of captain under General Beauregard and was advanced to the post of major shortly before being mustered out with the Army of Northern Virginia. His title of colonel was conferred some years ago as official recognition from the United Confederate Veterans, he having served as a colonel and aide on the staff of each succeeding commander since General Vance's tenure in office.

Losing a thumb in the Battle of Gettysburg and carrying 31 other scars of wounds received in battle, he was not only orphaned but suffered the loss of his four brothers in the cause of the south. His father and brothers were killed or died of wounds received at Gettysburg.

South Carolina Monument. Gettysburg. NMP. *Jill Ogline-Titus.*

NEVER LEFT THE FIELD

RANSOM F. WINGO
13TH SOUTH CAROLINA INFANTRY
Waco, Texas

Was slightly wounded at the second battle of Manassas and also at Gettysburg, but did not leave the field in either case. Was taken prisoner at Falling Water, on the Potomac, on the retreat from Gettysburg, and was taken to Baltimore jail, and from there to Point Lookout, Md., and was never exchanged. The last fight I was in was at Gettysburg.[48]

FORMER ENEMIES, FOREVER FRIENDS

W. E. Winston
7th Alabama Infantry
Nacogdoches, Texas
Nacogdoches Daily Sentinel
June 29, 1918

Foes In Civil War, Friends For Life, Rest Side By Side

Frank Robbins, a Union soldier, and W. E. Winston, a Confederate soldier, old firm friends, sleep

---

48   Yeary, *boys in gray*, p. 812.

side by side in the Oak Grove cemetery here. Both wounded and left for dead on the Gettysburg battlefield, recovered in the same hospital and were discharged. They returned to their homes, Winston to Texas and Robbins to Ohio, making a vow that they would seek each other if the time ever came when either was in need.

Winston built up a good foundry business at Nacogdoches. Twenty years after Gettysburg a man walked into his shop and said he was down and about. It was Frank Robbins. Winston gave him work. The two men remained firm friends and neither ever married. One day Winston bought out a lot in Oak Grove cemetery. It must be large enough for two graves – himself, and Robbins, and there the two old timers, friends in life, inseparable in death now rest side by side, double tombstone carrying their names, birth and date of death.

A SOLDIER OF THE LOST CAUSE

DREW B. WOOD
9TH ALABAMA INFANTRY
Dallas, Texas
Sunday Gazetteer
March 10, 1907

There was a chapter in this man's life that should give him a seat among the saints. It is this: He was a soldier of the last cause. He was one of those brave spirits that on that fateful day charged with Pickett up the hill at Gettysburg and sought glory at the cannon's mouth. Many a night in the glare of the campfire in the Boggy Woods and at Allen Bayou he told that dreadful experience. The *Dallas News* says that he will sleep his last sleep in the Confederate burial ground. This is truly a brave man; he will find plenty of company there. Peace to his ashes.

A STAFF COURIER

W. B. WOODY
WRIGHT'S ARTILLERY BATTERY
Rockdale, Texas
Polk County Enterprise
January 1, 1914

Editor Reporter: Having noticed your liberal proposition offering to publish the war records of all the members of our Camp, I am sending you today under separate cover a newspaper cut of myself, which I happen to have and which will save you the expense of having a new plate made. This plate was made for the Grand Army of the Republic at Gettysburg. It seems that the Commander of the G. A. R. wanted to get the pictures of all the staff of General Young who attended this year's reunion, for what purpose I know not. But the plate was made and I am sending same to you.

Now as to my war record will state briefly that I ran away from home when I was sixteen but was so light in weight that the War Department would not have me, but I managed to get in with General Bushrod Johnson as staff courier, and finally was permitted to join Wright's Battery, and was later assigned to General John B. Gordon as staff courier. I was with the army until it was disbanded at Appomattox on April 9, 1865.

Some few years after the war was over at the time the Confederate Veterans Association was organized and General J. B. Gordon was elected Commander, he put me on his staff, ranking me as "Colonel," and I have been retained as such ever since with the same rank, and as such was at the Gettysburg reunion this year with present Commander, General B. H. Young.

Now as to some of the things I did cause these various promotions I had rather others would say, and I leave that up to you.

I think Camp Sam Davis should not only accept the kind offer of The Reporter, but should feel grateful to you as well. The Reporter still fills the desire of my homesick heart each Monday morning when I am in Atlanta, but this summer I was four months away from Georgia and missed its weekly visits sadly.

Yours truly,
W. B. Woody

MINNIE BALL FROM GETTYSBURG EXTRACTED YEARS LATER

JUSTUS WOOLWORTH
2ND LOUISIANA INFANTRY

Panola County, Texas
Austin Weekly Statesman
December 3, 1885

County Treasurer Justus Woolworth is now in New Orleans, where he has just had extracted from his thigh a minnie ball received at the Battle of Gettysburg, and which has caused him great suffering and made him a cripple for over twenty years.

REMINISCENCE OF THE FIRST DAY'S FIGHTING

D. T. WOOTTON
12TH NORTH CAROLINA INFANTRY

Rockdale, Texas
Rockdale Reporter and Messenger
July 3, 1913

Interesting Reminiscence of the First Day's Fighting at Gettysburg
Mr. Editor:

Being in a reminiscence mood and it being fifty years today since the first day of the Battle of Gettysburg when I was wounded, I thought a little sketch might be interesting to the younger generation.

On the night before the battle next day, we camped about three miles from the battlefield. We were the advance brigade of Rhodes' division. Ewell's corps. We reached the battlefield about nine o'clock the next day and were immediately thrown in line of battle. Archer's brigade of Hill's corps had already opened the fight. It was not until between 12:00 and 1:00 o'clock that we began to charge. Just as the command to charge was given, I was detailed to fill the canteens, but by the time I reached the well in a nearby yard the minnie-balls were beginning to sing the sad requiem of death. Walking in the yard was a woman with three or four small children about her, all of them crying. I said to her, "Madam, we are going to have a dreadful battle in a few minutes; if I were you I would go to the rear." To which she replied, "Lord, Mister, which way is that?" I pointed to the west road, the one over which we had come that morning.

By the time I had the canteens filled, my brigade began the charge. The command from our officers was: "When you get to those Yankees, charge them." We did not go far before we commenced to fire upon them." During the charge our company was separated by a cross fence and four men were left on one side away from their comrades. All these four were shot during the fight: one man receiving two balls, another four; and another six, while the fourth man was killed. Our companies numbered twenty-four men before the fight but in five minutes after the firing began fourteen of us were down and both officers wounded. About this time I looked to the left where three regiments of our men had stood, but now the line of battle was marked by the windrows of dead. Not one was left. The first relief sent us was Daniel's North Carolina Brigade. This was their first fight. There was a battery of fifteen guns playing on them as they came, but with one volley accompanied by the rebel yell, they had those guns in their possession. That evening our regiment and the other remnants of the other three regiments in our brigade cut off twelve hundred Yankees from their army and captured the whole lot. I was wounded at one o'clock and laid on the battlefield until sundown so I did not have a hand in their capture.

Right here I want to correct one error in the *Houston Post* of July 1st. It stated that the cavalry on that day was commanded by General Wheeler, whereas, Generals Hampton and Stuart were in command. General Wheeler was never in command of the Virginia cavalry. This same charge of ten thousand men is very vividly described by General Gordon in Gordon's History.

If this communication is too long you may prune it down to suit yourself.
Respectfully,
D. T. Wootton.

In the hands of the enemy at Gettysburg. *Library of Congress.*

COULD NOT BE REMOVED FROM THE BATTLEFIELD

D. T. WOOTTON
12TH NORTH CAROLINA INFANTRY
Rockdale, Texas
Rockdale Reporter and Messenger
December 18, 1913

Daniel T. Wotton of Rockdale and member of Camp Sam Davis U. C.V. was born in Prince Edward County, Virginia, June 23, 1843. He enlisted in Warrenton, N. C., April 18, 1861, in Company

F, 12 North Carolina Infantry. During the first year of the war he was in service at Norfolk participating in the battle of Peats Turnout. After the seven days fight around Richmond and second Manassas his command was placed in Jackson's Corps and he was in the capture of Harper's Ferry and the battles of Sharpsburg, Fredericksburg, Chancellorsville and Gettysburg. At the last battle he was so severely wound on the first day he could not be removed when General Lee retired into Virginia and house was captured with all others wounded as himself. When he was able he was removed to prison at David's Island, N. Y., from where he was exchanged in January of '64, getting back to his command in time to engage in the battle of the Wilderness and Spotsylvania Court House. At this latter battle he was again captured and confined first in the military prison of Point Lookout and then Elmira, N. Y., at which place he reached until the close of the war, further exchanges being refused by the Federal government.

A Virginian in a North Carolina Regiment

D. T. Wootton
12ᵀᴴ North Carolina Infantry
Rockdale, Texas
Rockdale Reporter and Messenger
June 14, 1917

He was raised in Virginia but when the war between the North and South broke out, he was in North Carolina, and being anxious to do his duty as he saw it, cast his lot with the Confederacy by volunteering in Company F, 12th N. C. Infantry, where he served for the entire war and how well he did his part can better be told by the three wounds his body has carried ever since, two of which he received on that field made so world-wide by reason of the great Pickett's charge at Gettysburg.

It was both pain and pleasure this Camp took part in placing some never fading flowers at his grave, dealing with only facts regarding this good faithful soldier's history.

These last rites took place some nine miles south of Rockdale at his family burial ground on the 24th day of April, 1917. We wept but not all those without hope in the great resurrection when all the faithful shall be taken up to meet our Lord in Glory, and our prayer is that we may all meet him with all the rest of our comrades who have died in the faith, then death will have been but a rest from this world's toils and cares.

And now may our Heavenly Father guide us all to the end that we may have a home beyond the grave promised to all who put their trust in our Savior.

Done by request of this Camp and submitted to you this 12th day of May, 1917.
W. B. Woody.
A.P. Perry,
Committee.

Could Have Walked on Dead Men

W. L. Young
17ᵀᴴ Mississippi Infantry
Dallas, Texas

At Gettysburg, I was in Longstreet's Corps, with Pickett's Division, resting on our right. We were in the center of Lee's Army. I think this was the 2ⁿᵈ day of July, the day of the great battle. We were ordered in line about 2 p. m. We moved on the enemy, the Seventeenth and Thirteenth in the front, with the Eighteenth and Twenty-first Mississippi Regiments supporting us. As I was First Sergeant I knew how many guns we had and know that we went into battle with 416 men and came out with

67 unhurt. My regiment took 13 pieces of cannon and held them, but we could have walked on dead men for quite a distance. We had three color bearers killed that day and I had one man killed on each side of me in less time than it takes to write this. I can never forget that day. On the next day our entire artillery was brought to bear and they fought a duel for three hours; and, strange to say, that while we supported the artillery that day, we did not lose a man. The earth fairly shook, but there was so much smoke that there was much wild shooting. I have been in many hard fought battles but this was the most heart-rending of any that I ever witnessed.[49]

82nd Illinois Cavalry Monument. Gettysburg NMP.
Tom Miller.

A FINAL VISIT TO GETTYSBURG

LOUIS ZOELLNER
82ND ILLINOIS INFANTRY
San Antonio, Texas
San Antonio Express
August 6, 1916

Pioneer Merchant, Dies On Way Home.
Excessive Heat Cause Heart Failure –
In Business Near Half a Century.
Had Gallant War Record.

On his way home here from a purchasing trip to New York and Boston, death overtook Louis Zoellner, aged 78, of 522 Foster Street, and a pioneer business man of San Antonio. A dispatch to The Express from Logansport, Ind., last night stated that Mr. Zoellner was found dead in a Pullman berth on a Pennsylvania train when it reached Logansport. The coroner returned a verdict of death from heart failure, presumably caused by the heat.

In spite of his advance years, Mr. Zoellner was active in business and was manager for the American Hat and Shoe Company. He was born in Germany, November 4, 1836, and came to America while in his twenties.

During the War Between the States he fought with the Illinois troops as a first sergeant of Company H, of the Eighty-second Volunteer Infantry Regiment. He was captured at Gettysburg and imprisoned in Richmond, Va. Sometime later, however, he was exchanged and returned to his own regiment.

Saved Regimental Flag.

When the battle of Chancellorsville was raging at its hottest the regimental flag of the Eighty-second was ripped from its staff by a shell, the silken banner itself torn almost to shreds. Sergeant Zoellner snatched the remnants from the ground and bore them above his head throughout the thickest part of the fight. When the battle was over, he found some of the pieces of the flag in his pocket. In his excitement he had probably thrust them there, as the precious folds were gradually being torn to pieces. Three small stripes of his flag he kept and framed in his home.

He was given an honorable discharge from the army as a Second Lieutenant, June 8, 1865.

At the conclusion of the war he went to New Orleans, but a year or two later settled in Galveston.

---

49   Ibid., p. 834

Here he was married to Miss Emma Stissell, moving to San Antonio, several years later.

Mr. Zoellner always followed the mercantile business. He was one of the pioneer merchants of Commerce Street and opened his first store in this city, near the Commerce Street bridge, upon the site of the Riverside Building.

He remained there for five years, selling out his business at that time to enter the employ of A. B. Frank & Co., with whom he was connected for over twenty-five years. He then became manager for the American Hat and Shoe Company.

Translated Lincoln's Address.

Mr. Zoellner was a scholar and a great reader. He possessed a splendid library, but was particularly partial to German literature. In fact, the translation of English to German of the Gettysburg Address of President Lincoln of whom he was extremely proud.

Mr. Zoellner is survived by his widow and two daughters, Misses Essle and Victoria, and by one son, Ike Zoellner. A telegram was received by the family from Logansport, Ind., late last night stating that the body will be sent to San Antonio at noon today. It is expected that it will arrive here Tuesday morning, and in event the funeral will take place Wednesday.

RALLY ROUND THE FLAG

Corsicana Daily Sun
June 13, 1927

At Gettysburg 63 per cent of those present were killed or wounded. At one time during the heaviest firing the men seemed for a moment to waver. Human nature was exhausted and could stand no more – incessant marching and fight wand want of sleep; the men were becoming dazed and when half the command was down, dead or wounded, there came a time when it seemed that the brave line would give way. Colonel Henry J. Madill (commanding officer of the 141^s Pennsylvania,) quietly took the flag from the hands of the color bearer, and planting the staff in the ground, with his hand on the bunting, he burst into song with:

> *"Rally round the flag, boys,*
> *Rally round the flag.*
> *Shouting the battle cry of freedom."*

The men took up the refrain; new life animated the tired souls. Without another word the line braced up, and many men fell with the song on his lips.

Eternal Peace Memorial. *Gettysburg NMP.*

BOOKS

A Memorial and Biographical History of McLennan, Falls, Bell and Coryell Counties, (book) 1893.

Armstrong County Historical Society: *A Collection of Memories, A History of Armstrong County, 1876-1965*, (book), 1965.

Gammel, Hans, *The Laws of Texas, 1913-1914,* [Volume 16].

Johnson, Frank White, *A History of Texas and Texans*, (Chicago, IL & New York, NY), 1914.

Lindsley, Philip, *A history of greater Dallas and vicinity, vol. 2*, (Chicago, IL: American Historical Society). 1909.

Yeary, Mamie, *Reminiscences of the boys in gray*, (Dallas, TX: Smith & Lamar), 1912.

Young, S. O., *True stories of old Houston and Houstonians: historical and personal sketches*, (Galveston, TX), 1913.

NEWSPAPERS

Abilene (TX) Daily Reporter
Abilene (TX) Reporter
Abilene (TX) Semi Weekly Farm Reporter
Austin (TX) American
Austin (TX) American-Statesman
Austin (TX) Weekly Statesman
Baltimore (MD) Sun
Bastrop (TX) Advertiser
Bastrop (TX) Advisor
Belton (TX) Journal
Brenham (TX) Weekly Banner
Bryan (TX) Daily Eagle
Bryan (TX) Eagle
Bryan (TX) Weekly Eagle
Caldwell (TX) News-Chronicle
Cameron (TX) Herald
Coleman (TX) Democrat-Voice
Corpus Christi (TX) Caller-Times
Corsicana (TX) Daily Sun
Cuero (TX) Daily Record
Dallas (TX) Daily Herald
Dallas (TX) News
Denton (TX) Record-Chronicle
Dublin (TX) Progress
El Paso (TX) Herald
Fort Worth (TX) Daily Gazette
Galveston (TX) Daily News

Grapevine (TX) Sun
Honey Grove (TX) Journal
Houston (TX) Daily Post
Houston (TX) Post
Houston (TX) Post-Dispatch
Jacksboro (TX) News
Lockhart (TX) Post-Register
McKinney (TX) Courier-Gazette
McKinney (TX) Democrat
McKinney (TX) Weekly Telegraph-Gazette
Meridian (TX) Tribune
Nacogdoches (TX) Daily Sentinel
Pampa (TX) Daily News
Rockdale (TX) Reporter and Messenger
San Antonio (TX) Daily Express
San Antonio (TX) Express
San Antonio (TX) Light
Sherman (TX) Daily Democrat
Stephenville (TX) Empire
Taylor (TX) Daily Press
Temple (TX) Daily Telegram
Temple (TX) Weekly Times
Waco (TX) Times-Herald
Waxahachie (TX) Daily Light
Weimar (TX) Mercury
Wichita Falls (TX) Daily Times

JOURNALS/LETTERS/MANUSCRIPTS

Letter, Jno. H. Hunsethal to Nicholas Weeks Sr., July 8, 1863, Nicholas Weeks, Jr., Papers, 1861-1865, 1901-1903, Dolph Briscoe Center for American History, The University of Texas at Austin.

Letter, R. W. Downs to Mother, November 1863, J. T. Downs, Sr., Collection, 1843, 1861-1929, Dolph Briscoe Center for American History, The University of Texas at Austin

William A. Edwards, "Autobiography, or some incidents in my life. Reverend William A. Edwards, Fate, Texas 1847 and 1925, with epilogue by his daughter, Mrs. George C. Cochran," in *Dallas Genealogical Society, The Dallas Journal, vol. 44*, June 1998.

Letter E. Boyle to Nicholas Weeks Sr., July 18, 1863, Nicholas Weeks, Jr., papers, 1861-1865, 1901-1903, Dolph Briscoe Center for American History, The University of Texas at Austin.

Letter, Nicholas Weeks Jr. to Nicholas Weeks Sr., July 23?, 1863, Nicholas Weeks, Jr., papers, 1861-1865, 1901-1903, Dolph Briscoe Center for American History, The University of Texas at Austin.

Letter, Nicholas Weeks Jr. to Nicholas Weeks Sr., August 11, 1863, Nicholas Weeks, Jr., papers, 1861-1865, 1901-1903, Dolph Briscoe Museum for American History, The University of Texas at Austin.

Letter, Nicholas Weeks Jr. to Nicholas Weeks Sr., August 11, 1863, Nicholas Weeks Jr, papers, 1861-1865, 1901-1903, Dolph Briscoe Museum for American History, The University of Texas at Austin.

Telegraph, Nicholas Weeks Jr. September 29, 1863, 1861-1865, 1901-1903, Dolph Briscoe Museum for American History, The University of Texas at Austin.

WEBSITES

Handbook of Texas Online, George B. Dealey, "Belo, Alfred Horatio," accessed January 3, 2017, http://www.tshaonline.org/handbook/online/articles/fbe44.

Index